North Carolina

Private laws of the State of North-Carolina (1866 1867)

PRIVATE LAWS

OF THE

STATE OF NORTH CAROLINA,

PASSED BY THE

GENERAL ASSEMBLY

AT THE

SESSIONS OF 1866-'67.

RALEIGH:
WM. E. PELL, STATE PRINTER,
1867

PRIVATE LAWS

OF

NORTH CAROLINA.

1866-'67.

CORPORATIONS.

CHAPTER I.

AN ACT TO INCORPORATE THE TOWN OF FRANKLINSVILLE, IN THE COUNTY OF RANDOLPH.

SECTION 1. *Be it enacted by the General Assembly of the State of North Carolina, and it is hereby enacted by the authority of the same,* That the corporate limits of the town of Franklinsville shall be included within the following boundaries, to-wit: Beginning at the water-fence on Deep River, below the Island Ford Factory House, and running thence North forty degrees East to a poplar on the East bank of the branch, below Ryder's dwelling house, thence North to a little pine, back of Ryder's field in the woods, thence West to a red oak on the West side of the Greensboro' road, above Jasper York's dwelling, thence South, passing through the rock quarry on the Cedar Falls Road, to a large pine near the bank of Deep River, thence down the various courses of Deep River to the beginning.

Corporate limits.

Sec. 2. *Be it further enacted,* That it shall be lawful for the citizens resident within these limits, on the first Monday in May, in every year, to elect a Town Magistrate and three Commissioners, to serve as such for one year from the day of election, and in case there shall be no election on the day prescribed, to continue in office until their successors are appointed: *Provided,* That no one shall be eligible to the appointment of Town Magistrate or Commissioner, unless he has resided in said town six months immediately preceding his election, nor unless he is at the time of his election, and has been for six months previous thereto, seized and possessed of at least one lot or part of a lot, within the limits of said Town; nor shall any one be entitled to vote for such Town Magistrate and Commissioners, unless he has attained the age of twenty-one years, has paid a public tax, has been a resident of said Town for six months immediately preceding aid election, and shall have all the other qualifications essential to constitute a legally qualified voter for members of the General Assembly.

Sec. 3. *Be it further enacted.* That the Sheriff, or his lawful deputy, of Randolph county, shall hold said elections for Town Magistrate and Comissioners, under the same regulations that elections are now held for members of the General Assembly, and shall determine who is elected. He shall immediately furnish the Town Clerk with a certificate, stating who is elected Town Magistrate, and who are elected Commissioners, which said certificate the Town Clerk shall enter in a book to be kept for that purpose; and the said certificate, on entry thereof in the Clerk's book, shall be held and deemed conclusive of the election of such persons to the offices therein specified.

Sec. 4. *Be it further enacted,* That the said Commissioners, after they are thus elected, and shall have taken an oath faithfully to perform their duty, shall be deemed and held a body politic and corporate, by the name and style of the Commissioners of Franklinsville; and, as such, may sue and be sued, plead and be impleaded, have and use a common seal, and the same change at pleasure, and have perpetual succesion; and they, together with the Town Magistrate, shall also have power to adopt all such rules, by-laws and regulations as they, or a majority of them, may deem necessary for the good order and government of said Town: *Provided,* The same shall not be inconsistent with the laws or Constitution of this State, or of the United States. They shall also have power to appoint a Town Constable and a Town Clerk; the Clerk to act as Treasurer, and to hold their office for one year, and till others are chosen; and to appoint a patrol of all white males over twenty-one, and under fifty, years of age, and to prescribe the rules under which they shall act; and any person appointed a patrol as aforesaid, who shall refuse to act, shall forfeit the sum of ten dollars, to be recovered by warrant, in the name of the Commissioners of Franklinsville, before the Town Magistrate, and be applied as other taxes levied by the Town Magistrates and Commissioners.

SEC. 5. *Be it further enacted,* That the said Town Magistrate and Commissioners, or a majority of them, on or before the first Monday of July, in each and every year, if they deem it necessary, are hereby authorized and empowered to levy and collect a tax on the property and inhabitants of said Town not exceeding forty cents on the hundred dollars in any one year, on each poll, and fifteen cents on the hundred dollars worth of real estate; and also a tax, not exceeding two dollars per annum, on each merchant, grog-seller, or other dealer in goods, wares and merchandise; and each menagerie, company of circus-riders, equestrian performers, tumblers, rope-dancers and other actors of like character, who exhibit for reward; and any person failing to give in a full and fair list of the property for which he is liable under this Act for taxes, shall be subject to a double tax, to be collected in the same manner as other Town taxes; and all the taxes levied under the provisions of this section, shall, when collected, be applied to the improvement and repairs of the streets of said Town, and to such other purposes as the Town Magistrate and Commissioners may deem necessary for its advancement and prosperity.

Commissioners may levy tax for municipal purposes not exceeding a certain limit

SEC. 6. *Be it further enacted,* That the Commissioners, or a majority of them, shall have power to levy and collect a tax, not exceeding two dollars, on each and every person liable to work the streets under this charter, for the purpose of keeping the streets in repair, instead of calling the hands out to work.

Special tax for keeping streets in repair.

SEC. 7. *Be it further enacted,* That the Town Magistrate, who shall be a Justice of the Peace of said county, shall preside in all meetings of Commissioners, and shall have power to call them together whenever he may deem it necessary; he shall have power to issue warrants in the name of the Commissioners of Franklinsville against all persons who may violate the laws of the corporation, and shall try and determine the same; it shall also be his duty to have a general supervision over the corporation, to superintend all improvements and works ordered by the Commissioners, and see that the laws are observed and good order preserved.

Town Magistrate.

SEC. 8. *Be it further enacted,* That it shall be the duty of each person residing in said Town, to deliver to the Town Magistrate, on or before the first Monday in August, in each and every year, a statement or account of the number of taxable polls for which he or she may be by law bound to pay Town tax, and also a statement of Town property which he or she may own within the limits of said Town, and the value thereof; and any person failing to give either of the said statements shall incur a forfeiture of ten dollars, to be recovered by warrant, in the name of the Commissioners of Franklinsville, before the Town Magistrate, and be applied as taxes levied by said Town Magistrate and Commissioners.

Taxable polls and property.

SEC. 9. *Be it further enacted,* That the Town Constable shall give bond and security for the performance of his duty, as other Constables are now required by law to do, and shall have the same privileges and powers, and be subject to the same liabilities, as other Constables. He shall also give bond and security, in the sum of one thousand dollars, payable to the State of North Carolina, faithfully to collect and pay over all town taxes and penalties col-

Town Constable.

lected by him; he shall collect from each person in said Town the amount of tax imposed by the Town Magistrate and Commissioners, whenever he shall be furnished with a list of said amount, and shall be required so to do, and pay the same to the Town Clerk; and to enable the Town Constable especially to collect said tax, he is hereby authorized and empowered to have, use and exercise all lawful ways and means, which are usually had, used and exercised by the several Sheriffs of this State, in the collecting of the public Revenue, whether it may be by distress, warrrant or otherwise.

SEC. 10. *Be it further enacted,* That it shall be the duty of the Town Clerk, who shall be a citizen of said Town, but not a Commissioner or Magistrate, to record in a book kept for that purpose, all the proceedings of the said Magistrate and Commissioners, all ordinances, rules and regulations adopted by them for the government of said Town; to act as Treasurer, and to receive and disburse, under the direction of said Magistrate and Commissioners, all the taxes and monies of the corporation; to advertise all the ordinances, laws, rules and regulations of said corporation, at two or more public places in said Town; to submit annually to the Magistrate and Commissioners, a full statement of the receipts and expenditures of the year, and publish the same at two or more public places in said Town, and to perform whatever other acts and duties may be required of him by the Magistrate and Commissioners; and for said service he shall receive such compensation as said Magistrate and Commissioners may allot to him.

Town Clerk.

SEC. 11. *Be it further enacted,* That the Town Magistrate and Commissioners are hereby authorized to appoint an overseer, and enroll all hands within said corporation, liable to work on the public roads, to work on the streets of said town, and said hands shall not be liable to work on any other roads.

Overseer of streets.

SEC. 12. *Be it further enacted,* That no ordinance or regulation of said corporation shall be in force until the same shall have been advertised by the Town Clerk for the space of twenty days, at two or more public places in said Town.

Ordinances and regulations must be advertised for 20 days.

Penalty for Sheriff's failing to hold elections.

SEC. 13. *Be it further enacted,* That if the Sheriff shall fail to hold said election for Town officers, as prescribed in this Act, he shall forfeit the sum of fifty dollars, to be recovered by warrant in the name of the State, to be applied as the Commissioners of said Town may direct; and the Sheriff shall receive the sum of two dollars for each and every day that he may attend, holding said election.

Penalty for allowing str'ts to remain out of order.

SEC. 14. *Be it further enacted,* That if the said Magistrate and Commissioners shall permit the roads or streets, within the limits of said corporation, to get out of order and remain so, so as to become a nuisance, or shall permit any other nuisance to exist in said limits, which they have authority to remove, they shall be liable to indictment, and, on conviction, shall be fined at the discretion of the Court.

SEC. 15. *Be it further enacted,* That all laws and clauses of laws coming within the meaning and purview of this Act, be, and the same are hereby, repealed.

SEC. 16. *Be it further enacted,* That 'this act shall be in force from and after its ratification.

Ratified the 25th day of February, A. D., 1867.

CHAPTER II.

AN ACT TO INCORPORATE THE JONES COUNTY SAVINGS INSTITUTION.

SECTION 1. *Be it enacted by the General Assembly of the State of North Carolina, and it is hereby enacted by the authority of the same,* That for the purpose of establishing a Savings Institution in the town of Kinston, in the county of Lenoir, Jacob F. Scott, John H. Coward, A. J. Murrill,

Board of Commissioners.

F. M. Rountree, J. H. Dibble, R. F. Bright, Daniel Perry, John H. Everett, shall constitute a Board of Commissioners, who shall, after giving ten day's notice of the time and place by them or a majority of them agreed upon, cause books to be opened for receiving subscription to the capital stock of the company, and cause the same to be kept open for thirty days, unless the capital stock hereinafter mentioned shall be sooner subscribed.

SEC. 2. *Be it further enacted,* That the subscribers aforesaid and such others as may thereafter become members of the company shall be and are hereby created and made a body politic and corporate, by the name and style of the Jones County Savings Institution, to be located in said town of Kinston, and by that name shall have succession, and be capable in law and equity to hold and dispose of real and personal estate and property, by will, deed, or any other means, to sue and be sued, plead and be impleaded, and to answer and be answered in all courts either in law or equity, and to receive and make all deeds or conveyances that any individual could make and have, and use a common seal, and the same to change and renew at pleasure, and generally to do any other act necessary to accomplish the purposes and provisions of this act: *Provided,* the said corporation shall hold only such land as shall be requisite for the transaction of its business, or shall have been mortgaged to it by any way of security, or conveyed to it in satisfaction of debts previously contracted in the course of its dealings, or purchased at sale under executions which shall have been obtained for such debts.

Corporate powers.

Restrictions.

SEC. 3. *Be it further enacted,* That upon the subscription of the capital stock aforesaid, the commissioners, or a majority of them, shall notify the subscribers, and appoint a time and place for them to assemble and take upon themselves the corporate powers and privileges, and then annually thereafter, as the by-laws of the institution shall provide, five directors shall be chosen for the management of the business of the institution for the ensuing year, or until their successors shall be elected according to the by-laws of the company.

Five Directors to be chosen.

SEC. 4. *Be it further enacted,* That the directors for the time being, or a majority of them, shall have power to elect a President from their own body, or from the other members of the company, to appoint all such officers, agents, attorneys, as they may deem necessary, to transact the business of said Institution, to fix the compensation, in their

President and other officers.

Bonds required.

discretion to dismiss them; to provide for the taking of bonds to said Institution from all or any of the officers, agents, or attorneys, or servants, by them so appointed, with security, on such conditions and in such form as they shall prescribe, for the faithful performance of their several duties, and to secure the corporation from loss; to regulate the manner of making and receiving deposits, the form of certificates to be issued to depositors, and the manner of transferring stock in said Institution, of the funds of the corporation, in such manner as they shall deem most safe and beneficial; to provide for the admission of members, and furnishing proof of such admission; to provide for paying all necessary expenses incurred in conducting the affairs of the corporation, and to pass such by-laws as shall or may be necessary to the exercise of the said power vested in said corporation by this charter, and the same by-laws to alter and repeal: *Provided, however*, that the stockholders in any general meeting may modify, or change, or repeal any of the by-laws of said Institution as made by the directors as aforesaid, and may pass others which shall be binding upon the said directors: *Provided, further*, That no by-law of the Institution shall be made incompatible with the constitution and laws of this State or of the United States.

Privileges.

SEC. 5. *Be it further enacted*, That said corporation shall be capable of receiving from any person or persons, or bodies corporate or politic, any deposit or deposits of money, and it shall have power to invest its funds in notes, bonds, bills of exchange, gold and silver coin, State bonds, or State securities, United States Bonds, or securities of the United States, at the discretion of the directors, in a manner, by them, deemed most safe and beneficial, and the same to sell and buy, as they may deem most advisable: *Provided*, That nothing herein contained shall be construed to authorize the corporation to issue any certificate of deposit, or bill, or note, or other device in the nature of a bank note, or any bill intended to circulate as money.

Deposits.

SEC. 6. *Be it further enacted*, That such deposits shall be repaid to such depositors when required, at such times, and with such interest, and under such regulations as the Board of Directors shall, from time to time, prescribe, which regulations shall not be altered so as to affect any one who may have deposited with said institution at the time of such alteration, and all certificates or evidences of deposit made by the proper officer shall be affected to bind the institution as fully as if attested by the seal of the corporation and company.

SEC. 7. *Be it further enacted,* That when any deposit shall be made by any person being a minor, the said corporation may pay to such depositor, any such sum or sums of money, as may be due to him or her, at their discretion, not exceeding two hundred and fifty dollars, although no guardian shall have been appointed for such minor, and the receipt or acquittance of such minor shall be as valid as if the same were executed by a guardian of such minor. Deposits by minors.

SEC. 8. *Be it further enacted,* That it shall be the duty of the Directors, at least once in every six months, to appoint five competent members of said corporation, as a Committee of Examination, whose duty it shall be to investigate the business and affairs of the corporation, and make and publish a report in one or more newspapers in the State; and it shall be the duty of said Directors to make and declare, at least semi-annually, dividends of its profits, whenever the profits of the company will justify it, and the same to pay over to the Stockholders, or their attorneys, agents, or their legal representatives, within ten days thereafter, if called on. Committee of examination.

SEC. 9. *Be it further enacted,* That no Stockholder, who is a debtor to the corporation, shall be permitted to transfer his stock until such debt be paid, or otherwise secured to the satisfaction of the Directors, who are hereby authorized to sell and transfer the same, if the debt is not paid, first giving thirty days notice, in writing, to such Stockholder, of their intention so to do. Debtors to the corporation may not transfer their stock, until such debts be paid.

SEC. 10. *Be it further enacted,* That in all discounts or loans made by said corporation, it shall not take more than the rate of interest established by the Legislature of North Carolina, and it shall be lawful for the corporation to take such interest in advance at the time of making such loan. Interest on Discounts and Loans.

Individual property not bound for the debts, &c., of the Corporation.

SEC. 11. *Be it further enacted,* That the individual property or estate of the stockholders of the corporation shall not be bound for the debts, or contracts, or liabilities of the corporation.

Books, &c., to be open for inspection.

SEC. 12. *Be it further enacted,* That the books and business of the corporation shall, at all times, be subject to the inspection of the Treasurer of the State, or any person or agent that the Governor or Legislature may appoint, to make such inspection and examination.

Capital Stock.

SEC. 13. *Be it further enacted,* That the capital stock of said corporation shall not be more than two hundred and fifty thousand dollars, to be divided into shares of one hundred dollars each, unless an additional capital shall hereafter be authorized by the Legislature.

SEC. 14. *Be it further enacted,* That this Act shall be in force from and after its ratification.

Ratified the 28th day of February, A. D., 1867.

CHAPTER III.

AN ACT TO INCORPORATE THE NEW BERNE MEMORIAL ASSOCIATION.

Corporators.

WHEREAS, A number of ladies of the city of New Berne, to-wit: Mistresses J. P. Daves, J. E. Nash, J. P. Dillingham, W. P. Moore, C. S. Primrose, Julia Lewis, J. M. F. Harrison and Misses Harriett Lane, Annie M. Slover and Henrietta A. Dewey, have associated themselves together for the purpose of collecting the remains of those who died in the service of the Confederate States, of re-interring the same, and erecting suitable memorials over the spot: *And whereas,* it is deemed advisable, for the accomplishment of their object and for the continuance and protection of such memorials as may be raised, that the Association should have a corporate existence: Therefore,

SECTION 1. *Be it enacted by the General Assembly of the State of North Carolina, and it is hereby enacted by the au-*

thority of the same, That the aforesaid ladies, and all others who may from time to time be associated with them, shall be and are hereby created, constituted and declared to be a body politic and corporate in law, and in fact, by the name and style of the New Berne Memorial Association, and by this name shall be capable of taking by purchase, devise or donation, real and personal estate to the amount of ten thousand dollars, and of holding and conveying the same, shall have a common seal, may sue and be sued, plead and be impleaded in all Courts of law and equity, and shall have and enjoy perpetual succession in these and all other needful powers and privileges for the attainment of the object aforesaid and for none other.

_{Name, powers and privileges.}

SEC. 2. *Be it further enacted,* That the Association shall have power to appoint such officers as may be deemed needful for carrying out the purposes of the corporation, and make all such rules, regulations and laws as may be thought proper for the government of the same: *Provided,* they are not inconsistent with the laws of the State or the United States.

_{Association may make all necessary by-laws, &c.}

SEC. 3. *Be it further enacted,* That this Act shall be in force from and after its ratification.

Ratified the 18th day of February, A. D., 1867.

CHAPTER IV.

AN ACT TO INCORPORATE THE BLADEN MANUFACTURING COMPANY, IN THE COUNTY OF BLADEN.

SECTION 1. *Be it enacted by the General Assembly of the State of North Carolina, and it is hereby enacted by the authority of the same,* That John A. McDowell, Joseph C. Abbott, Duncan Cromartie, Alfred M. Waddell, George Z. French, L. G. Estes, Daniel Clark, John L. Kelly and George S. Hanson, and their associates, successors and assigns, be, and they are hereby, created a corporation and a body politic, in law and in fact, by the name and style of

_{Corporators.}

Objects and privileges. the Bladen Manufacturing Company, for the purpose of manufacturing cotton, wool and other articles in the county of Bladen ; and by that name and style, may sue and be sued, plead and be impleaded in any Court of Record, contract and be contracted with, have perpetual succession and a common seal, and acquire, possess, enjoy and retain real and personal estate, and also goods and merchandise, to enable them to carry on their business with advantage and profit, and shall so continue for thirty years; and, during said period, and at the expiration thereof, may sell, barter, exchange and dispose of the real and personal estate acquired in a corporate character, as also all the articles manufactured and owned by them.

SEC. 2. *Be it further enacted,* That said corporation shall have power to make all necessary by-laws and regulations, **Powers.** not inconsistent with the laws and Constitution of North Carolina, for its government, and to alter and amend the same at pleasure, and to appoint officers and agents to transact their business and conduct their operations.

SEC. 3. *Be it further enacted,* That the capital stock of **Capital stock:** said Company or corporation shall be two hundred thousand dollars, in shares of one hundred dollars each; at least thirty thousand dollars of which shall be actually paid in before the company shall proceed, under this charter, to manufacture, and the capital stock may, at the discretion of the Company, be increased to five hundred thousand dollars.

SEC. 4. *Be it further enacted,* That the Stockholders, at their first general meeting, shall proceed to organize, by the election of such number of Directors and officers, as in **Organization.** their judgment may be necessary to properly attend to and conduct the business of the Company ; and in their by-laws shall prescribe their general duties, and provide for their re-election, and for the general meetings of Stockholders, and also prescribe the mode of election, manner and scale of voting, and the manner of issuing certificates of stock, and the mode of transferring and assigning the same. All officers, when once elected by said Company, shall continue in office until their places are filled by others duly chosen, and the regular term of office shall not be less than one year. If the election of officers, and filling vacancies, be omitted on the day prescribed, the same may be done on any subsequent day, without forfeiting any of the rights or privileges of the Company

SEC. 7. *Be it further enacted,* That this Act shall be in force from and after its ratification.

Ratified the 26th day of January, A. D., 1867.

CHAPTER V.

AN ACT TO INCORPORATE THE AMERICAN AGRICULTURAL AND MINERAL LAND COMPANY.

SECTION 1. *Be it enacted by the General Assembly of the State of North Carolina, and it is hereby enacted by the authority of the same,* That Joseph A. Brauner, Robert V. Welch, John B. Love, James R. Love, and their associates, successors and assigns, be and they are hereby declared to be a body politic and corporate, by the name and style of the American Agricultural and Mineral Land Company; and as such shall have the rights and privileges conferred, and be subject to all the restrictions imposed, on corporations by the twenty-sixth (26th) chapter of the Revised Code of North Carolina, so far as the same are not inconsistent with the Act. The persons named in this section, or any two them, or their associates and assigns, shall be authorized to receive subscriptions of stocks, and provide for the organization of the Company in such manner, and upon such notice to the subscribers, as they may deem reasonable. Corporators.
Powers and privileges.

SEC. 2. *Be it further enacted,* That said Company shall have power to purchase and hold real and personal property, sell and mortgage the same, and, for the purpose of its charter, may advance money upon real personal security at such rate of interest, not exceeding eight per cent., as the by-laws of the Company may direct. Further Powers and Privileges.

250 LAWS OF [Sessions

Company may issue bonds, in aid of its object.

SEC. 3. *Be it further enacted,* That said Company shall have power, for the purpose of raising an Agricultural and Mineral fund, to develope the real estate of said Company, to issue bonds which shall be done under the corporate seal of said Company, and shall bear interest at a rate not exceeding eight per cent., and whenever so expressed upon the face of the bond, be a lien upon the real estate of said Company without the execution of a formal mortgage.

Capital.

SEC. 4. *Be it further enacted,* That the capital stock of said Company shall not exceed two millions of dollars, in shares of fifty or one hundred dollars each, to be paid and secured as may be provided for under such rules as the by-laws of the Company may direct.

SEC. 5. *Be it further enacted,* That this Act shall be in force from and after its ratification, and for the space of sixty years.

Ratified the 26th day February, A. D., 1867.

CHAPTER VI.

AN ACT TO INCORPORATE THE ROCKY POINT MANUFACTURING COMPANY, IN THE COUNTY OF CUMBERLAND.

Corporators.

SECTION 1. *Be it enacted by the General Assembly of the State of North Carolina, and it is hereby enacted by the authority of the same,* That Col. David Gillis, Duncan Shaw, Daniel McNutt, Thos. S. Lutterloh, their associates, successors and assigns, be and they are hereby constituted a body corporate and politic, under the name and style of the Rocky Point Manufacturing Company, and by that name may sue and be sued, shall have power to purchase, hold, possess and enjoy real and personal estate.

Powers, &c.

SEC. 2. *Be it further enacted,* That the said corporation shall have power to make all such by-laws, rules and regulations as may be necessary to the ordering and well-governing the same, not inconsistent with the laws of the State or United States.

SEC. 3. *Be it further enacted,* That the capital stock of said corporation shall not exceed fifty thousand dollars, in shares of fifty dollars each, to be paid in such manner and under such rules and regulations as may be necessary.

<small>Capital.</small>

SEC. 4. *Be it further enacted,* That the corporation named in first section shall have power and authority to open books of subscription to the capital stock of said corporation, at such times and places, and under the direction of such persons, as the corporation may determine, and that the Stockholders may elect such officers as they may deem necessary for the proper management of the business of the same: That they shall have full power and authority to manufacture cotton goods, yarns, shirting and sheetings of every kind and description whatsoever, and to deal in goods, wares and merchandise of every kind.

<small>May open books of subscription.</small>

<small>Corporate objects.</small>

SEC. 5. *Be it further enacted,* That this Act shall be in force from and after its ratification.

Ratified the 4th day of March, A. D., 1867.

CHAPTER VII.

AN ACT TO INCORPORATE "THE CRANBERRY MINING AND MANUFACTURING COMPANY."

SECTION 1. *Be it enacted by the General Assembly of the State of North Carolina, and it is hereby enacted by the authority of the same,* That E. Nye Hutchison, T. J. Sumner, R. F. Hoke, G. W. Swepson, T. D. Carter, William J. Brown, J. C. Smyth and P. B. Chambers, and their associates, successors and assigns be, and they are hereby, created and constituted a body politic and corporate, under the name and style of the "Cranberry Mining and Manufacturing Company," for the purpose of working, mining and exploring for iron and all other metals and minerals in the counties of Mitchell, Yancey and Watauga, and for mining, manufacturing and vending the same, and espe-

<small>Corporators.</small>

cially for the purpose of converting iron into steel; and said Company shall have power to purchase, hold, sell, or convey real or personal property, and to borrow money upon mortgages, mortgage bonds or other evidence of indebtedness, such as to create a lien on all the estate, real and personal, of the Company.

Powers and privileges.

SEC. 2. *Be it further enacted,* That the capital stock of said Company shall not exceed two millions, divided into shares of one hundred dollars each; and said Company may provide for the sale and transfer of shares in such manner and form as said corporation shall, from time to time, deem expedient, and may levy and collect assessments, forfeit and sell delinquent's shares, declare and pay dividends on the shares, in such manner as their by-laws shall direct.

Capital.

SEC. 3. *Be it further enacted,* That there shall be such number of Directors of said Company as the Stockholders in their by-laws may direct, and such other officers as they may, in the same manner, create; and that said corporation shall exist for sixty years.

Directors, &c.

SEC. 4. *Be it further enacted,* That this Act shall be in force from and after its ratification.

Ratified the 4th day of March, A. D., 1867.

CHAPTER VIII.

AN ACT TO INCORPORATE THE HOOVER HILL MINING COMPANY.

SECTION 1. *Be it enacted by the General Assembly of the State of North Carolina, and it is hereby enacted by the authority of the same,* That Joseph A. Worth, Wm. J. Brown, J. F. E. Hardy, Joseph A. McDowell, N. W. Woodfin, Joseph R. Osborne and Thomas W. Patton, or a majority of them, and their associates, successors and assigns be, and they are hereby, constituted a body corporate and politic, under the name and style of the Hoover Hill Mining Company, and as such shall have succession, and may have and use a common seal, and change the same at pleasure, and shall

Corporators.

be capable to sue and be sued, to plead and be impleaded in any Court of Law or Equity, and may also have, use, exercise and enjoy all the powers and privileges of opening and working of mines, and of buying, holding and selling and conveying mines, and shall have power to purchase and hold, to sell and convey all such property, real and personal, as may be necessary for the purposes aforesaid. The said Company shall have power, for the purposes aforesaid, to make such by-laws and regulations as may be necessary, and which shall be binding on the Company: *Provided*, That they be consistent with the Constitution and laws of the State. Powers and privileges.

SEC. 2. *Be it further enacted*, That the capital stock of the said Company shall be three hundred thousand dollars, to be divided into shares of one hundred dollars each, and the said corporation shall have power to increase their capital stock to one million of dollars, whenever they shall deem it advisable, and the lands, mines, machinery and other property of said Company shall constitute a part of the capital stock, at such price as shall be agreed on by the owners thereof, on the one part, and those who may associate with them and constitute the aforesaid corporation by subscribing for stock payable in money, on the other. Capital.

SEC. 3. *Be it further enacted*, That the subscription of the said capital stock shall be made at such times and places, and in such manner, as the said Joseph A. Worth, Wm. J. Brown, J. F. E. Hardy, Joseph A. McDowell, N. W. Woodfin, Joseph R. Osborne and Thomas W. Patton, or a majority of them, shall designate, and the stockholders shall be entitled, at all their meetings, to one vote for each share of stock so held in person or by proxy, and the shares in said corporation shall be transferable in such manner as may be provided by by-laws of said Company, and shall be considered as personal property. Subscriptions to Stock.

SEC. 4. *Be it further enacted*, That the affairs of said Company shall be managed by a Board of Directors, not less than five nor more than nine, one of whom shall be appointed President, all to be chosen by the stockholders, Directors.

and shall serve one year, and until their successors are chosen; and the failure to elect at any time shall not work a forfeiture or dissolution of this corporation, and until the first election of Directors shall be held, the said Joseph A. Worth, Wm. J. Brown, J. F. E. Hardy, Joseph A. McDowell, N. W. Woodfin, Joseph R. Osborne and Thomas W. Patton, or a majority of them, shall have full power to manage the affairs of said Company, under such rules and regulations as they may make for their own government; and this Act shall be in force and the rights hereby granted continue for sixty years from its ratification.

Ratified the 26th day of January, A. D., 1867

CHAPTER IX.

AN ACT TO INCORPORATE THE TRUSTEES OF THE "LOWELL COLORED SCHOOL SOCIETY," IN THE COUNTY OF WASHINGTON.

Corporators. SECTION 1. *Be it enacted by the General Assembly of the State of North Carolina and it is hereby enacted by the authority of the same,* That John C. Guyther, Theophilus Ashe, Alexander Fagan, Prosper Armistead, Frank James, Frank Fessenden, Willie Johnson, Aaron Gaylord, John Bell, George W. Jones, George Parmerlee, and Virgil Nicholls, shall be, and they are hereby declared to be, a body politic and corporate, by the name, style and title of the "Trustees of the Lowell Colored School Society," to have continuance thirty years, and, by the name and title aforesaid, to have succession and a common seal, and be

Powers and privileges. able and capable in law to take, receive and hold all manner of lands, tenements and other hereditaments which shall, at any time or times, be granted, sold, released, devised, or otherwise conveyed to them and their successors, by any person or persons, or bodies corporate or politic; and, further, that the said Trustees and their successors, under the corporate name aforesaid, shall be able and capable, in law, to take, receive and possess all monies, goods and chattels that shall be given, sold or released or bequeathed, by any person or persons, for the use of said Society, and the same to apply according to the will of the donor.

SEC. 2. *Be it further enacted,* That the said Trustees and their successors, by the name aforesaid, shall be able and capable in law, to bargain, sell, grant, convey and confirm to the purchaser or purchasers, such lands, tenements and hereditaments aforesaid, when the condition of the grant to them, or the will of the devisee, does not forbid it. Further powers.

SEC. 3. *Be it further enacted,* That the said Trustees, and their successors by the name aforesaid, shall be able and capable in law, to sue and be sued, to plead and be impleaded, answer and be answered, in all Courts of Record whatever, in all manner of suits, complaints, pleas, matters and demands. Further powers.

SEC. 4. *Be it further enacted,* That the said Trustees and their successors shall be, and are hereby, authorized and empowered, to make, ordain and establish such by-laws, ordinances and regulations, for the government of said Society, as are usual, and to them seem necessary: *Provided,* The same be not repugnant to the Constitution and laws of this State, or of the United States. By-laws, &c.

SEC. 5. *Be it further enacted,* That the Trustees named in this Act, or a majority of them, shall have power to fill all vacancies occurring by death, resignation or otherwise.

SEC. 6. *Be it further enacted,* That the real estate held by the Trustees aforesaid, in the State of North Carolina, shall, at no time, exceed in quantity five hundred acres. Real estate held not to exceed 500 acres.

SEC. 7. *Be it further enacted,* That this Act shall take effect and be in force from and after its ratification.

Ratified the 26th day of February, A. D., 1867.

CHAPTER X.

AN ACT TO INCORPORATE THE WADESBORO' SAVINGS INSTITUTION.

Commissioners.

SECTION 1. *Be it enacted by the General Assembly of the State of North Carolina, and it is hereby enacted by the authority of the same,* That for the purpose of establishing a Savings Institution in the Town of Wadesboro', Messrs. S. W. Cole, James A. Leak, George W. Little, W. P. Kendall, S. S. Arnold, H. A. Crawford, W. G. Smith, J. M. Scales, W. C. Smith, shall constitute a Board of Commissioners, who shall, after giving ten day's public notice of the time and place by them or a majority of them agreed upon, cause books to be opened for receiving subscription to the capital stock of the Company, and cause the same to be kept open for thirty days, unless the capital stock hereinafter mentioned shall be sooner subscribed.

Books of subscription.

Corporate powers, &c.

SEC. 2. *Be it further enacted,* That the subscribers aforesaid, and such others as may thereafter become members of the Company, shall be, and hereby are created and made, a body politic and corporate, by the name and style of "The Wadesboro' Savings Institution," to be located in said town, and by that name shall have succession and be capable in law to hold and dispose of real and personal property by deed or otherwise, to sue and be sued, plead and be impleaded, and to answer and be answered in all Courts of Law or Equity, and to receive and make all deeds, transfers and conveyances whatsoever, and to make, have and use a common seal, and the same to change and renew at pleasure, and generally to do every other act or thing necessary to accomplish the purposes and provisions of this Act: *Provided,* That said corporation shall purchase and hold only such lands, tenements and hereditaments as shall be requisite for the convenient transaction of its business, or shall have been *bona fide* mortgaged to it by way of security, or conveyed to it in satisfaction of debts previously contracted in the course of its dealings, or purchased at sales upon judgments which shall have been obtained for such debts.

SEC. 3. *Be it further enacted,* That upon the subscription of the capital stock aforesaid, the said Commissioners, or a majority of them, shall notify the said subscribers, and appoint a time and place for them to assemble and take upon themselves their corporate powers and privileges, and then, and annually thereafter, as the by-laws of said Institution shall provide, five Directors shall be chosen for the management of the affairs of the Institution for the ensuing twelve months, or until their successors shall be elected, according to the by-laws of the Company. Election of Directors.

SEC. 4. *Be it further enacted,* That the Directors for the time being, or a majority of them, shall have power to elect a President from their own body, or from the other members; to appoint all such officers, agents and servants as they shall deem necessary to transact the business of said Institution; to fix their compensation, and, in their discretion, to dismiss them; to provide for the taking of bonds to said Institution from all or any of the officers, agents or servants by them so appointed, with security conditioned in such form as they shall prescribe for the faithful execution of their several duties, and to secure the corporation from loss; to regulate the manner of making and receiving deposits; the form of certificates to be issued to depositors, and the manner of transferring stock in said Institution; to provide for the investment of the funds of the corporation in such manner as they shall deem most safe and beneficial; to provide for the admission of members, and furnishing proof of such admission; to provide for paying all necessary expenses incurred in conducting the affairs of the corporation, and generally to pass all such by-laws as shall or may be necessary to the exercise of said powers, and of the powers vested in said corporation by this charter, and the same by-laws to alter and repeal: *Provided, however,* That the Stockholders in any general meeting may modify, alter, or repeal any of the by-laws of said Institution so made by the Directors as aforesaid, and President and other officers.

may pass others which shall be binding upon the said Directors: *Provided further*, That no by-laws of the Institution shall be made incompatible with the Constitution and laws of this State, or of the United States.

Concerning deposits.
SEC. 5. *Be it further enacted,* That said corporation shall be capable of receiving from any person or persons, or bodies politic or corporate, any deposit or deposits of money, and it shall have power to invest its funds in notes, bonds, bills of exchange, gold and silver, public stocks, or other securities, at the discretion of the Directors, in the manner by them deemed most safe and beneficial, and the same to sell and levy, as they may deem most advisable : *Provided,* That nothing herein contained shall be construed to authorize the corporation to issue any certificate of deposit, or bill, or note, or other device, in nature of a bank note.

Certificates of deposit.
SEC. 6. *Be it further enacted,* That such deposits shall be repaid to each depositor, when required, at such times and with such interest, and under such regulations, as the Board of Directors shall, from time to time, prescribe, which regulations shall not be so altered as to affect any one who may have deposits with said institution at the time of such alteration ; and all certificates, or evidences of deposit, made by the proper officer, shall be effectual to bind the institution as fully as if attested by the company.

Deposits of minors.
SEC. 7. *Be it further enacted,* That when any deposit shall be made by any person being a minor, the said corporation may pay to such depositor any such sum or sums as may be due to him or her, at their discretion, not exceeding two hundred and fifty dollars, although no guardian shall have been appointed for such minor, and the receipt or acquittance of such minor shall be as valid as if the same were executed by a guardian of such minor.

Semi-annual Board of Examination.
SEC. 8. *Be it further enacted,* That it shall be the duty of the Directors, at least once in every six months, to appoint five competent members of said corporation, as a Committee of Examination, whose duty it shall be to investigate the affairs of the corporation, and make and publish a report in one or more newspapers published in said town of Wadesboro', if any, and, if none, then in the newspaper pub-

lished nearest to said town ; and it shall be the duty of said Directors to make and declare, at least semi-annually, dividends of its profits, whenever the profits and situation of the Company will justify it, and the same to pay over to the Stockholders, or their legal representatives, within ten days thereafter, if called on.

SEC. 9. *Be it further enacted,* That no stockholder, who is a debtor to the corporation, shall be permitted to transfer his stock until such debt be paid or otherwise secured to the satisfaction of the Directors, who are hereby authorized to sell and transfer the same if the debt is not paid, first giving ten days prior notice in writing to such stockholders of their intention so to do. *Concerning tranfers of stock by debtors.*

SEC. 10. *Be it further enacted,* That in all discounts or loans to be made by said Institution, it shall not take more than the rate of interest established by the laws of the State of North Carolina, but it shall and may be lawful to take such interest, in advance, at the time of making such loans. *Discounts and Loans.*

SEC. 11. *Be it further enacted,* That the concerns of the Institution shall, at all times, be subject to the inspection of the Treasurer of the State, or of such other officers or agents of the State as may be selected for that purpose by the General Assembly. *Affairs of Institution open for inspection.*

SEC. 12. *Be it further enacted,* That the capital stock of said corporation shall not exceed the sum of one hundred thousand dollars, to be divided into shares of one hundred dollars each, unless and until an additional capital shall hereafter be authorized by the General Assembly. *Capital.*

SEC. 13. *Be it further enacted,* That this Act shall be in force from and after its ratification.

SEC. 14. *Be it further enacted,* That said corporation shall continue for thirty years.

Ratified the 25th day of February, A. D., 1867.

CHAPTER XI.

AN ACT TO INCORPORATE THE CHARLOTTE MERCHANTS' AND PLANTERS' BENEFIT ASSOCIATION.

Corporators.

SECTION 1. *Be it enacted by the General Assembly of the State of North Carolina and it is hereby enacted by the authority of the same,* That John L. Morehead, C. D. Vernon, John H. McAden, and their associates, successors and assigns be, and the same are hereby, constituted and appointed a body corporate and politic, under the style and name of the "Charlotte Merchants' and Planters' Association," and by that name shall be entitled to all the rights and privileges granted to corporations by the laws of North Carolina.

Make advancements on growing crops, when lien shall attach.

SEC. 2. *Be it further enacted,* That said corporation shall have power to make advancements of money upon growing crops of every kind and description, and that a lien shall attach upon said crops for the amount advanced, including interest and commissions, as agreed upon by the parties.

May make advances to assist planting interests. Lien to attach.

SEC. 3. *Be it further enacted,* That the said corporation shall have power to advance money to any and all persons for the purpose of entering into the business of planting all kinds of crops, and of purchasing and improving land and other business, and the amount so advanced, including interest and commissions, agreed upon by the parties, shall attach, as a lien, upon the crop or crops, and the lands on which said crops are grown, until such sums are paid, the said lien being as binding, in law, as if the same was duly registered according to the laws of this State: *Provided, however,* That this lien shall be postponed in favor of the landlord, when advancements may have been made to tenants.

Proviso.

Powers and privileges.

SEC. 4. *Be it further enacted,* That said corporation shall have authority to deal in gold and silver coin, bonds, promissory notes, bills of exchange, and all kinds of securities, and to take mortgages for the same, according to law; and that the capital stock of said company shall be subject to the same taxe imposed on the capital stock of other like incorporated Companies, and that the corporate privileges herein granted shall continue for thirty years, and the capital stock shall not exceed three hundred thousand dollars.

SEC. 5. *Be it further enacted,* That this act shall be in force from and after its ratification.

Ratified the 4th day of March, A. D., 1867.

CHAPTER XII.

AN ACT TO INCORPORATE THE RALEIGH MEMORIAL ASSOCIATION.

WHEREAS, A number of ladies of the city of Raleigh, (to-wit:) Mistresses L. O'B. Branch, President, Dr. Lacy, R. G. Lewis, Il. L. Evans, H. W. Miller, Vice Presidents; Miss S. H. Partridge, Secretary, and Annie M. Mason, Treasurer; Hon. G. W. Mordecai, Gen. W. R. Cox, Mr. William Grimes, P. F. Pescud, H. Husted, and Major B. Manly, President's council, and their successors in office, have associated themselves together for the purpose of collecting the remains of those who died in the service of the Confederate States, of re-interring the same, and erecting suitable memorials over the spot: *And whereas,* it is deemed advisable, for the accomplishment of this object, and for the continuous protection of such memorials as may be raised, that the Association should have a corporate existence: Therefore,

Corporators.

SECTION 1. *Be it enacted by the General Assembly of the State of North Carolina, and it is hereby enacted by the authority of the same,* That the aforesaid ladies, and all others who may from time to time be associated with them, shall be, and are hereby, created, constituted and declared to be a body politic and corporate, in law and in fact, by the name and style of the "Raleigh Memorial Association,"

Powers and privileges.   and by that name shall be capable of taking by purchase, devise or donation, real and personal estate, to the amount of ten thousand dollars, and of holding and conveying the same; shall have a common seal, may sue and be sued, plead and be impleaded in all Courts of Law and Equity, and shall have and enjoy perpetual succession, in these and all other needful powers and privileges, for the attainment of the object aforesaid, and for none other.

Officers and by-laws.   SEC. 2. *Be it further enacted*, That the Association shall have power to appoint such officers as may be deemed needful for carrying out the purposes of the corporation and make all such rules and regulations and by-laws as may be thought proper for the government of the same: *Provided*, They are not inconsistent with the laws of the State and of the United States.

SEC. 3. *Be it further enacted*, That this Act shall be in force from and after its ratification.

Ratified the 4th day of March, A. D., 1867.

CHAPTER XIII.

AN ACT AUTHORIZING THE FORMATION OF THE DURHAM NORTH CAROLINA INDUSTRIAL ASSOCIATION IN THE COUNTY OF ORANGE.

Corporators.   SECTION 1. *Be it enacted by the General Assembly of the State of North Carolina and it is hereby enacted by the authority of the same*, That John R. Green, John W. Cheek, and their associates, are hereby constituted a body politic and corporate, under the name and style of the Durham North Carolina Industrial Association, for the purpose of

Objects.   purchasing, holding and disposing of the same, of carrying on the Manufacturing, Mining, Agricultural and the mechanical and [other] business necessary to a full development and successful prosecution of a large enterprise, embracing the above named branches of industry, and to continue for

Powers.   a period of thirty years, with power to make and use a common seal, and to alter and change [illegible] and to make such by-laws, not inconsistent with [illegible] of this State and the laws of the United States, [illegible] deem useful and necessary; to sue and be sued, to plea be impleaded, to hold, buy, purchase or otherwise, and dis[pose] of the same in any way, all real estate and personal proper[ty] which may be deemed useful and necessary for the carrying on their operations or which they may become possessed of in the prosecution of their said business.

SEC. 2. *Be it further enacted*, That the capital stock of said corporation shall be one hundred thousand dollars, and shall be divided into shares of twenty-five dollars each. Capital.

SEC. 3. *Be it further enacted*, That the said corporators and their associates shall have the right to invest such portion of the capital stock of the said corporation in real estate and personal property, as they may deem for the best interest of the corporation, and such property may be received by them in payment for subscription to said capital stock. The subscription to the capital stock of the company may be obtained by opening books for general subscription, or by private and personal solicitation, as the said corporation may deem most desirable. May invest capital in real estate, &c or receive subscriptions in the same.

SEC. 4. *Be it further enacted*, That the said corporation shall have an office for the transaction of business in the county or district where their operations are carried on, and they may have offices in other places, if they deem it for the interest of the Company to establish them. Offices of Corporation.

SEC. 5. *Be it further enacted*, That all subscribers to the capital stock, who shall not have paid their subscriptions according to the terms agreed upon, shall be liable to the creditors of the said corporation for all amounts remaining unpaid on their said subscriptions, and may be proceeded against in the usual way and manner for collection of the same. Delinquent subscribers.

SEC. 6. *Be it further enacted*, That the business of the said corporation shall be managed by a Board of Directors of not less than five, nor more than nine, one of whom shall be President; the Directors shall be elected annually, when the number of Directors for the year shall be determined Directors.

by a vote of the Stockholders, but a failure to elect shall not work a forfeiture of the charter, but the Directors and officers of the previous year shall continue in office until others are elected in their stead. At all meetings of the Stockholders, each share of stock shall entitle the holder to one vote, which may be voted in person or by proxy; the place of meeting of Stockholders to be fixed by the Board of Directors, and due notice given of the same.

SEC. 7. *Be it further enacted,* That the stock of this Company shall be taken and regarded as personal property, and taansferable on the books of the Company as the by-laws shall prescribe.

Ratified the 4th day of March, A. D., 1867.

CHAPTER XIV.

AN ACT TO INCORPORATE HOLSTON ANNUAL CONFERENCE OF THE METHODIST EPISCOPAL CHURCH, SOUTH.

SECTION 1. *Be it enacted by the General Assembly of the State of North Carolina, and it is hereby enacted by the authority of the same,* That the Reverends Thomas K. Catlett, Joseph Askew, Thomas K. Munsey, Timothy Sullins, James Atkins, Ephraim E. Wiley, D. D., Wm. G. E. Cun-

Corporators. ningham, Carroll Long, James S. Kennedy, James W. Dickey, John H. Branner, William M. Kerr, John Bouney, Jacob Brilhart, Henry C. Neal, and others associated with them, under the name and style of "Holston Annual Conference of the Methodist Episcopal Church, South," and their successors, duly chosen according to the rules and regulations of said Church, be, and they are hereby, constituted a

Powers and body politic and corporate, by the name and style aforesaid, privileges. and shall be able and capable to take and hold all such estate, property and effects as may be acquired by gift, purchase, devise or bequest, to aid and enable said Annual Confer-

Objects. ence to undertake and carry on the work of Christian education, of Foreign and Domestic Missions, of the publication of such books, tracts and papers as are connected with the diffusion of religious literature and learning, and of building up and supporting churches of their faith and worship in the United States of America: *Provided,* That the property, real or personal, held or possessed by said corporation, shall not exceed two million dollars.

<small>Restriction.</small>

SEC. 2. *Be it further enacted,* That the members of said Annual Conference, and their successors, shall have and use a common seal, and alter the same at their pleasure, and may, through their officers or regularly appointed agents, sue and be sued, plead and be impleaded, receive and make all deeds, transfers and conveyances, and do every other act necessary to accomplish the purposes hereinbefore indicated : *Provided,* That no act of the said Annual Conference, or its agent, be done in violation of the Constitution and laws of this State or of the United States.

<small>Further powers and privileges.</small>

SEC. 3. *Be it further enacted,* That the General Assembly reserve to itself the right to amend the charter hereby granted, by restricting or enlarging its privileges.

SEC. 4. *Be it further enacted,* That this act shall be in force from and after its ratification.

Ratified the 4th day of March, A. D., 1867.

CHAPTER XV.

AN ACT TO INCORPORATE THE "KITTRELL'S SPRINGS FEMALE COLLEGE," IN THE COUNTY OF GRANVILLE.

SECTION 1. *Be it enacted by the General Assembly of the State of North Carolina, and it is hereby enacted by the authority of the same,* That the Rev. Cornelius B. Riddick, Rev. James H. Riddick and Henry Riddick, with such other persons as they may associate with them, be and they are hereby created and constituted a body corporate, to be known by the name and style of "The Board of Trustees of the Kittrell's Springs Female College," and by that name shall have succession and a common seal, and shall

<small>Corporators.</small>

Powers, &c. be able and capable, in law, of purchasing, holding and selling real and personal estate to the value of five hundred thousand dollars, for the use and benefit of the said College, and of suing and being sued, pleading and being impleaded in their corporate name.

Trustees and Faculty may confer degrees &c. SEC. 2. *Be it further enacted*, That the said Trustees, or a majority of them, shall have power to fill all vacancies in said Board, and, together with the Faculty, to confer such degrees, diplomas and marks of literary distinction as are usually conferred in Colleges and Seminaries of learning, and the said Board of Trustees shall possess, use and enjoy all other powers, privileges and immunities pertaining to bodies corporate of like nature, and the said corporation may exist for the period of fifty years.

SEC. 3. *Be it further enacted*, That this Act shall be in force from and after its ratification.

Ratified the 28th day of February, A. D., 1867.

CHAPTER XVI.

AN ACT TO REPEAL AN ACT ENTITLED AN ACT TO AMEND THE CHARTER OF THE WASHINGTON TOLL BRIDGE COMPANY.

SECTION 1. *Be it enacted by the General Assembly of the State of North Carolina, and it is hereby enacted by the authority of the same*, That the said recited Act, ratified December 11th, 1866, be and the same is hereby repealed.

SEC. 2. *Be it further enacted*, That this Act be in force from and after its ratification.

Ratified the 26th day of February, A. D., 1867.

CHAPTER XVII.

AN ACT TO AMEND SECTION 4TH, OF AN ACT PASSED DURING THE SESSION OF 1858–'59, ENTITLED AN ACT TO AUTHORIZE THE ROANOKE NAVIGATION COMPANY TO DISCONTINUE THE USE OF THEIR CANAL AROUND THE GRAND FALLS OF THE ROANOKE RIVER, AND TO MAKE SALE OF THEIR REAL ESTATE, WATER-POWER AND OTHER PRIVILEGES BETWEEN THE TOWNS OF GASTON AND WELDON, IN THE STATE OF NORTH CAROLINA.

SECTION 1. *Be it enacted by the General Assembly of the State of North Carolina, and it is hereby enacted by the authority of the same,* That the 4th Section of an Act, passed by the General Assembly of the State of North Carolina, during the session of 1858–'9, entitled an Act to authorize the Roanoke Navigation Company to discontinue the use of their Canal around the grand falls of the Roanoke River, and to make sale of their real estate, water-power and other privileges, between the towns of Gaston and Weldon, in the State of North Carolina, be amended, to read as follows, to-wit: That the place and terms of sale of the said property be left to the discretion of the stockholders of the Company, in general meeting assembled, including the States of Virginia and North Carolina by their proxies. **Amendment.**

SEC. 2. *Be it further enacted,* That this Act shall be in force from and after its ratification.

Ratified the 27th day of February, A. D., 1867.

CHAPTER XVIII.

AN ACT TO INCORPORATE THE NORTH CAROLINA AGRICULTURAL AND MANUFACTURING COMPANY.

SECTION 1. *Be it enacted by the General Assembly of the State of North Carolina, and it is hereby enacted by the au-*

thority of the same, That J. A. Leland, Eleazer C. Taylor, Silas L. Biglow, and their associates, successors and assigns, be, and they are hereby, created a corporation and body politic, in law and in fact, the name and style of the North Carolina Agricultural and Manufacturing Company, for the purpose of carrying on a general business of Agriculture in the State of North Carolina, to raise cotton and wool, and to manufacture the same into cloth or yarns, to produce and manufacture naval stores, and to engage in the general business of buying and selling, or bartering, in the produce of said State; to buy and sell merchandise; and, by said name and style, may sue and be sued, plead and be impleaded in any Court of Record, contract and be contracted with, have succession and a common seal, and acquire, possess, lease, sell, dispose of real and personal estate, and generally to do anything necessary to enable them to carry on their said business with advantage and profit; and shall continue for thirty years, and during said period shall sell, barter, exchange and dispose of the real and personal estate acquired in a corporate character; may own and employ and manage ships, steam vessels for the purpose of promoting emigration into the State of North Carolina, and for any other purpose connected with their business.

Corporators.
Objects.
Powers and privileges.

Sec. 2. *Be it further enacted,* That said corporation shall have power to make all necessary by-laws and regulations, not inconsistent with the Constitution of the State or the United States, for its government, and to alter and amend the same at pleasure, and to appoint such officers and agents to transact and conduct their business, and to fix the salaries thereof, as they shall from time to time deem proper.

Further powers and privileges

Sec. 3. *Be it further enacted,* That the capital stock of said corporation shall be one hundred thousand dollars, in shares of one hundred dollars each, and the capital stock of the Company may, at its discretion, be raised to one million.

Capital.

Sec. 4. *Be it further enacted,* That whenever the sum of twenty five thousand dollars is subscribed and actually paid as part of the capital stock of said company, they may organize, and may then elect such officers and directors as

Company may organize, when?

they may deem proper to the due management of their business, and may prescribe the time and manner of such elections at their first general meeting, and also when and how future general or special meetings shall be called, the scale of votes, manner of voting, the manner of issuing certificates of stock, and the mode of transferring and assigning the same. All officers, when once duly elected by said Company, shall continue until another election, or until their successors shall be appointed; the term of all officers shall not be less than one year, but any officer may, for good and sufficient cause, be removed by the President and Directors, and a successor appointed by them, to continue in office until the next regular election.

SEC. 5. *Be it further enacted,* That this Act shall be in force from and after its ratification.

Ratified the 4th day of March, A. D., 1867.

CHAPTER XIX.

AN ACT TO INCORPORATE THE NATIONAL LOAN AND TRUST COMPANY.

SECTION 1. *Be it enacted by the General Assembly of the State of North Carolina, and it is hereby enacted by the authority of the same,* That Richard B. Haywood, Richard C. Badger and James B. Johnston, of the city of Raleigh, and such other persons as may hereafter be associated with them, and their successors, are hereby created a body corporate, under the name of the National Loan and Trust Company, and by that name shall have perpetual succession, and may sue and be sued in any Court whatever, with powers and privileges as are hereinafter provided.

SEC. 2. *Be it further enacted,* That the capital stock of said Company shall not exceed one million of dollars, in shares of one hundred dollars each; but when one hundred thousand dollars shall have been actually subscribed, and

Corporators.

Capital.

fifty thousand dollars paid in cash, the said Company may organize and proceed to business under this Act.

SEC. 3. *Be it further enacted,* That the said Company shall have power to guarantee the payment, punctual performance and collection of promissory notes, bills of exchange, contracts, bonds, accounts, claims, rents, annuities, mortgages, choses in action, evidences of debt, and certificates of property, real or personal, upon such terms as may be established by the Board of Directors of said Company; to receive upon storage, deposit or otherwise, merchandise, bullion, specie, plate, stocks, bonds, moneys, promissory notes, certificates and evidences of debt, contracts or other property, and to take the necessary management, custody and charge of real and personal estate, and property in trust or otherwise, and to advance moneys, securities and credits, upon any property, real or personal, on such terms as may be established by the Directors of said Company; but no rate of interest to exceed seven per cent. per annum shall be charged or received by said Company in any transaction.

<small>Objects and purposes of Corporation.</small>

SEC. 4. *Be it further enacted,* That the business and corporate powers of said Company shall be exercised by a Board of Directors, consisting of such number of persons, not less than five and not exceeding twenty-one, as may be prescribed by the by-laws of said Company, to be elected annually, by a majority in interest of the stockholders, voting at an election to be held at such time and place as may be prescribed by the by-laws of said Company; and it shall be lawful for the said Company, by a vote of two-thirds of the said Board of Directors, with the consent of three-fourths of the stockholders, to permit dealers with the Company to participate in the profits of the business of the Company, on such terms as may be prescribed by the Board of Directors, and also to provide for the issue of script for such profits, and how far such script shall be liable for losses to be sustained by said Company, and in what manner such script shall be redeemed and paid off: *Provided,* That no dividend or payment by said Company to or on account of such script shall be made so as to impair the cash capital of the said Company

<small>Board of Directors.</small>

SEC. 5. *Be it further enacted*, That Richard B. Haywood and Richard C. Badger, shall be, and they are hereby appointed, Commissioners, to open books of subscription to the capital stock of said Company, at such time and place as they, or a majority of them, shall deem proper, and for such amounts as, in their judgment, the business of the Company may require, but for no less amount of subscription than one hundred thousand dollars, as hereinbefore provided. The persons named in the first section of this Act shall be Directors of said Company for one year after passage of this Act, and until others shall be elected in their stead; the remaining Directors for the same period shall be elected by a majority in interest of the stockholders, voting at an election to be held under the inspection of said Commissioners, within twenty days from the closing of the subscription called for by them, and all the Directors must be stockholders in said Company.

Commission ers to open Books of subscription, &c.

SEC. 6. *Be it further enacted*, That it shall be lawful for said Company to lease, purchase, hold and convey all such real or personal estate as may be necessary to carry on their business, as well as such real and personal estate as they may deem it necessary to acquire in the enforcement or settlement of any claim or demand arising out of their business transactions, and to sell or exchange the same for other property as they may determine, or the interest of the Company require, and the said Company are hereby authorized to make, execute and issue, in the transaction of their business, all necessary receipts, certificates and contracts, which receipts, certificates and contracts shall bear the impress or stamp of the seal of the Company, and shall be signed by the President and counter-signed by the Secretary or Treasurer thereof.

Powers and privileges.

SEC. 7. *Be it further enacted*, That in case any property deposited with said Company, upon which any advance shall have been made by them, shall, before the maturity of the contract, from any cause, decrease in value from the price originally fixed, said Company may give notice, in writing, to the owner of such property or his agent, to perform the conditions of the contract, or make good the de-

Proceedings in case of depreciated property, upon which advances may be made.

ficiency caused by such decrease in value, within thirty (30) days, and in default thereof may sell and dispose of such property at public sale, and out of the proceeds thereof retain the amount due then under the contract, together with the cost, charges and expenses; but nothing in this Act contained shall be held or construed to limit or affect the liability or obligation of the corporation hereby created, as the same is fixed by the common law or by Statute, any further than the same is limited or affected by the express terms of the contract in this section mentioned.

Transfers of Stock. SEC. 8. *Be it further enacted,* That the stock of said Company shall be transferable only on the books of the Company.

Liable to taxes and required to make exhibit. SEC. 9. *Be it further enacted,* That this corporation shall be liable to taxes imposed by the State on similar institutions; and for this purpose may be required to make such returns and exhibit as will enable such taxes to be laid; and this charter shall not continue longer than twenty years.

Ratified the 4th day of March, A. D., 1867.

CHAPTER XX.

AN ACT TO INCORPORATE PERQUIMANS MALE AND FEMALE ACADEMY, IN THE TOWN OF HERTFORD, COUNTY OF PERQUIMANS.

Corporators SECTION 1. *Be it enacted by the General Assembly of the State of North Carolina, and it is hereby enacted by the authority of the same,* That Willis H. Bagley, Joseph S. Granberry, Charles W. Wood, Arthur Smith Jordan and Darien B. Daughtry, and their successors, be, and they are hereby, incorporated and made a body politic, under the name and style of the Trustees of Perquimans Male and Female Academy, in the town of Hertford, county of Perquimans, with the usual rights and powers and privileges, and subject to the usual restrictions of such corporations.

SEC. 2. *Be it further enacted,* That said Trustees shall have power to fill all vacancies in said Board that may happen by death or otherwise.

SEC. 3. *Be it further enacted,* That this Act shall be in force from and after its ratification.

Ratified the 18th day of February, A. D., 1867.

CHAPTER XXI.

AN ACT TO INCORPORATE THE "PIGEON RIVER MINING AND MANUFACTURING COMPANY OF HAYWOOD COUNTY."

SECTION 1. *Be it enacted by the General Assembly of the State of North Carolina and it is hereby enacted by the authority of the same,* That William A. Dozier, John G. Eve, Samuel L. Love, Matthew H. Love, William B. Love and Alexander Calder, and their associates, successors and assigns, are hereby created and constituted a body politic and corporate, by the name and style of the "Pigeon River Mining and Manufacturing Company of Haywood county," for the purpose of working, mining and exploring for gold, copper, silver, lead, and all other minerals and metals, and for mining, vending, smelting and working the same, and for working and manufacturing metals or chemicals; and by that name may sue and be sued, plead and be impleaded, appear, prosecute and defend, in any Court of Law or Equity in this State whatsoever, in all suits and actions; may have a common seal, and the same alter at pleasure, and may enjoy all the privileges and powers incident to mining, smelting and manufacturing corporations; and may also purchase, hold and convey and mortgage any real and personal property or estate, held as capital stock, to the amount of one million of dollars.

SEC. 2. *Be it further enacted,* That said corporation shall have power to erect all necessary machinery, mills, stamping machines, build and repair roads to and from places of mining and manufacturing, to the nearest place of public Railway, either in this State or Tennessee.

<small>Stock</small>

SEC. 3. *Be it further enacted,* That said corporation may divide their stock into such number of shares, and provide for the sale and transfer thereof, in such manner and form as said corporation shall, from time to time, deem expedient, and may levy and collect assessments, forfeit and sell delinquent shares in such manner as the by-laws may direct, and shall issue scrip for the shares of stock, and each share shall entitle the holder thereof to one vote in meetings of Stockholders; and, also, said corporation shall have power to enact and pass such by-laws and regulations as they may deem necessary, not repugnant to the laws of this State and the United States.

<small>President and Directors.</small>

SEC. 4. *Be it further enacted,* That it shall be lawful for the corporation to be managed by a President and three or five Directors, who shall be stockholders, and have power to fill vacancies in their own body, shall continue in office until others are elected or appointed, and also to exercise all such rights as by this Act are conferred or granted; but the stockholders shall have power to elect said Directors annually, two of whom shall be actual residents of this State.

<small>Corporators shall be Directors until others are chosen</small>

SEC. 5. *Be it further enacted,* That the aforesaid W. A. Dozier, John G. Eve, Samuel L. Love, Matthew H. Love, William B. Love, and Alexander Calder, shall manage the affairs of said corporation as Directors, until others are elected or appointed, shall meet and organize by choosing one of their own body a President, and appoint a Secretary and other employees, make such by-laws as, for the time being, they shall deem expedient, and may then proceed to business.

<small>Directors.</small>

SEC. 6. *Be it further enacted,* That this corporation shall exist for fifty years from the passage of this Act; and that this Act to be in force from and after its passage.

Ratified the 18th day of February, A. D., 1867.

CHAPTER XXII.

AN ACT TO INCORPORATE THE MECKLENBURG FEMALE COLLEGE, IN THE CITY OF CHARLOTTE.

SECTION 1. *Be it enacted by the General Assembly of the State of North Carolina, and it is hereby enacted by the authority of the same,* That Rev. A. M. Shipp, D. D., W. A. Gamewell, J. W. North, C. Murchison, S. Lander, N. Aldrich, W. C. Power, A. G. Stacy, Prof. G. F. Round, Hon. Z. B. Vance, J. H. Wilson, Esq., Dr. C. J. Fox, W. J. Yates, C. Dowd, T. H. Brem, John Wilkes, M. L. Wriston, W. M. Mills, C. M. Ray, W. T. Shipp, J. T. Bryce and T. D. Gillespie, be and they are hereby created and constituted a body corporate, to be known by the name and style of "The Board of Trustees of the Mecklenburg Female College;" and by that name shall have succession and a common seal, and shall be able and capable in law of purchasing, holding and selling real and personal property to the value of five hundred thousand dollars, ($500,000) for the use and benefit of said College; and of suing and being sued, pleading and being impleaded in their corporate name.

Corporators.

Powers, &c

SEC. 2. *Be it further enacted,* That the said Trustees, or a majority of them, shall have power to fill all vacancies occurring in said Board, and, together with the faculty, to confer such degrees, diplomas and marks of literary distinction as are usually conferred in Colleges and Seminaries of learning; and the said Board of Trustees shall enjoy all other powers, privileges and immunities belonging to bodies corporate of the like nature, and the said corporation may exist for the period of ninety-nine (99) years.

Trustees and Faculty may confer Degrees, &c.

SEC. 3. *Be it further enacted,* That this Act shall be in force from and after its ratification.

Ratified the 27th day of February, A. D., 1867.

CHAPTER XXIII.

AN ACT TO INCORPORATE THE TOWN OF NAHUNTA, IN THE COUNTY OF WAYNE.

Name.

SECTION 1. *Be it enacted by the General Assembly of the State of North Carolina and it is hereby enacted by the authority of the same,* That the Town of Nahunta, in the county of Wayne, be, and the same is hereby incorporated by the name and style of "The Town of Nahunta," and shall be subject to all the provisions contained in the one hundred and eleventh (111th) chapter of the Revised Code.

Corporate limits.

SEC. 2. *Be it further enacted,* That the corporate limits of said Town shall be as follows: Beginning at a post on the Wilmington and Weldon Rail Road, eighty (80) poles north of the warehouse, and runs south seventy-two, east forty poles to a post, then south eighteen, west one hundred and sixty poles to a post, then north eighteen east, one hundred and sixty poles to a post, then south seventy-two west, crossing the Rail Road eighty poles to a post, then north eighteen, east one hundred and sixty poles to a post, then south seventy-two east forty poles to the beginning.

SEC. 3. *Be it further enacted,* That this Act shall be in force from and after its ratification.

Ratified the 18th day of February, A. D., 1867.

CHAPTER XXIV.

AN ACT TO AUTHORIZE THE DISMAL SWAMP CANAL COMPANY TO ISSUE EIGHT PER CENT. BONDS.

SECTION 1. *Be it enacted by the General Assembly of the State of North Carolina, and it is hereby enacted by the authority of the same,* That it may and shall be lawful for the

Dismal Swamp Canal Company to issue Coupon Bonds bearing interest at the rate of eight per cent. per annum, the principal to be paid at such time and place as may be deemed by the Company most expedient, and the interest to be paid semi-annually at such place as may be determined on for the payment of the principal of such bonds: *Provided*, That the whole amount of bonds which shall be issued under this Act shall not exceed the sum of two hundred thousand dollars. Character of Bonds.

SEC. 2. *Be it further enacted*, That the said Company be and they are hereby authorized to sell and dispose of the bonds authorized by this Act, in such mode and on such terms as they may deem advisable, and to give such security for the punctual payment of the said bonds as they may deem expedient. Power to dispose of Bonds.

SEC. 3. *Be it further enacted*, That this Act shall be in force from and after its ratification.

Ratified the 11th day of December, A. D. 1866.

CHAPTER XXV.

AN ACT TO INCORPORATE THE TOWN OF DURHAM IN THE COUNTY OF ORANGE.

SECTION 1. *Be it enacted by the General Assembly of the State of North Carolina, and it is hereby enacted by the authority of the same,* That the Town of Durham, in the county of Orange, be and the same is hereby incorporated by the name and style of the Town of Durham, and shall be subject to all the provisions contained in the 111th chapter of the Revised Code. Name.

SEC. 2. *Be it further enacted,* That the corporate limits of said Town shall extend one-half mile in all directions from the ware-house of the North Carolina Rail Road in said Town. Limits.

SEC. 3. *Be it further enacted,* That this Act shall be in force from and after its ratification.

Ratified the 22d day of December, A. D., 1866.

CHAPTER XXVI.

AN ACT TO AMEND SECTION 2ND OF AN ACT TO INCORPORATE THE TOWN OF MARSHALL.

Change of time of municipal election.

SECTION 1. *Be it enacted by the General Assembly of the State of North Carolina, and it is hereby enacted by the authority of the same,* That the 2nd section of an Act incorporating the town of Marshall, in Madison county, ratified the — day of March, 1863, be so amended as to allow an election, for the purposes mentioned in said Act, to take place, for the present year only, on the Saturday immediately preceding the first term of the County Court, for said county, to be held in the year 1867.

SEC. 2. *Be it further enacted,* That this Act shall be in force from and after its ratification.

Ratified the 22nd day of December, A. D., 1866.

CHAPTER XXVII.

AN ACT TO INCORPORATE THE COLLINS GOLD MINING COMPANY IN THE COUNTY OF FRANKLIN.

SECTION 1. *Be it enacted by the General Assembly of the State of North Carolina, and it is hereby enacted by the authority of the same,* That Thomas K. Thomas, S. G. Sturgis, James H. Platt, Dr. Ellis Malone, and Charles H. Thomas, and their associates, successors and assigns, be and they are hereby enacted and constituted a body politic and corporate, by the name and style and title of the "Collins Gold Mining Company," for the purpose of working, mining and exploring for gold, copper and other minerals and metals, in the county of Franklin, and for mining, smelting, working and vending the same, with power to pur-

Corporators.

Objects.

Powers.

chase, take, hold, sell, mortgage, lease, or convey real or personal estate, with a capital stock not to exceed five hundred thousand dollars.

SEC. 2. *Be it further enacted,* That said corporation may divide their stock into shares of not less than fifty dollars each, issue certificates therefor, elect a President, Directors and all other necessary officers, have succession and a common seal, and make and adopt rules, regulations and by-laws for the government of said Company, and be entitled to all the rights, privileges and immunities and subject to all the restrictions contained in chapter twenty-six (26) of the Revised Code, entitled "Corporations." Stock, Directors, &c.

SEC. 4. *Be it further enacted,* That this Act shall be in force from and after its ratification.

Ratified the 22d day of December, A. D., 1866.

CHAPTER XXVIII.

AN ACT TO INCORPORATE THE THOMAS GOLD MINING COMPANY, IN THE COUNTY OF FRANKLIN.

SECTION 1. *Be it enacted by the General Assembly of the State of North Carolina, and it is hereby enacted by the authority of the same,* That Thomas K. Thomas, S. G. Sturgis, James H. Platt, Dr. Ellis Malone and Charles H. Thomas, and their associates, successors and assigns, be, and they are hereby, created a body politic and corporate, by the name, style and title of the "Thomas Gold Mining Company," for the purpose of working, mining and exploring for gold, copper and all other metals and minerals, in the county of Franklin, and for mining, smelting, working and vending the same, with the power to purchase, take, hold, sell, mortgage, lease or convey real or personal estate, with a capital stock not to exceed five hundred thousand dollars. Corporators.

Objects.

Powers, &c.

SEC. 2. *Be it further enacted,* That said Corporation may divide their stock into shares of not less than fifty dollars each, issue certificates therefor, elect a President, Directors and all other necessary officers; have succession and a com- Stock, Directors, &c.

mon seal, and make and adopt rules, regulations and by-laws for the government of the said Company, and be entitled to all the rights, privileges and immunities, and subject to all the restrictions contained in chapter twenty-six, (26) of the Revised Code, entitled "Corporations."

Sec. 3. *Be it further enacted,* That this Corporation shall exist for thirty years, and that this Act shall be in force from and after its ratification.

Ratified the 22nd day of December, A. D., 1866.

CHAPTER XXIX.

AN ACT TO INCORPORATE THE STURGIS GOLD MINING COMPANY, IN THE COUNTY OF FRANKLIN.

Section 1. *Be it enacted by the General Assembly of the State of North Carolina, and it is hereby enacted by the authority of the same,* That Thomas K. Thomas, S. G. Sturgis, James H. Platt, Dr. Ellis Malone and Charles H. Thomas, and their associates, successors and assigns, be, and they are hereby, created and constituted a body politic and corporate, by the name, style and title of the "Sturgis Gold Mining Company," for the purpose of working, mining and exploring for gold, copper, and all other metals and minerals, in the county of Franklin, and for mining, smelting, working and vending the same, with power to purchase, hold, sell, mortgage, lease or convey, real or personal estate, with a capital not to exceed five hundred thousand dollars.

Sec. 2. *Be it further enacted,* That said corporation may divide their stock into shares, not less than fifty dollars each, issue certificates therefor, elect a President, Directors and all other necessary officers, have succession and a common seal, and make and adopt rules, regulations and by-laws, for the government of said Company, and be entitled to all the rights, privileges and immunities, and subject to all the restrictions, contained in chapter twenty-six, (26,) Revised Code, entitled "Corporations."

SEC. 3. *Be it further enacted*, That this corporation shall exist for thirty years, and that this Act shall be in force from and after its ratification.

Ratified the 22d day of December, A. D., 1866.

CHAPTER XXX.

AN ACT TO INCORPORATE WILSON LODGE, NO. 226, OF FREE AND ACCEPTED MASONS.

SECTION 1. *Be it enacted by the General Assembly of the State of North Carolina, and it is hereby enacted by the authority of the same,* That Perry Tomlin, Charles R. Jones, D. B. White, Henry A. Mowbray, G. W. Clegg, T. M. Gill, Charles Howell, John F. Foard, and other officers and members of the Lodge of Free and Accepted Masons, at Olin, in Iredell county, with their successors, are hereby incorporated by the name and style of Wilson Lodge, number two hundred and twenty-six, subject to the provisions of chapter twenty-six, of the Revised Code. *Corporators* *Name.*

SEC. 2. *Be it further enacted,* That this Act shall be in force from and after its ratification.

Ratified the 18th day of February, A. D., 1867.

CHAPTER XXXI.

AN ACT TO INCORPORATE THE ST. PHILLIP'S SINGING SOCIETY OF NEW BERNE.

SECTION 1. *Be it enacted by the General Assembly of the State of North Carolina and it is hereby enacted by the authority of the same,* That the Trustees which at present are, or in future may be, of the St. Phillip's Episcopal Singing Society, in the city of New Berne, be and the same are hereby incorporated and declared to be a body politic and corporate, under the name and style of the St. Phillip's *Name.*

Powers.

Objects.

Episcopal Singing Society, and by such name and style shall have succession and a common seal, sue and be sued, plead and be impleaded, acquire and transfer property, real and personal, to the value of five thousand dollars, and pass all such by-laws and regulations as may be necessary and proper for the promotion of their objects (improvement in Church music) and which shall not be inconsistent with the laws of this State and of the United States.

Ratified the 18th day of February, A. D., 1867.

CHAPTER XXXII.

AN ACT TO INCORPORATE THE ROCKFORD MALE AND FEMALE SEMINARY, AT ROCKFORD, SURRY COUNTY.

Corporators.

SECTION 1. *Be it enacted by the General Assembly of the State of North Carolina, and it is hereby enacted by the authority of the same,* That M. Y. Folger, T. J. Williams, W. M. Norman, P. H. Dobson, R. S. Folger, L. C. Turner and L. H. Burns, be, and they are hereby, constituted a body politic and corporate, by the name and style of the "Trustees of Rockford Male and Female Seminary," and by that name may sue and be sued, plead and be impleaded; shall have perpetual succession and a common seal; may acquire by purchase, gift or otherwise, to them and their successors, estates, real and personal, for the use of said Seminary; and enjoy all other powers, privileges and immunities incident to bodies corporate of a like nature.

Powers, privileges, &c.

Quorum.

SEC. 2. *Be it further enacted,* That any three of said Trustees may constitute a quorum for the transaction of business, and in case of any vacancy by death, removal, resignation or otherwise, any three of said Trustees shall have power to fill vacancies thereby occasioned.

Spirituous liquors not to be retailed within 2 miles of Seminary.

SEC. 3. *Be it further enacted,* That no license to retail spirituous liquors, at the site or within two miles of said Seminary, shall be granted, and, if granted, the same shall be void.

Sec. 4. *Be it further enacted*, That no person in the State, without permission in writing from the Principal of said Seminary, shall sell or deliver to any student of the said Seminary, or to any other person, any spirituous liquors, for the purpose of being used, or with the knowledge that the same will be used, at said Seminary, or within two miles thereof, by any student. *Further regarding spirituous liquors.*

Sec. 5. *Be it further enacted*, That any person who shall offend against any of the provisions of this Act, shall be deemed guilty of a misdemeanor. *Penalty.*

Sec. 6. *Be it further enacted*, That this act shall be in force from and after its ratification.

Ratified the 18th day of February, A. D., 1867.

CHAPTER XXXIII.

AN ACT TO INCORPORATE THE MERCHANTS' AND PLANTERS' MUTUAL BENEFIT COMPANY.

Section 1. *Be it enacted by the General Assembly of the State of North Carolina, and it is hereby enacted by the authority of the same*, That Robert H. Cowan, Edward D. Hall and James W. Lippitt, of the city of Wilmington, and their associates, are hereby constituted and appointed a body corporate and politic, under the style and name of the "Merchants' and Planters' Mutual Benefit Company." *Corporators*

Sec. 2. *Be it further enacted*, That said Company shall have power to make advancements of money upon growing crops of every kind and description, and that a lien shall attach upon said crop to the amount advanced, including legal interest and commissions, subject, however, to the claim of registration hereafter set forth. *May make advancements on growing crops, when lien shall attach.*

Sec. 3. *Be it further enacted*, That said Company shall have power to advance money for the purpose of entering into the business of planting crops, and that a lien shall attach from the time of casting of said crops, until the amount so advanced, with interest and commissions agreed *Advance money for planting interests, when lien shall attach.*

upon between the parties, are satisfied and paid, subject to the claim of registration hereafter set forth: *Provided, however,* that the lien shall be postponed in favor of the landlord, where advances may be made to tenants.

SEC. 4. *Be it further enacted,* That said Company shall have power to solicit investments by and through its Agents, or otherwise, for the purpose of this charter, and give and take such acquittance, receipts and vouchers, for the bonding, loaning and management of the same, as the by-laws of said company shall direct.

SEC. 5. *Be it further enacted,* That all receipts given by the parties receiving the money advanced, shall be registered in the county where the land is situate, upon which the crop or crops shall be grown, and that a lien shall take effect from the date of registration; and the corporate privileges herein granted shall continue for seven years.

Ratified the 12th day of February, A. D., 1867.

CHAPTER XXXIV.

AN ACT TO INCORPORATE WILMINGTON INSTITUTE IN THE CITY OF WILMINGTON, COUNTY OF NEW HANOVER.

SECTION 1. *Be it enacted by the General Assembly of the State of North Carolina, and it is hereby enacted by the authority of the same,* That Robert H. Cowan, Dr. Armand J. DeRosset, John Bauman, Claus Tierhen and Levi McGinney, and their successors in office, be, and the same are hereby, constituted a body politic and corporate, to be known and distinguished by the name and style of "The Trustees of Wilmington Institute," and by that name shall have succession and a common seal; and shall be able and capable, in law, of holding lands, tenements and chattels, sufficient for the purpose and design of the Institute; and of suing and being sued, and of pleading and being impleaded; with full power of making all needful rules and by-laws for the government of the said Institute, not incon-

Corporators.

Powers and Privileges.

sistent with the constitution of this State and of the United States; and they are hereby invested with all other powers and rights necessary or usually appertaining to municipal corporations.

SEC. 2. *Be it further enacted,* That this Act shall be in force from and after its ratification.

Ratified the 25th day of February, A. D., 1867.

CHAPTER XXXV.

AN ACT TO AMEND THE CHARTER OF THE TOWN OF MURFREESBORO', IN THE COUNTY OF HERTFORD.

SECTION 1. *Be it enacted by the General Assembly of the State of North Carolina, and it is hereby enacted by the authority of the same,* That no person or persons shall hereafter be granted, by the Justices of the County Court of Hertford, any license to sell at retail a less quantity than one-half gallon of any spir'tuous, fermented or malt liquors or wines, in or within two miles of the corporate limits of the town of Murfreesboro', in the county of Hertford, unless the persons applying therefor, in addition to the other requirements of the law as it now exists, shall exhibit the consent in writing of the Commissioners in said Town, in general meeting assembled, under the penalty of one hundred dollars for each and every offence, to be recovered by warrant or writ before any person or persons having jurisdiction over the same; said sum, when collected, to be applied and accounted for as other money by the Commissioners of said Town.

Consent of Commissioners necessary to obtaining license to retail spirituous liquors.

SEC. 2. *Be it further enacted,* That this Act shall be in force from and after its ratification.

Ratified the 11th day February, A. D., 1867.

CHAPTER XXXVI.

AN ACT TO INCORPORATE THE TUCKASEEGE GOLD AND COPPER MINING COMPANY.

SECTION 1. *Be it enacted by the General Assembly of the State of North Carolina, and it is hereby enacted by the authority of the same,* That Robert G. A. Love, Samuel L. Love, Henry Platt, W. H. Thomas and Thomas P. Love, and their associates, successors and assigns, be, and they are hereby, created and constituted a body corporate and politic, by the name and style of "The Tuckaseege Gold and Copper Mining Company," and, as such, shall have succession, and may have and use a common seal, and change the same at pleasure ; may sue and be sued, plead and be impleaded, in any Court of Law and Equity ; have power to make all such by-laws and regulations (not inconsistent with the laws and constitution of this State) as may be deemed necessary for the government of the said Company, which shall be binding thereon ; and shall have, exercise and enjoy, all the rights and privileges of a body corporate, necessary to carry on the business of mining, smelting and manufacturing, and of transporting and vending their products, and shall also have the power to purchase, lease, hold, dispose of and convey any estate, real, personal or mixed : *Provided,* That the said Company shall, at no time, hold more than five thousand acres of land.

SEC. 2. *Be it further enacted,* That the capital stock of said Company may be divided into such number of shares and of such amount for each share as the stockholders thereof may, in general meetings, direct : *Provided,* That the capital stock shall not exceed one million of dollars, which shares shall be considered as personal property, and certificates therefor may be issued, and the same made transferable and assignable, and liable to assessment, for-

Corporators.

Powers and privileges.

Restriction.

Capital stock.

feiture and sale, by the Board of Directors, in such manner as the by-laws of the Corporation shall prescribe.

SEC. 3. *Be it further enacted,* That the affairs of said Company shall be managed by a Board of Directors, one, at least, of whom shall be a citizen of this State, who must be stockholders, composed of such number, and elected by the stockholders, in such manner as the by-laws shall direct, and they shall choose one of their number to be President of the Board and of the Company. Three of the Board of Directors shall be a quorum to transact business, of whom the President, or one appointed by him to fill the place, shall always be one; they shall have power to fill any vacancies that may happen in their body, and, until the first election of Directors shall be held by the stockholders, the said Robert G. A. Love, Samuel L. Love, W. H. Thomas, Thomas P. Love and Henry Platt shall constitute the Board of Directors of said Company, with full power and authority to exercise all the corporate powers thereof.

Directors.

SEC. 4. *Be it further enacted,* That general meetings of the stockholders in said Company may be called and held as the by-laws shall prescribe; to constitute a meeting, there must be present, in person or by proxy, (the proxy being a stockholder) those who hold a majority of the stock, each share of which shall entitle the holder to one vote; and every act shall require the sanction of a majority of the votes which may be present.

General meetings.

SEC. 5. *Be it further enacted,* That this Act shall not be so construed as to give to the said Company any banking privileges or to exempt the lands and other property of the Corporation from taxation.

Banking privileges forbidden. Liability to taxes.

SEC. 6. *Be it further enacted,* That this Act shall take effect and be in force from and after its ratification, and continue in force for the period of thirty years.

Ratified the 19th day of February, A. D., 1867.

CHAPTER XXXVII.

AN ACT TO AUTHORIZE THE FORMATION OF THE ENGLISH AND AMERICAN WOOL AND VINE GROWING, MANUFACTURING, MINERAL AND AGRICULTURAL ASSOCIATION IN THE UNITED STATES OF AMERICA.

SECTION 1. *Be it enacted by the General Assembly of the State of North Carolina, and it is hereby enacted by the authority of the same,* That G. B. Tennent, N. W. Woodfin, R. B. Vance, S. M. Hatch, George S. Cameron, Robert McDowell, Geo. C. Bogart, Lyman W. Gilbert, P. Kimberly, and their associates, are hereby constituted a body politic *Corporators* and corporate, under the name and style of " The English and American Wool and Vine growing, Manufacturing, Mining and Agricultural Association, in the United States of America," for the purpose of purchasing lands, holding and disposing of the same, of carrying on the wool and vine growing, manufacturing, mining, agricultural, mechanical, and other business necessary to a full develop- *Powers and privileges.* ment and successful prosecution of a large enterprise, embracing the above named branches of industry, and to continue in existence for a period of thirty years, with power to make and use a common seal, and to alter and change the same at pleasure; and to make such by-laws, not inconsistent with the laws of the State and of the United States, as they may deem useful and necessary, to sue and be sued, plead and be impleaded, to hold, by purchase or otherwise, and dispose of the same in any way which may be deemed useful and necessary for carrying on their operations, or which may become possessed of in prosecution of their business.

Capital. SEC. 2. *Be it further enacted,* That the capital stock of said corporation shall be one million of dollars, with the privilege of increasing it to such sum as the Company may deem essential to the vigorous prosecution of their business, and shall be divided into shares of one hundred dollars each. The amount of capital stock may be increased at any annual meeting of the Stockholders, or at any special meeting of the same, called for that purpose.

SEC. 3. *Be it further enacted,* That the said corporators, and their associates, shall have the right to invest such portion of the capital stock of the said corporation in real estate and personal property, as they may deem for the best interest of the corporation, and such property may be received by them in payment for subscriptions of said capital stock. The subscriptions to the capital stock of the Company may be obtained by opening books of subscription, or by private and personal solicitation, as the said corporation may deem most desirable. May invest capital in real estate, &c., or receive subscriptions in the same.

SEC. 4. *Be it further enacted,* That the said corporation shall have an office for the transaction of business in the county or district where their operations are carried on. and they may have offices in other places, if they shall deem it for the interest of the Company to establish them. Offices of the corporation.

SEC. 5. *Be it further enacted,* T at all subscribers to the capital stock, who shall not have paid their subscriptions according to the terms agreed upon, shall be liable to the creditors of the said corporation for all amounts remaining upon their said subscriptions, and may be proceeded against in the usual way and manner for the collection of the same. Delinquents

SEC. 6. *Be it further enacted,* That the business of said corporation shall be managed by a Board of Directors, of not less than five nor more than thirteen, one of whom shall be President. The Directors shall be elected annually, when the number of the Directors for the year shall be determined by a vote of the Stockholders; but a failure to elect shall not work a forfeiture of the charter, but the Directors and officers of the previous year shall continue in office until others are elected in their stead: *Provided,* That one or more of said Directors shall be residents of the State of North Carolina. At all meetings of the Stockholders, each share of stock shall entitle the holder to one vote, which may be voted in person or by proxy The place of Directors.

19

meeting of Stockholders, to be fixed by the Board of Directors, and due notice given by the same.

Transfers of stock.
SEC. 7. *Be it further enacted,* That the stock of this Company shall be taken and regarded as personal property, and transferable on the books of the Company, as the by-laws shall prescribe.

SEC. 8. *Be it further enacted,* That this Act shall be in force from and after its ratification.

Ratified the 28th day of February, A. D., 1867.

CHAPTER XXXVIII.

AN ACT TO INCORPORATE THE SOUTH UNION MANUFACTURING COMPANY OF RICHMOND COUNTY.

Corporators.
SECTION 1. *Be it enacted by the General Assembly of the State of North Carolina, and it is hereby enacted by the authority of the same,* That Robert J. Steele, Jr., and John Shortridge, their associates, successors and assigns, be and they are hereby created a corporation and body politic, in law and in fact, by the name and style of the South Union Manufacturing Company of Richmond county, and in that

Privileges and powers.
name and style may sue and be sued, plead and be impleaded in any Court of Record, contract and be contracted with, have perpetual succession and a common seal, and acquire, own and possess real and personal estate, and shall so continue for the term of thirty years.

Objects.
SEC. 2. *Be it further enacted,* That the said corporation shall have power to establish factories and mills for the manufacture of cotton, wool, hemp, flax, leather, iron and other like materials, upon Hitchcock Creek, in the county of Richmond, and for no other purpose.

SEC. 3. *Be it further enacted,* That within ninety days after the passage of this Act, that any three of the Stockholders in the Company may call a general meeting of the Company, at any convenient place in Rockingham, and proceed to elect three Directors, requiring a majority of the votes present to make a choice, and the Directors thus chosen shall, from among themselves, choose a President, provided that a majority of the stock be represented in said meeting; and annually thereafter the Stockholders shall meet in Rockingham, at such place as the Board of Directors shall designate, for the purpose of electing three Directors, which Directors, thus chosen by a majority of votes present, shall appoint one of their number President; the Directors having appointed a President, the President and the other Directors shall be termed the Board of Directors, which Board of Directors shall appoint the other officers who may be required, and make such rules, regulations and by-laws for the same, as may be deemed necessary, and manage the business of the concern for one year: *Provided, always*, That a majority of the stock shall be represented at such meeting, and the Board of Directors shall be considered in office until other Directors are chosen. A majority of the Board of Directors shall be capable of transacting business, and, in case of the absence of the President, appoint a President *pro tem*.

<small>Directors &c.</small>

SEC. 4. *Be it further enacted*, That the Board of Directors may, at any time, call a general meeting of the Stockholders, and the Stockholders, or as many of them as hold or represent one-fourth of the whole, may at any time call a general meeting of the Stockholders, and at such meeting, a majority of the votes thereto agreeing, all officers and Directors of the Company may be removed and others appointed in their stead; and such general meeting may, if necessary, do and perform whatever may be done and performed at the annual meeting of the Stockholders in furtherance of the general welfare of the corporation.

<small>General Meetings.</small>

SEC. 5. *Be it further enacted*, That the capital stock of said corporation shall consist of two hundred and fifty shares of one hundred dollars each, and that the Stockholders may have power to increase said capital stock to seven hundred and fifty shares, whenever the business of said corporation may require it, the necessity of such increase of stock and the amount to be determined by a general meeting of the

<small>Capital.</small>

Stockholders, a majority of the capital stock already subscribed being represented in said general meeting.

SEC. 6. *Be it further enacted*, That the stock of said Company shall be deemed and taken as personal estate and may be transferred in such manner as the Board of Directors may, from time to time, point out.

Transfers of stock.

SEC. 7. *Be it further enacted*, That the said corporation, through their Board of Directors, may make contracts or become bound by instruments, security or agreement in writing, signed by the President or any other person duly authorized by him; but the legal estate in the lands, tenements, hereditaments claimed by the Company shall pass to the purchaser only by deed under the corporate seal of the corporation and the signature of the President.

SEC. 8. *Be it further enacted*, That any legal process against the corporation may be served on the President, and in case he is not in the State or avoids service, the service of the same on any of the Directors shall be deemed sufficient.

SEC. 9. *Be it further enacted*, That the Stockholders at the general meeting shall appoint a Chairman, who shall preside for the time being; the meeting shall keep a fair record of their proceedings upon all questions; each Stockholder shall be entitled to one vote for each share by him held, and may vote in person or by proxy in such manner as shall be, from time to time, prescribed by the Board of Directors. It shall require Stockholders representing a majority of the stock to form a general meeting.

Scale of voting.

SEC. 10. *Be it further enacted*, That the President shall convene the Board of Directors whenever he may deem it necessary, or whenever two of the Directors may require him to do so, and that all transactions in meetings of the Board of Directors shall be determined by a majority vote.

Board of Directors.

SEC. 11. *Be it further enacted*, That the Board of Directors shall, when deemed expedient, declare semi-annually dividends of the nett profits of the Company.

Dividends.

SEC. 12. *Be it further enacted*, That this Act shall be in force from and after its ratification.

Ratified the 11th day of February, A. D., 1867.

CHAPTER XXXIX.

AN ACT TO INCORPORATE THE TOWN OF SCOTLAND NECK, IN THE COUNTY OF HALIFAX.

SECTION 1. *Be it enacted by the General Assembly of the State of North Carolina, and it is hereby enacted by the authority of the same,* That a town is hereby established in the county of Halifax, by the name and style of Scotland Neck, the corporate limits of which said town of Scotland Neck shall be as follows, to-wit: Beginning on the south side of the road leading through the village of Greenwood, seven hundred and sixty feet from the centre of the road leading to Clarksville; thence North 12½ W. 1750 feet, thence N. 14, E. 6440 feet, thence S. 76, W. 2280 feet, thence S. 14, W. 6440 feet, thence S. 12½, E. 1050 feet, thence S. 86, W. 2100 feet to the beginning. Corporate limits.

SEC. 2. *Be it further enacted,* That the government of the said Town of Scotland Neck shall be vested in the following named persons, to-wit: John Nichols, Eli C. Biggs and N. B. Josey, and their successors in office. Commissioners.

SEC. 3. *Be it further enacted,* That the Commissioners aforesaid, to-wit: John Nichols, Eli C. Biggs and N. B. Josey, and their duly appointed successors in office, as hereinafter provided, shall be, and they are hereby, incorporated and constituted a body politic and corporate, by the name and style of the Commissioners of the town of Scotland Neck, and by that name and style shall have perpetual succession and a common seal, with all the rights, privileges, immunities and powers granted to and vested in corporations, by virtue of chapter one hundred and eleven, of the Revised Code of North Carolina. Corporate powers and privileges.

SEC. 4. *Be it further enacted,* That an election shall be held once in each and every year, on the first Monday of January, by the inhabitants of said town of Scotland Neck, who have been domiciled within the corporate limits of Annual elections.

said Town for three months immediately preceding the day of election, qualified to vote for members of the House of Commons of the General Assembly of North Carolina, for five Commissioners of the aforesaid Town, who shall hold their office for or e year, or until their successors are elected and qualified.

SEC. 5. *Be it further enacted*, That the Commissioners, to-wit: John Nichols, Eli C. Biggs, and N. B. Josey, appointed by this Act, shall be and continue such, until their successors are elected and qualified.

SEC. 6. *Be it further enacted*, That this Act shall be in force from and after its ratification.

Ratified the 21st day of February, A. D., 1867.

CHAPTER XL.

AN ACT TO INCORPORATE THE COLORED EDUCATIONAL ASSOCIATION, OF NORTH CAROLINA.

Corporators.

SECTION 1. *Be it enacted by the General Assembly of the State of North Carolina, and it is hereby enacted by the authority of the same,* That James H. Harris, Handy Lockhart, Moses Patterson, W. H. Anderson, John R. Caswell, W. H. Matthews, Robert Wyche, Wilson Morgan, J. E. O'Hara, colored persons and residents of the county of Wake, and their successors and associates, are hereby incorporated into a body politic, under the name and style of "The Colored Educational Association of North Carolina," with power and for the purpose of establishing Schools and encouraging and promoting generally Education among the colored children of the State, and may, for such purpose, receive donations and acquire and hold estate of any kind, not exceeding one hundred thousand dollars in value.

Objects.

SEC. 2. *Be it further enacted,* That the persons hereby incorporated may, in their discretion, and whenever they deem it advisable, associate with them so many other colored persons, in the State, as may be sufficient to keep ten members in the county of Wake, and five or a less number in each or any of the other counties of the State, and every person becoming a member shall signify the same in writing, filed among the archives of the corporation, and the corporation shall have all the powers that may be proper for the purpose of the Association, and be subject to all the provisions set forth in chapter twenty-six, (26) of the Revised Code of this State.

SEC. 3. *Be it further enacted,* That whenever any person who may have been associated as a member for any particular county shall cease to be a resident of such county, he shall cease to be a member of the Corporation. Concerning residence of members.

SEC. 4. *Be it further enacted,* That this Act shall go into effect on its ratification.

Ratified the 2nd day of March, A. D., 1867.

CHAPTER XLI.

AN ACT TO AMEND AN ACT ENTITLED "THE NORTH CAROLINA JOINT STOCK PUBLISHING COMPANY."

SECTION 1. *Be it enacted by the General Assembly of the State of North Carolina, and it is hereby enacted by the authority of the same,* That the charter of the North Carolina Joint Stock Publishing Company be amended as follows, to-wit: In section 1st. striking out "Christian Advocate Joint Stock;" making the title of the Company "The North Carolina Publishing Company." Also in same section, after the words, "divided into shares," strike out "one hundred dollars," and insert, instead thereof, the words, "as shall be prescribed in the by-laws of said Company." Amendment.

Ratified the 14th day of February, A. D., 1867.

CHAPTER XLII.

AN ACT TO INCORPORATE "THE WILMINGTON MANUFACTURING COMPANY."

SECTION 1. *Be it enacted by the General Assembly of the State of North Carolina, and it is hereby enacted by the authority of the same,* That Thomas E. Roberts, Henry H. Roberts, Edwin A. Keith, J. M. Motley, George C. Preston and T. M. Niven, and their associates, successors and assigns, are hereby created and constituted a body politic and corporate, by the name of "The Wilmington Manufacturing Company," for the purpose of manufacturing various kinds of articles, wood, iron and other ma crials, and may purchase and hold, sell, mortgage, lease or convey real and personal estate or property, with a capital not to exceed three hundred thousand dollars.

SEC. 2. *Be it further enacted,* That said corporation may divide their stock into shares of not less than one hundred dollars, issue certificates therefor, elect a President, Directors, and all other necessary officers, and make and adopt rules, regulations and by-laws for the government of said Company, and be entitled to all the rights, privileges and immunities, and subject to all the restrictions, contained in chapter twenty-six, of the Revised Code, entitled "Corporations."

SEC. 3. *Be it further enacted,* That this corporation shall exist for thirty years, and this Act be in force from and after its ratification.

Ratified the 26th day of February, A. D., 1867.

Corporators

Objects.

Capital.

Powers and privileges.

CHAPTER XLIII.

AN ACT TO INCORPORATE THE NEW BERNE LODGE, NO. 245, ANCIENT YORK MASONS.

SECTION 1. *Be it enacted by the General Assembly of the State of North Carolina, and it is hereby enacted by the authority of the same,* That James O. Whitmore, P. B. Rice, John Fair, Jr., C. W. Gunn, George L. Campbell, T. M. Cowles, W. H. S. Sweet, and other officers and members of New Berne Lodge, No. 245, of Free and Accepted Masons, at New Berne, in Craven county, and their successors, are hereby incorporated a body politic, by the name and style of "New Berne Lodge, number two hundred and forty-five," subject to the provisions of chapter twenty-six of the Revised Code.

Corporators.

SEC. 2. *Be it further enacted,* That this act shall be in force from and after its ratification.

Ratified the 4th day of February, A. D., 1867.

CHAPTER XLIV.

AN ACT TO INCORPORATE THE TOWN OF COLUMBIA, IN THE COUNTY OF TYRRELL.

SECTION 1. *Be it enacted by the General Assembly of the State of North Carolina, and it is hereby enacted by the authority of the same,* That William D. Carsturpton, John McCleese, S. S. Hassell, E. Lee and William Happer, and their successors in office, be, and they are hereby, appointed and constituted a body politic and corporate, under the name and style of "The Commissioners of the Town of Columbia," and by that name may have succession and common seal, sue and be sued, and have and enjoy all t rights and privileges enumerated in chapter one hundred

Corporators.

Powers, &c.

and eleven, (111) of the Revised Code, entitled "Towns," and the said Commissioners or their successors, if at any time there should be a failure to elect at the time appointed, shall remain in office until their successors are elected and duly qualified.

SEC. 2. *Be it further enacted,* That the said Town of Columbia shall be embraced within the following boundaries, in the county of Tyrrell, to-wit: Beginning at the Ferry wharf, on the east side of Scuppernong River, and running up the said river south fifty poles, then east one hundred and twenty-five poles, then west one hundred and twenty-fives poles to the said river, then along the said river to the beginning.

<small>Limits.</small>

SEC. 3. *Be it further enacted,* That all laws and clauses of laws that may come in conflict with this Act be and they are hereby repealed, and that this Act shall be in force from and after its ratification.

Ratified the 2nd day of March, A. D., 1867.

CHAPTER XLV.

AN ACT TO INCORPORATE THE NORTH CAROLINA LAND AGENCY FOR THE ENCOURAGEMENT OF IMMIGRATION.

SECTION 1. *Be it enacted by the General Assembly of the State of North Carolina, and it is hereby enacted by the authority of the same,* That R. C. Badger, C. B. Root, Jas. Litchford, jr., F. G. Foster and J. G. Hester, and their associates and successors, are hereby constituted a body corporate and politic, under the name and style of "The North Carolina Land Agency for the encouragement of Immigration," and, as such, shall have succession, use a common seal, may sue and be sued, plead and be impleaded, and shall have all other powers necessary and incident to corporate bodies, and shall and may hold, possess and acquire, all such real and personal estate as shall be proper

<small>Corporators.</small>

<small>Powers & privileges.</small>

and necessary to carry out the purposes of the said Company as hereinafter provided.

SEC. 2. *Be it further enacted,* That said Company may pass all such by-laws as may be necessary to the complete organization of the same, and may elect such officers, and for such terms, as shall be prescribed in such by-laws, and may require and take from such officers, entrusted with the monies of the said Company, such bond as the said by-laws shall prescribe. Further powers.

SEC. 3. *Be it further enacted,* That the capital stock of said Company shall not exceed five hundred thousand dollars, and the shares shall be each one hundred dollars, and may be subscribed at such time and place as shall be prescribed by the officers thereof. Capital.

SEC. 4. *Be it further enacted,* That for the encouragement of immigration and the settlement of the uncultivated lands of this State, said Company shall have the power to divide the property, placed in their hands for sale, into such a number of shares as shall cover the total amount of said property, such shares to be of such amount as shall be prescribed by the by-laws of said Company, which shares may be sold to the share-holders; and when the whole number of said shares are sold, the property, together with the list of said share-holders, are to be placed in the hands of the Committee of Division hereafter provided for, who shall at once proceed to divide such property by lot amongst said share-holders. Purposes and manner of operation.

SEC. 5. *Be it further enacted,* That said Agency shall have the power to appoint a committee of five, to be styled the Committee of Division, three of whom shall have the power to act, and whose duties shall be as provided in the preceding section. Committee of Division.

SEC. 6. *Be it further enacted,* That whenever such real estate or personal property shall be placed in the hands of said Agency for sale, it shall be lawful for said Agency to advance to the owner thereof as much as fifty per cent. of the value of such property, at a rate of interest not exceeding eight per cent., taking, as a security therefor, a mortgage, with power of sale, from said owners. May make advances on property.

Charitable provision. SEC. 7. *Be it further enacted,* That two shares in every division made as provided for in the third section of this Act, shall be given to the relief and benefit of the poor in this State, said shares being divided among the different counties of the State by lot.

SEC. 8. *Be it further enacted,* That the privileges herein granted shall be subject to the same restrictions as are contained in chapter 26, Revised Code.

Ratified the 1st day of March, A. D., 1867.

CHAPTER XLVI.

AN ACT TO AMEND AN ACT PASSED BY THE GENERAL ASSEMBLY, AT THE SESSION OF 1838–'39, ENTITLED AN ACT TO INCORPORATE THE TRUSTEES OF GREENSBORO' FEMALE COLLEGE, IN THE COUNTY OF GUILFORD.

Powers and privileges of Trustees. SECTION 1. *Be it enacted by the General Assembly of the State of North Carolina, and it is hereby enacted by the authority of the same,* That said Trustees be and are hereby authorized and empowered to form a Joint Stock Company, by converting such a portion of the real and personal estate belonging to said corporation, as they may deem necessary, into capital stock, and also to issue certificates of stock in said corporation, under such rules and regulations as may be adopted by them, (with the power to issue such certificates of stock in redemption of the present indebtedness of said corporation,) to the extent of two hundred thousand dollars, consisting of shares of fifty dollars each; and they are hereby clothed with authority to make sale of such certificates of stock, with the understanding that said Trustees may redeem such certificates by refunding to the purchaser the cost price thereof, with interest thereon from the time of purchase until redeemed, at the rate of six per cent. per annum, subject to a reduction of any dividend which may have been received by such Stockholders upon his certificate of stock aforesaid.

SEC. 2. *Be it further enacted,* That this Act shall take effect from and after its ratification.
Ratified the 13th day of February, A. D., 1867.

CHAPTER XLVII.

AN ACT TO AMEND THE CHARTER OF OLIN HIGH SCHOOL.

SECTION 1. *Be it enacted by the General Assembly of the State of North Carolina, and it is hereby enacted by the authority of the same,* That the Acts of the General Assembly of the State of North Carolina, passed at its session of 1855 and '56, entitled an Act to incorporate the Trustees of the New Institute, in Iredell county, and an Act to amend the same, by which the style of the Trustees of the New Institute was changed to that of "Olin High School," ratified the 24th day of January, A. D., 1857, be amended as hereinafter provided.

SEC. 2. *Be it further enacted,* That the Trustees of Olin High School shall be invested with all the rights, privileges and immunities granted to them by virtue of both the above recited Acts, and, in addition thereto, shall hereafter be known by the name and style of the Olin Agricultural and Mechanical College; and by the name and style of the "Olin Agricultural and Mechanical College," shall be capable of purchasing, holding and receiving by gift, donation or otherwise, real and personal property of every kind and description whatsoever, and by that name and style may sue and be sued, and shall have perpetual succession and a common seal. *Additional powers and privileges conferred.*

Change of name.

SEC. 3. *Be it further enacted,* That O. G. Foard, John F. Foard and James Southgate, be, and they are hereby, constituted a Board of Commissioners of the said Olin Agricultural and Mechanical College, with full power and authority to open books of subscription to the capital stock of said corporation, at such times and places and under the direction of such persons as they may name, and keep open *Commissioners to open books of subscription.*

Capital. the same until the said capital stock shall reach the sum of one hundred and twenty-five thousand dollars, if they shall desire to increase said capital stock to that amount.

Directors, &c. SEC. 4. *Be it further enacted,* That said stockholders shall have power to elect or appoint, from the body of stockholders, seven Directors, whose duty it shall be to elect a President of said College, and make all such by-laws, rules and regulations as may be necessary for the well ordering and governing said College, not inconsistent with the laws of the State or of th United States.

May confer degrees, &c. SEC. 5. *Be it further enacted,* That said corporation shall have full power and authority to adopt such measures as may be necessary to enable them to establish a Literary, Agricultural and Mechanical College of the highest grade; that they may grant diplomas and confer degrees, in any and all the departments of learning that can be taught in any Institution of learning in this or any other State, where the arts and sciences are taught.

Work-shops, &c. SEC. 6. *Be it further enacted,* That the said corporation may, from time to time, build work-shops of all kinds, for wood-work, carpenter shops, blacksmith shops and tan yards.

Model farm. SEC. 7. *Be it further enacted,* That the said corporation may purchase and conduct a model farm on which all the agricultural sciences may be taught.

Prohibition of sale of spirituous liquors within 2½ miles of said College. SEC. 8. *Be it further enacted,* That the County Court of Iredell county be, and the same is hereby, prohibited from granting license to retail spirituous liquors, by a measure less than a quart, to any person whatsoever, within two miles and a half of said College; and any person who shall sell any quantity, within the said limits, shall be deemed guilty of a misdemeanor, and upon conviction, in any of the Courts of such county, may be punished at the discretion of the Court.

SEC. 9. *Be it further enacted,* That this act shall be in force and take effect from and after its ratification.

Ratified the 26th day of February, A. D., 1867.

CHAPTER XLVIII.

AN ACT TO INCORPORATE THE NORTH CAROLINA ORPHAN ASYLUM.

SECTION 1. *Be it enacted by the General Assembly of the State of North Carolina, and it is hereby enacted by the authority of the same,* That N. Aldrich, J. F. Wilson, J. E. N. Hutchison, M. S. Wriston, W. A. Williams, W. J. Yates, Jas. J. Blackwood, J. P. Bruin, D. Parks, J. R. Blake, J. M. Hutchison, R. F. Hoke, W. Eaton, J. T. Sumner, Jesse H. Lindsay, George Davis, J. G. Shepherd, Z. B. Vance, Thos. E. Skinner, W. J. Palmer, Jos. J. Davis, A. T. Summey, George Green, and their associates, be and they are hereby ordained and constituted a perpetual body corporate, to be known by the name of the "Directors of the North Carolina Orphan Asylum," to be located in or near Charlotte, in Mecklenburg county, North Carolina; and by that name shall have perpetual succession, and they and their successors, or a majority of them, by the name aforesaid, shall be able and capable in law to sue and be sued, plead and be impleaded, and shall take, receive and hold any property, real or personal, and any moneys or other things whatsoever, which have been or shall be given, purchased or granted, for the use and benefit of said Asylum, and the same to apply accordingly, and by gift, purchase, devise or otherwise, to take, have and possess, receive, enjoy and retain, to them and their successors forever, any lands, rents or tenements of whatsoever nature or kind soever, to be applied or held for the benefit of said Asylum.

SEC. 2. *Be it further enacted,* That the said Directors, or a majority of them, shall have power to appoint from time to time such Superintendent and other officers as to them shall appear necessary, also a Treasurer and Secretary, upon such conditions and with such restrictions as they may deem proper, and the said Directors or a majority of them shall have power to make all such laws and regulations for the management and support of said Asylum, and for the preservation of order and discipline therein, as they may deem necessary.

Sec. 3. *Be it further enacted,* That upon the death, removal, inability or refusal to act, or resignation of any of the Directors above named in the first section of this Act, it shall be lawful for the remaining Directors, or a majority of them, to elect other Director or Directors in the room as such as die, remove, refuse to act or resign.

<small>Vacancies in Board of Directors.</small>

Sec. 4. *Be it further enacted,* That said Directors, or a majority of them, shall have power to make such regulations and by-laws as may be necessary for their own government, and the successful management of the Asylum.

Sec. 5. *Be it further enacted,* That this Act shall be in force from after its ratification.

Ratified the 28th day of February, A. D., 1867.

CHAPTER XLIX.

AN ACT TO CHANGE THE NAME OF THE CAROLINA JOINT STOCK INSURANCE AND TRUST COMPANY.

Sec. 1. *Be it enacted by the General Assembly of the State of North Carolina, and it is hereby enacted by the authority of the same,* That the name of the Carolina Joint Stock Insurance and Trust Company, which was incorporated by an Act, ratified the 6th day of March, 1866, be, and the same is hereby, changed to the "American Joint Stock Insurance and Trust Company."

<small>"American Joint Stock Insurance and Trust Company."</small>

Sec. 2. *Be it further enacted,* That this Act shall be in force from and after its ratification.

Ratified the 21st day of December, A. D., 1866.

CHAPTER L.

AN ACT TO INCORPORATE THE NEW BERNE STEAM FIRE ENGINE COMPANY, NO. 1.

SECTION 1. *Be it enacted by the General Assembly of the State of North Carolina, and it is hereby enacted by the authority of the same,* That Andrew Collins, Andrew J. Pool, Thomas Powers, C. P. Loomis, Henry J. Meninger, D. W. Wardrup, Phineas Merwin, Samuel T. Jones, J. Edwin West, J. F. Robertson, James O. Whittemore, and other persons who shall be associated with them, for the object intended, and those successors duly elected and chosen according to the by-laws of the Company, shall constitute a body politic and corporate, by the name and style of the Newberne Steam Fire Engine Company, No. 1., for the purpose of more united and efficient action in the extinguishment of fires in the city of New Berne, and by this name and style shall have power to acquire a Steam Fire Engine, or Engines, and such real estate as may be needful for their proper care and custody, the value of which shall at no time exceed the sum of $15,000.

Corporators.

Objects.

SEC. 2. *Be it further enacted,* That said Company shall, by the name and style aforesaid, have succession, sue and be sued, plead and be impleaded, have a common seal, and alter the same at pleasure, and make all by-laws and rules necessary for the proper government of the Company and the management of its funds, not inconsistent with the laws of the State; and in all matters do and perform what is customary and proper for fulfilling the object of the association.

Powers and privileges.

SEC. 3. *Be it further enacted,* That members in the actual service of the Company, performing duties when required, shall be exempt, during the continuance of such service, from jury and militia duty, and, after the faithful performance of required duties in the Company, for the term of seven years, a certificate thereof shall exempt for life, the

Members exempt from jury and militia duty, &c.

holder from jury and militia duty, and from all taxes on the poll.

Sec. 4. *Be it further enacted,* That this Act shall be in force from and after its ratification.

Ratified the 20th day of December, A. D., 1866.

CHAPTER LI.

AN ACT TO INCORPORATE THE "MC'LEAN FIRE ENGINE COMPANY, NO. ONE," IN THE TOWN OF FAYETTEVILLE.

Section 1. *Be it enacted by the General Assembly of the State of North Carolina, and it is hereby enacted by the authority of the same,* That John H. Robinson, Charles P. Mallett, Jes e R. Kyle, E. P. Powers, W. F. Campbell, Charles Haigh, William Widdefield, and their associates, in the town of Fayetteville, shall be, and they are hereby, constituted a body politic and corporate, by the name and style of the "McLean Fire Engine Company, No. One," and by that name they may sue and be sued, plead and be impleaded, shall have a succession and common seal, and exercise other powers incident to corporate bodies.

Corporators.

Sec. 2. *Be it further enacted,* That a majority of the members of said Fire Company shall have power and authority to adopt a constitution and pass such by-laws, rules and regulations for their government as to them may seem best, for the better regulation of their body, not inconsistent with the constitution and laws of the United States and of this State, and that all fines and penalties, which may be collected by said Company of their members for any infringement of their laws, shall enure to the use of said Company.

Powers, &c.

Sec. 3. *Be it further enacted,* That the members of said Fire Company shall at no time exceed one hundred and twenty-five members and while they shall continue members of said Company, they shall be exempt from the pay-

Limit as to members. Exemptions.

ment of town poll taxes, and also from the performance of military duty, except in case of insurrection and invasion.

SEC. 4. *Be it further enacted,* That this Act shall be in force from and after its ratification.

Ratified the 18th day of December, A. D., 1866.

CHAPTER LII.

AN ACT TO AMEND THE 122ND CHAPTER OF THE ACTS OF 1858–'59, ENTITLED " AN ACT TO INCORPORATE THE BINGHAM COAL MINING COMPANY."

SECTION 1. *Be it enacted by the General Assembly of the State of North Carolina, and it is hereby enacted by the authority of the same,* That the 122d chapter of the Acts of 1858–'59, entitled "An Act to incorporate the Bingham Coal Mining Company," be so amended as to authorize said Company to subscribe to the capital stock of the Western Rail Road Company and to that of the Cheraw & Coal Field Rail Road Company, or to the stock of either of them, and this bill shall be in force from and after its ratification. Amendment

Ratified the 12th day of February, A. D., 1867.

CHAPTER LIII.

AN ACT TO AMEND AN ACT TO INCORPORATE THE TOWN OF JEFFERSON, IN THE COUNTY OF ASHE.

SECTION 1. *Be it enacted by the General Assembly of the State of North Carolina, and it is hereby enacted by the authority of the same,* That section (4) four of said Act be amended as follows: In 5th line of said section, strike out (50) fifty cents and insert one dollar. In 6th line of said section, strike out (12½) twelve and a-half cents, and insert Amendments.

(25) twenty-five cents. In 8th line of said section, strike out ($3) three dollars and insert ($6) six dollars. In 9th line, strike out (50) fifty cents and insert ($1) one dollar. In 10th line, strike out ($2) two dollars, and insert ($5) five dollars. In 11th line, strike out ($1) one dollar and insert ($5) five dollars. In 12th line, strike out ($1) one dollar and insert ($5) five dollars; and that section 5th of said Act be so amended as to read, after the last word in said section, that "said Commissioners be authorized and empowered to lay off and open such additional streets, as in their judgment they may deem expedient and necessary."

Sec. 2. *Be it further enacted,* That all parts or clauses of said Act, coming in conflict with this Act, shall be, and the same are hereby, repealed, and that this Act shall be in force from and after its ratification.

Ratified the 26th day of February, A. D., 1867.

CHAPTER LIV.

AN ACT TO AUTHORIZE THE PRESIDENT AND DIRECTORS OF THE BLOUNT'S CREEK MANUFACTURING COMPANY, OF THE TOWN OF FAYETTEVILLE, TO BORROW MONEY TO REBUILD THEIR FACTORY.

May borrow $30,000 and issue bonds therefor.

Section 1. *Be it enacted by the General Assembly of the State of North Carolina, and it is hereby enacted by the authority of the same,* That for the purpose of rebuilding the factory of the Blount's Creek Manufacturing Company, of the town of Fayetteville, destroyed by order of General Sherman, that the President and Directors of said Company are hereby authorized and empowered to borrow the sum of thirty thousand dollars; to issue therefor the coupon bonds of said Company, or other evidences of debts, payable at such time, and with such rate of interest, as they may determine, and in such manner and form as they may prescribe; and, to secure the payment of the same, may execute a mortgage on all the property of the Company which they may now possess, or hereafter acquire, or any part thereof; or the said President and Directors may, with the consent of the present Stockholders, reduce the value and number of shares, to represent the present value of the property, and receive additional Stockholders, who shall make payments to them for the number of new shares issued, or may issue preferred stock, in such manner and form as the Company, or President and Directors thereof, may determine.

Sec. 2. *Be it further enacted,* That this Act shall be in force from and after its ratification.

Ratified the 22nd day of December, A. D., 1866.

CHAPTER LV.

AN ACT TO AMEND THE CHARTER OF THE TOWN OF WILSON.

Section 1. *Be it enacted by the General Assembly of the State of North Carolina, and it is hereby enacted by the authority of the same,* That the present limits of the Town of Wilson shall be extended so as to embrace all the lands within the following boundaries, to-wit: Beginning at a post on the west side of the Wilmington and Weldon Rail Road in the rear of Albert Farmer's lot; thence directly up said Rail Road, ten chains to a post; thence north 39½, west 121 poles to a post; thence south 86½, west 74 poles to a post; thence south 51½, west 124 poles to a post; thence south 39¾, east 252 poles to the Rail Road; thence 65½, west 54 poles to a post; thence north 24½, east 162 poles to a post; thence north 65½, east 54 poles to the beginning. *New limits*

Sec. 2. *Be it further enacted,* That said corporation shall, in future, be governed by the provisions of the chapter 111, Revised Code, and the general laws of the State now in force and which may hereafter be enacted in reference to Towns. *Ch. 111. Rev. Code.*

Sec. 3. *Be it further enacted,* That in addition to the powers granted above, the Commissioners of said Town shall have authority to lay and collect annual taxes for *Additional powers.*

municipal purposes on all persons and subjects within the corporate limits, which may be taxed for State and county purposes : *Provided,* such taxes shall be uniform on all subjects, and shall be equal to the wants and necessities of said Town.

Taxes.

Sec. 4. *Be it further enacted,* That said Commissioners shall be further empowered to impose and collect, in addition to any annual taxes, a monthly tax on persons or companies who shall be engaged in the following trades, professions or callings in said Town, to-wit

1st. On persons keeping horses or vehicles for hire a tax not exceeding five dollars.

2nd. On hotels a tax not exceeding ten dollars.

3rd. On drinking saloons a tax not exceeding twenty-five dollars.

4th. On drays, carts and wagons, for hire, a tax not exceeding ten dollars.

5th. On billiard tables and bowling alleys a tax not exceeding five dollars.

6th. On persons or firms engaged in buying and selling goods, wares, merchandise, produce or other articles, a tax on the amount of sales not exceeding one per centum, to be given in on oath before the Mayor or Town Clerk.

7th. On eating saloons, cook-shops and oyster houses, a tax not exceeding three dollars.

8th. On lawyers, physicians and dentists, a tax not exceeding five dollar .

9th. On butchers, daguerreans, photographers, auctioneers, commission or forwarding merchants, soda water and ice cream venders, a tax not exceeding five dollars.

10th. On express companies, having an office in Town, a tax not exceeding ten dollars.

11th. On every circus, menagerie, theatrical company, concert, minstrel or exhibition, (except for benevolent purposes, to be judged of by the Mayor,) a tax not exceeding twenty-five dollars for each exhibition

License to retail spirituous liquors.

Sec. 5. *Be it further enacted,* That the County Court of Wilson county shall not have power to grant license to retail spirituous liquors in said town, nor in one mile of the corporate limits, unless the person applying for the same shall produce to the Court a written recommendation from a majority of the Commissioners of said Town.

SEC. 6. *Be it further enacted,* That it shall be the duty of the Sheriff of Wilson county to hold an election at the court house, in the town of Wilson, on the first Thursday in April, in each and every year, for a Mayor and five Commissioners, twenty days notice of such election having previously been given by him in any newspaper published in said Town.

Elections.

SEC. 7. *Be it further enacted,* That it shall be the duty of the Commissioners to keep the streets of said Town in order, and they shall have power to lay out and open any new street, or widen or straighten those already made; and if the owners of property affected by the said streets, so opened, straightened or widened, shall claim damages, it shall be lawful for the said Board of Commissioners to choose three disinterested persons, and the person claiming damages to choose three disinterested persons, as arbiters, whose duty it shall be, after being duly sworn by the Mayor or some Justice of the Peace, to fairly and impartially assess damage sustained by opening or widening said streets, taking into consideration the enhanced value of the property by such widening and opening; and should the arbitrators thus chosen, fail to agree, they shall have power to call in an umpire. The award of the arbitrator, thus chosen, shall be conclusive, unless the party aggrieved shall choose to appeal to the Superior Court of said county, (both parties,) and shall be returned under their hands and seals to the Board of Commissioners, which shall be entered at length on the book of the proceedings of the Board.

Streets.

SEC. 8. *Be it further enacted,* That the Commissioners of said Town may adopt such ordinances as they may deem proper, to enforce the powers and authority hereby vested in them.

SEC. 9. *Be it further enacted,* That this Act shall be in force from and after its ratification.

Ratified the 22nd day of December, A. D., 1866.

CHAPTER LVI.

AN ACT TO REGULATE THE RETAILING OF SPIRITUOUS LIQUORS IN THE TOWN OF WILLIAMSTON.

Consent of Mayor and Commissioners necessary.

SECTION 1. *Be it enacted by the General Assembly of the State of North Carolina, and it is hereby enacted by the authority of the same,* That the Court of Pleas and Quarter Sessions of Martin county shall not grant a license to retail spirituous liquors, by the small measure less than a quart, in the town of Williamston, to any person, unless such person shall produce to the Court of Pleas and Quarter Sessions a recommendation from the Mayor and Commissioners of said town, signed by the Mayor.

SEC. 2. *Be it further enacted,* That this Act be in force from and after its ratification.

Ratified the 18th day of February, A. D., 1867.

CHAPTER LVII.

AN ACT TO INCORPORATE THE ROCKY MOUNT MANUFACTURING COMPANY.

Corporators.

SECTION 1. *Be it enacted by the General Assembly of the State of North Carolina, and it is hereby enacted by the authority of the same,* That W. S. Battle, W. R. Cox, and T. W. Battle, their associates, successors and assigns, are hereby constituted a body politic and corporate, under the name of the Rocky Mount Manufacturing Company, with a capital stock of one hundred and fifty thousand dollars,

Capital.

with liberty to increase the same to five hundred thousand dollars. The said Company shall be authorized to carry on any kind of Manufacturing and Milling business, and,

Objects.

to that end, shall have all the incidents and powers conferred under the provisions of the 26th Chapter of the Revised Code, entitled "Corporations," or Corporations organized under the provisions thereof.

SEC. 2. *Be it further enacted*, That this Act shall be in force from and after its ratification.

Ratified the 12th day of February, A. D., 1867.

CHAPTER LVIII.

AN ACT TO INCORPORATE "FRANKLIN LODGE, NO. 109," OF FREE AND ACCEPTED MASONS, IN THE TOWN OF BEAUFORT.

SECTION 1. *Be it enacted by the General Assembly of the State of North Carolina, and it is hereby enacted by the authority of the same*, That Samuel S. Dill, T. P. Whiting, H. H. Willis, John A. Hedrick, Wm. P. Daughtry, Wm. F. Hatsel, Wm. S. Robinson, Jacob S. Gibble, David M. Jones, and J. B. Whitehurst, of the town of Beaufort, and their successors in office, be, and they are hereby, incorporated a body politic and corporate, under the name and style of "Franklin Lodge, No. 109," and by that name may have succession perpetually, and a common seal, sue and be sued, plead and be impleaded in any Court of Record, or before any Justice of the Peace in this State, contract and be contracted with, acquire, hold and dispose of personal property for the benefit of said Lodge, and also such real estate as may be necessary for the transacting and carrying on the business of said Lodge.

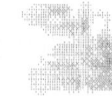

Corporators

Powers and privileges.

SEC. 2. *Be it further enacted*, That the said corporation shall have power to pass all necessary by-laws and regulations for its own government, which may not be inconsistent with the Constitution of the United States, nor with the Constitution of the State of North Carolina.

SEC. 3. *Be it further enacted*, That this Act shall be in force from and after its ratification.

Ratified the 18th day of February, A. D., 1867.

CHAPTER LIX.

AN ACT TO INCORPORATE THE HIBERNIAN BENEVOLENT SOCIETY, OF THE CITY OF WILMINGTON.

Corporators.

SECTION 1. *Be it enacted by the General Assembly of the State of North Carolina, and it is hereby enacted by the authority of the same,* That Jno. Dawson, Jas. Reiley, Stephen Kelly and Walter Furlong, and their associates and successors, are hereby incorporated by the name and style of "The Hibernian Benevolent Society, of the City of Wilmington," and by that name, may have succession and a common seal, sue and be sued, plead and be impleaded in any Court in this State, hold and dispose of personal estate, and also such real estate as may be necessary for the convenient transaction of the business of said corporation, and to promote the object of said Society, and enjoy all the rights and privileges which are conferred upon Corporations by chapter 26th, Revised Code, entitled "Corporations."

Powers, &c.

SEC. 2. *Be it further enacted,* That this Act shall be in force from and after its ratification.

Ratified the 12th day of February, A. D., 1867.

CHAPTER LX.

AN ACT TO AUTHORIZE THE SALE OF THE ACADEMY IN THE TOWN OF ELIZABETH CITY.

SECTION 1. *Be it enacted by the General Assembly of the State of North Carolina, and it is hereby enacted by the authority of the same,* That W. W. Griffin, Timothy Hunter, John J. Grandy and Rufus K. Speed, only survivors of the Trustees of Elizabeth City Academy, in the county of Pasquotank, or their successors, or any three of them, be, and they are hereby, authorized and empowered to sell the Academy lot, in said town, at such time and upon such terms as they may deem to the interest of said Academy, and, with the proceeds of such sale, may purchase other property and improve the same, for the use specified in the charter of the said Elizabeth City Academy, and for no other purpose.

SEC. 2. *Be it further enacted,* That this act shall be in force from and after its ratification.

Ratified the 26th day of February, A. D., 1867.

CHAPER LXI.

AN ACT TO INCORPORATE THE ROCKY POINT ACADEMY, IN THE COUNTY OF NEW HANOVER.

SECTION 1. *Be it enacted by the General Assembly of the State of North Carolina, and it is hereby enacted by the authority of the same,* That D. S. Durham, H. E. Carr, S. S. Satchwell, T. P. Armstrong, James S. Hines, James Durham and Calvin V. Hines, be, and they are hereby, created a body politic and corporate, in the State of North Carolina, under the name and style of " The Trustees of Rocky Point Academy," and as such corporation shall have and enjoy all the privileges, rights and immunities granted to corporations in chapter twenty-six, Revised Code, entitled " Corporations." — Trustees.

SEC. 2. *Be it further enacted,* That said corporation shall have the lawful right to establish a school, under the said name of Rocky Point Academy, [at] or near the Rocky Point Depot, in the county of New Hanover, and State of North Carolina, and to adopt all necessary rules and by-laws and regulations for the government and maintenance of the same. — Objects and powers.

SEC. 3. *Be it further enacted,* That it shall be unlawful for any person or persons, to erect, keep, maintain or have,

Prohibition as to retailing spirituous liquors. at Rocky Point Academy, or within three miles thereof, any tippling house, establishment, or place for the sale of wines, cordials, spirituous or malt liquors, and any person or persons offending against the provisions of this Act shall be guilty of a misdemeanor, and, upon conviction of the offence in a Court of competent jurisdiction, shall suffer the penalties imposed for misdemeanors.

SEC. 4. *Be it further enacted,* That this Act shall be in force from and after its ratification.

Ratified the 4th day of March, A. D., 1867.

CHAPTER LXII.

AN ACT TO AUTHORIZE THE TRUSTEES OF VINE HILL ACADEMY, IN THE COUNTY OF HALIFAX, TO SELL A PART OF THE LANDS BELONGING TO THE INSTITUTE.

SECTION 1. *Be it enacted by the General Assembly of the State of North Carolina, and it is hereby enacted by the authority of the same,* That the Trustees of the Vine Hill Academy, in the county of Halifax, be and they are hereby authorized and empowered to sell and make title to such portion of the land belonging to said Instiution, as in their judgment may be to the advantage of the Institution.

SEC. 2. *Be it further enacted,* That this Act shall be in force from and after its ratification.

Ratified the 21st day of February, A. D., 1867.

CHAPTER LXIII.

AN ACT TO AMEND THE CHARTER OF THE OCEANIC HOOK AND LADDER COMPANY OF THE TOWN OF BEAUFORT.

SECTION 1. *Be it enacted by the General Assembly of the State of North Carolina, and it is hereby enacted by the authority of the same,* That the Ocianic Hook and Ladder Company of the Town of Beaufort, during their actual and legal connection with said Company, and no longer, shall be exempt from jury and militia duty.   *Exemptions.*

SEC. 2. *Be it further enacted,* That this Act shall take effect from and after its ratification

Ratified the 14th day of February, A. D., 1867.

CHAPTER LXIV.

AN ACT TO AMEND THE CHARTER OF THE CAPE FEAR BOAT COMPANY.

SECTION 1. *Be it enacted by the General Assembly of the State of North Carolina, and it is hereby enacted by the authority of the same,* That said Company are hereby authorized to increase their capital stock to fifty thousand dollars, instead of thirty thousand, as limited by their charter granted on the 29th January, 1849.   *Increase of capital.*

SEC. 2. *Be it further enacted,* That this Act shall be in force immediately after its ratification.

Ratified the 18th day of February, A. D., 1867.

CHAPTER LXV.

AN ACT TO CHANGE THE NAME OF WAYNE FEMALE COLLEGE.

Change.
SECTION 1. *Be it enacted by the General Assembly of the State of North Carolina, and it is hereby enacted by the authority of the same,* That Wayne Female College Company, chartered by Letters Patent, dated 1st May, A. D., 1857, the name of which be and the same is hereby changed to that of Goldsboro' Female College.

Debts.
SEC. 4. *Be it further enacted,* That all debts outstanding against, and all debts in favor of, Wayne Female College, may be collected by suit in the name of Goldsboro' Female College.

SEC. 2. *Be it further enacted,* That this Act shall be in force from and after its ratification.

Ratified the 18th day February, A. D., 1867.

CHAPTER LXVI.

AN ACT TO INCORPORATE THE WAYNESVILLE BAPTIST COLLEGE IN THE COUNTY OF HAYWOOD, AND TO APPOINT TRUSTEES THEREOF.

Trustees.
SECTION 1. *Be it enacted by the General Assembly of the State of North Carolina, and it is hereby enacted by the authority of the same,* That E. B. Herren, Walter Brown, R. N. Welch, S. W. Welch, D. B. Nelson, C. B. Mingers, J. P. Osborne, Hiram McCracken, David Platt and Samuel L. Love, be and they are hereby incorporated by the name and style of the Trustees of Wayneville Baptist College,

Powers, &c.
and by that name shall be able and capable in law to sue and be sued, plead and be impleaded, acquire by purchase, gift or otherwise, to them and their successors, real and

personal estate for the use of said College, and enjoy all other powers, privileges and immunities belonging to bodies corporate of the like nature.

SEC. 2. *Be it further enacted*, That the Faculty of said College, that is to say, the President, Professors and Teachers, by and with the consent of the Trustees, shall have the power of conferring all such degrees or marks of literary distinction or diplomas, as are usually conferred in Colleges and Seminaries of learning. Degrees.

SEC. 3. *Be it further enacted*, That in case of any vacancy occurring by death, resignation or otherwise, of said Trustees, the remainder, or a majority of them, may appoint successors to the same, who shall have the same powers and authorities as the Trustees constituted by this Act. Vacancies.

SEC. 4. *Be it further enacted*, That this Act shall be in force and take effect from and after its ratification.

Ratified the 18th day of February, A. D., 1867.

CHAPTER LXVII.

AN ACT TO INCORPORATE EDENBOROUGH MEDICAL COLLEGE, IN THE COUNTY OF ROBESON.

SECTION 1. *Be it enacted by the General Assembly of the State of North Carolina, and it is hereby enacted by the authority of the same*, That Dr. Hector M'Lean, of the county of Robeson, and such other persons as he may associate with him, be, and they are hreby, declared to be a body corporate and politic, by the name and style of the Edenborough Medical College, and by that name and style may sue and be sued, plead and be impleaded; that the said corporation may acquire, hold, possess and enjoy real and personal estate; that they may make all such rules, by-laws and regulations as may be necessary for the good government of the same; that they may elect or appoint a President and Directors or a Board of Managers, or a Board of Trustees; that they may acquire by purchase or donation Corporators.

Powers, &c.

all such real estate as may be necessary, and improve the same, from time to time, together with all such personal property as may be necessary to make said Institution a first class Medical College of the highest grade; that they may employ or associate with them all necessary teachers and professors, whose duty it shall be to deliver lectures and give instruction in all the various branches in Medical Science.

<small>Compensation, &c.</small>
SEC. 2. *Be it further enacted,* That said instructors may receive for their services, for the instruction of students in said Institution, such compensation as may be fixed or prescribed by by-laws, rules and regulations of said College, or fixed or agreed upon by the President, or Directors, or Board of Managers, or Board of Trustees, and may sue for and recover the same in any of the Superior Courts or Courts of Pleas and Quarter Sessions, or before any Justice of the Peace having jurisdiction of the same; that they shall have perpetual succession, and may have a common seal.

<small>Degrees and Diplomas.</small>
SEC. 3. *Be it further enacted,* That the said Edenborough Medical College may confer degrees and grant diplomas to practice medicine in any of the counties of this State, and such diplomas shall entitle the recipient to all the rights, privileges, immunities and advantages that can be given, granted or bestowed by any Medical College or Institution where the arts and sciences of medicine are taught; and that any graduate of said Institution, having received his diploma for the same, and having complied with all its requirements, may practice medicine in any of the counties of this State, subject to the same rules and regulations as are now required by the laws of North Carolina in such cases made and provided.

SEC. 4. *Be it further enacted,* That all laws and clauses of laws coming in conflict with the provisions of this Act, be and the same are hereby repealed.

SEC. 5. *Be it further enacted,* That this Act shall be in force and take effect from and after its ratification.

Ratified the 26th day of February, A. D., 1867.

CHAPTER LXVIII.

AN ACT TO AMEND CHAPTER 42, PRIVATE LAWS, 1866.

SECTION 1. *Be it enacted by the General Assembly of the State of North Carolina, and it is hereby enacted by the authority of the same,* That the said Act of incorporation be so amended as to change the name of the Company therein incorporated to the " American Joint Stock Insurance and Trust Company." *Change of name.*

SEC. 2. *Be it further enacted,* That the third section of the said Act be amended by inserting, after the words, " secured by pledges of personal property, as at common law," the words, " or by mortgages on real estate, with powers of sale." *Further change.*

SEC. 3. *Be it further enacted,* That this Act shall be in force from and after its ratification.

Ratified the 2nd day of March, A. D., 1867.

CHAPTER LXIX.

AN ACT TO INCREASE THE CAPITAL STOCK OF " THE CLARENDON BRIDGE COMPANY."

SECTION 1. *Be it enacted by the General Assembly of the State of North Carolina and it is hereby enacted by the authority of the same,* That the first section of " An Act to incorporate the Clarendon Bridge Company, and to invest powers therein," chapter 34, ratified 30th day of January, 1866, be, and the same is hereby, amended, so as to increase the capital stock of said company to a sum not exceeding fifty thousand dollars. *Increased to $30,000.*

SEC. 2. *Be it further enacted,* That this Act shall be in force from and after its ratification.

Ratified the 2nd day of March, A. D., 1867.

CHAPTER LXX.

AN ACT TO AMEND AND RE-ENACT THE ACT OF THE GENERAL ASSEMBLY OF THE STATE OF NORTH CAROLINA, RATIFIED THE 25TH DAY OF JANUARY, 1843, ENTITLED "AN ACT TO INCORPORATE THE ALBEMARLE SWAMP LAND COMPANY."

SECTION 1. *Be it enacted by the General Assembly of the State of North Carolina, and it is hereby enacted by the authority of the same,* That the Act of Assembly, ratified the 25th day of January, 1843, entitled "An Act to incorporate the Albemarle Swamp Land Company," shall be, and the same is hereby amended and re-enacted, to read as follows:

Corporators. That Richard N. Riddick, William B. Whitehead, Nathaniel Riddick and others, the present owners of the lands and other property of the Association, known as the Albemarle Swamp Land Company, and such other persons as may hereafter be associated with them, and their successors, be and they are hereby created a body politic and corporate, by the name and style of "The Albemarle Swamp Land Company;"

Powers, &c. and in their corporate name may sue and be sued, appear, prosecute and defend to final judgment and execution, in any Courts or elsewhere, have a common seal, which they may alter at pleasure, elect, in such manner as they shall determine to be proper, all necessary officers, and to fix their compensation, and define their duties and obligations, and make by-laws and regulations, consistent with the laws of the State, for their own government, and for the due and orderly conducting of their affairs, and the management of their property.

Capital. SEC. 2. *Be it further enacted,* That the capital stock of said corporation shall be not less than one hundred and forty thousand dollars, to be divided into shares of one hundred dollars each, and the said corporation shall have power to increase their capital stock to five hundred thousand dollars.

Sec. 3. *Be it further enacted*, That the said corporation shall have the power to operate and carry on their business in the counties of Beaufort and Washington, and the counties adjoining thereto, for the purpose of getting and dealing in lumber and timber, and transporting or selling the same, and may transport the same in their own, or the vessels of others; also in milling, merchandizing, canaling, making roads, draining, and improving and cultivating Swamp and other lands, and shall have all power and rights incident to corporate companies, which may be necessary to carry into effect the objects of said corporation. *Objects.*

Sec. 4. *Be it further enacted*, That there shall be not less than three, nor more than five, of the Stockholders Directors in said corporation, one of whom shall be President, and the said corporation may, by their by-laws, determine the manner of calling and conducting all meetings, the number of members that shall constitute a quorum, the number of shares that shall entitle the members to one or more votes, the mode of voting by proxy, the mode of selling shares for the non-payment of assessment, and the tenure of office of the several officers, and the manner in which vacancies in any of the offices shall be filled till a regular election, and they may annex suitable penalties to such by-laws for any one offence, not exceeding in any one case the sum of twenty dollars. *Directors.*

Sec. 5. *Be it further enacted*, That the shares which any member of said corporation may be entitled to, shall be represented by certificates of stock, to be issued by said corporation in such manner as they may direct, and all such shares or stock shall be deemed personal estate, and may be transferred by the party in person, or by power of attorney on the books of said corporation, or in such manner as they may direct by their by-laws. *Certificates of stock.*

Sec. 6. *Be it further enacted*, That the said corporation shall have full power at any time to close its operations, and surrender up its charter and corporate privileges, in which case all the estates, real, personal or otherwise, shall be vested in the holders of the stocks, according to their respective shares, and shall be divided accordingly, and the *Further powers.*

said corporation shall have power to hold their meetings within or without the State of North Carolina.

SEC. 7. *Be it further enacted,* That all the lands and property of the Association aforesaid, known as the Albemarle Swamp Land Company, shall, as soon as the corporation herein referred to shall accept this charter and organize under it by virtue thereof, become the property of this corporation in such portions as the same may now be owned by the members thereof, and persons representing two-thirds of the said property shall have power to accept and organize under this charter.

Acceptance of charter.

SEC. 8. *Be it further enacted,* That the said corporation may fix their number of shares so as the whole value thereof shall not be less nor more than the amounts named in section second; that this charter shall be for sixty years, unless terminated as hereinbefore provided for or forfeited by operation of law.

Duration.

SEC. 9. *Be it further enacted,* That the several provisions of the twenty-sixth chapter of the Revised Code, of North Carolina, shall be the law to govern this corporation as far as applicable, except as far as altered by this charter.

Chapter 26, Revised Code.

SEC. 10. *Be it further enacted,* That the acceptance of, and organizing under this charter, shall not operate to discontinue any suit now pending for or against the Association aforesaid; but the same may be prosecuted as pending, or in the name of the corporation, if the Court in which any such suit may be pending shall so order by entry made on the record of the Court, and all rights, privileges and remedies now possessed by the Association shall be vested in the said corporation, so soon as the same is organized under this charter.

Acceptance of this charter not to operate to discontinue pending suits, &c.

SEC. 11. *Be it further enacted,* That this Act shall be in force from and after its ratification.

Ratified the 19th day of February, A. D., 1867.

CHAPTER LXXI.

AN ACT TO INCORPORATE BLACK ROCK LODGE, NO. 135, IN THE COUNTY OF BRUNSWICK.

SECTION 1. *Be it enacted by the General Assembly of the State of North Carolina, and it is hereby enacted by the authority of the same,* That the Master and Wardens, and their successors in office, are hereby constituted a body corporate and politic, by the name and style of Black Rock Lodge, number one hundred and thirty-five, in the county of Brunswick, and by that name shall have perpetual succession and a common seal, may sue and be sued, plead and be impleaded, and in general exercise and enjoy all such rights and privileges as are usually incident to corporate bodies of like nature. *Powers, &c.*

SEC. 2. *Be it further enacted,* That this Act shall be in force from and after its ratification.

Ratified the 27th day of February, A. D., 1867.

CHAPTER LXXII.

AN ACT TO INCORPORATE THE TABLE ROCK SEMINARY, IN THE COUNTY OF BURKE.

SECTION 1. *Be it enacted by the General Assembly of the tate of North Carolina, and it is hereby enacted by the authority of the same,* That Robert Patton, Benjamin Galloway, H. H. Kincaid, J. G. Hetton and B. H. Lisk, be and they are hereby declared to be a body politic and corporate, to be known as the Trustees of the Table Rock Seminary, in the county of Burke, and by that name shall have succession and a common seal, may sue and be sued, plead and be impleaded in any Court of law in this State, *Corporators.* *Powers, &c.*

and may hold such lands and tenements, goods and chattels, as may be sufficient for all the purposes of said Seminary.

SEC. 2. *Be it further enacted,* That said Trustees shall have power to make such laws, rules and regulations as may be necessary for the good government of said Seminary, not inconsistent with the laws of the United States, or of this State, and may fill vacancies in the Board of Trustees occasioned by death or otherwise, and do and perform all such things as are usually performed by similar institutions.

Further powers.

SEC. 3. *Be it further enacted,* That said corporation shall continue and be in force for and during the term of thirty years.

SEC. 4. *Be it further enacted,* That this Act shall be in force from and after its ratification.

Ratified the 26th day of February, A. D., 1867.

CHAPTER LXXIII.

AN ACT TO INCORPORATE THE CHAMBER OF COMMERCE OF THE CITY OF WILMINGTON, NORTH CAROLINA.

WHEREAS, William L. DeRossett, Avon E. Hall and Joseph B. Russell, have formed themselves into an association in the city of Wilmington, for the better promotion and regulation of trade and commerce among the members of the same, to be called "The Chamber of Commerce of the city of Wilmington, North Carolina:"

Corporators.

SECTION 1. *Be it enacted by the General Assembly of the State of North Carolina, and it is hereby enacted by the authority of the same,* That the said William L. DeRossett, Avon E. Hall, Joseph B. Russell, and such other persons as are now and may hereafter become members of said association, be, and they are hereby, constituted a body politic and corporate, to be distinguished and known by the name of "The Chamber of Commerce of the city of Wilmington,

Powers, &c.

North Carolina," and by that name shall have succession and so continue for the term of thirty years, and have a common seal, and plead and be impleaded, acquire, hold and transfer property, real and personal, for the use of said Association, and may, by their by-laws and regulations, govern and control the same, as is now provided by law.

SEC. 2. *Be it further enacted,* That this Act shall go into effect from and after its ratification.

Ratified the 25th day of February, A. D., 1867.

CHAPTER LXXIV.

AN ACT TO AMEND "AN ACT TO INCORPORATE AND ESTABLISH THE HILLSBORO' ACADEMY, AT HILLSBORO," PASSED AT THE SESSION OF 1861.

SECTION 1. *Be it enacted by the General Assembly of the State of North Carolina, and it is hereby enacted by the authority of the same,* That an Act to incorporate and establish Hillsboro' Military Academy, passed at the session of 1861, be so amended as to change the corporate name of the Company to the "North Carolina Military and Polytechnic Academy." *Change of name.*

SEC. 2. *Be it further enacted,* That the Superintendent of said Academy shall be commissioned by the Governor as a Brigadier General of the North Carolina Militia, and the Professors not higher than Lieutenant Colonels, all to take rank in said Militia from the date of their commissions. *The Superintendent.*

SEC. 3. *Be it further enacted,* That it shall be lawful for the Governor to appoint, every year, a Board of Visitors, to consist of not more than seven persons, whose duty it shall be to attend the annual examination of said Academy, and who shall have the power to elect, at the first examination, or sooner, if requested to do so, by the Superintendent, from such number of names recommended to the Superintendent as may be submitted to them, eight young *Board of Visitors.*

Gratuitous instruction. men, one from each Judicial District, as now constituted, and said young men, so selected, shall be educated at said Academy, free of charge for tuition : *Provided, however,* That such beneficiaries shall pledge their honor to the Superintendent, on entering the Academy, to teach two years within the State of North Carolina after graduation.

Proviso.

Board to report to Governor. SEC. 4. *Be it further enacted,* That the Board of Visitors shall make a report to the Governor, after each examination, to be transmitted to the General Assembly at its ensuing session.

Corporate existence. SEC. 5. *Be it further enacted,* That General R. E. Colston and his associates, and their successors, being so constituted a body politic, under the name and style hereinbefore given, shall continue their corporate existence for ninety-nine years.

SEC. 6. *Be it further enacted,* That this Act shall not be so construed as to repeal any part of said Act, passed at the session of 1861, except so much as comes in conflict with the provisions of this Act.

SEC. 7. *Be it further enacted,* That this Act shall be in force from and after its ratification.

Ratified the 26th day of February, A. D., 1867.

CHAPTER LXXV.

AN ACT TO CONSOLIDATE THE FIRE COMPANIES OF THE CITY OF NEW BERNE.

Preamble. WHEREAS. The several Fire Companies of the city of New Berne have formed and adopted a constitution and by-laws for their general government, and have associated themselves under the name and title of the "Fire Department of the city of New Berne," the object of which association is the more effectual and harmonious action of all the fire companies, in the protection of the lives and property of the inhabitants of the city of New Berne, against destructive fires and conflagrations; *And, whereas,* the object of the said association will be best promoted by an Act of incorporation: Therefore,

SECTION 1. *Be it enacted by the General Assembly of the State of North Carolina, and it is hereby enacted by the authority of the same,* That Samuel Radcliff, Wm. H. Harvey, Martin McNamam, Andrew Collins, Joseph D. Myers, John Davis, Thomas Powers, J. L. Watkins, Henry J. Menninger, and J. E. Nash, firemen of the city of New Berne, and their associates, officers and members of "New Berne Steam Fire Engine Company," "Atlantic Engine Company," and "Holden Hook and Ladder Company," and all persons who are now or may hereafter become members of the several Fire Companies of the city of New Berne, be, and they are hereby, constituted and declared to be a body corporate and politic in law, by the name of "The Fire Department of the city of New Berne," and by such name they shall have succession and be persons in law capable of suing and being sued, pleading and being impleaded, answering and being answered unto, defending and being defended in all Courts of judicature whatsoever, and that they and their successors may have a common seal, make, enter into, and execute any contract or agreement touching or concerning the objects of said incorporation, and shall have full power and authority to make, form and adopt such form of constitution, and such by-laws and regulations for their government, not inconsistent with the Constitution and laws of this State or of the United States, as they shall think proper.

Corporators.

Powers, &c.

SEC. 2. *Be it further enacted,* That all the affairs, property and concerns of said corporation shall be managed and conducted by a Board of officers, consisting of one Engineer, one Foreman and assistant Foreman, and two representatives from each and every Fire Company, a majority of whom shall be a quorum, for the transaction of business, that they shall be citizens of this State, and they shall hold their office for one year, and until their successors shall be chosen.

Officers.

SEC. 3. *Be it further enacted,* That the Board of officers, thus constituted, may elect from among the engineers elected by the various Fire Companies, one Chief Engineer,

Chief Engineer.

who shall be the presiding officer of the board of officers, and that they may also elect, out of their own body, a Secretary and a Treasurer.

SEC. 4. *Be it further enacted*, That at all fires, and upon all occasions when the Fire Department may be assembled, the Chief Engineer shall have the general supervision, direction and control of the Fire Department.

SEC. 5. *Be it further enacted*, That in the absence of the Chief Engineer, all his authority, powers and duties shall devolve upon and be exercised by the senior Assistant Engineer; and, in the absence of the senior Assistant, by the next Assistant Engineer, according to his rank, and in the absence of all the Engineers, by the senior Foreman or other senior officer or member of the Fire Department.

Senior Assistant Engineer.

SEC. 6. *Be it further enacted*, That the Chief Engineer, or other officer acting in his stead and place, shall have all the powers, authorities and privileges heretofore granted to the Fire Wardens of the city of New Berne.

SEC. 7. *Be it further enacted*, That this Act shall be deemed a public Act, and shall take effect immediately.

Ratified the 25th day of February, A. D., 1867.

CHAPTER LXXVI.

AN ACT TO SET APART AND MAKE PERPETUAL THE MCINTYRE CEMETERY, IN THE COUNTY OF CUMBERLAND.

SEC. 1. *Be it enacted by the General Assembly of the State of North Carolina, and it is hereby enacted by the authority of the same*, That the land and premises known as the McIntyre Cemetery, in the county of Cumberland, bounded and described as follows: Beginning at a stone on the West side of Steward's creek on the South margin by the Morganton road, running thence South 28 degrees West, one chain and 57 links to a stone, then South 81 degrees West 27 links to a stone, then South 9 degrees East two chains and 82 links to a stone, then North 81 degrees East

Limits.

one chain to a stone, then North 9 degrees West two chains and 82 links to a stone, then North 28 degrees East one chain and 35 links to a stone in the South margin of said Morganton road, thence to the beginning, containing half an acre for the purpose of being preserved and kept sacred as a cemetery, be and the same is hereby vested in the Chairman of the County Court of Cumberland, and his successors in office, to be forever exempt from transfer, sale, or appropriation in any form or manner, or for any purpose whatever, other than as a cemetery, and shall be exempt from taxation and sale under execution. *Exempt from taxation.*

SEC. 2. *Be it further enacted,* That this Act shall be in force from and after its ratification.

Ratified the 26th day of February, A. D., 1867.

CHAPTER LXXVII.

AN ACT TO INCORPORATE THE AMERICAN INDUSTRIAL ASSOCIATION OF NORTH CAROLINA.

SECTION 1. *Be it enacted by the General Assembly of the State of North Carolina, and it is hereby enacted by the authority of the same,* That Lyman W. Gilbert, and his associates, are hereby constituted a body politic and corporate, under the name and style of the American Industrial Association, of North Carolina, for the purpose of purchasing lands, holding and disposing of the same, of carrying on the Wood and Vine Growing, Manufacturing, Mining, Agricultural, Mechanical and other business necessary to a full development and successful prosecution of a large enterprise, embracing the above named branches of industry, and to continue in existence for a period of (30) thirty years, with power to make and use a common seal, and to alter and change the same at pleasure ; and to make such by-laws, not inconsistent with the laws of this State, and of the United States, as they may deem useful and necessary ; to sue and be sued, to plead and be impleaded, to hold by pur- *Corporators.* *Purposes.* *Powers.*

chase or otherwise, and dispose of the same in any way, all real estate and personal property, which may be deemed useful and necessary for carrying on their operations, or which they may become possessed of in the prosecution of their said business.

Capital. SEC. 2. *Be it further enacted,* That the capital stock of said corporation shall be one million of dollars and shall be divided into shares of ten dollars each.

Further powers. SEC. 3. *Be it further enacted,* That the said corporator and his associates shall have the right to invest such portion of the capital stock of the said corporation in real estate and personal property, as they may deem for the best interest of the corporation, and such property may be received by them in payment for subscriptions to said capital stock. The subscriptions to the capital stock of said Company may be obtained by opening books for general subscription, or by private and personal solicitations, as the said corporators may deem most advisable.

Location of offices. SEC. 4. *Be it further enacted,* That the said corporation shall have an office for the transaction of business in the county or district where their operations are carried on, and they may have offices in other places if they shall deem it for the interest of the Company to establish them.

Delinquents SEC. 5. *Be it further enacted,* That all subscribers to the capital stock, who shall not have paid their subscriptions according to the terms agreed upon, shall be liable to the creditors of said corporation for all amounts remaining unpaid on their said subscriptions, and may be proceeded against in the usual way and manner for the collection of the same.

Directors, &c. SEC. 6. *Be it further enacted,* That the business of the said corporation shall be managed by a Board of Directors of not less than five or more than thirteen, one of whom shall be President. The Directors shall be elected annually, when the number of Directors for the year shall be determined by a vote of the stockholders, but a failure to elect shall not work a forfeiture of the charter, but the Directors and officers of the previous year shall continue in office until others are elected in their stead. At all meetings of the stockholders each share of stock shall entitle the owner to one vote, which may be voted in person or by proxy. The place of meeting of the stockholders to be fixed by the Board of Directors, and due notice given of the same.

SEC. 6. *Be it further enacted,* That the stock of this Company shall be taken and regarded as personal property, and transferable on the books of the Company, as the by-laws shall prescribe. Transfers of stock.

Ratified the 4th day of March, A. D., 1867.

CHAPTER LXXVIII.

AN ACT TO INCORPORATE THE "FLAT SWAMP, LOCK'S CREEK AND EVANS' CREEK CANAL COMPANY," OF THE COUNTY OF CUMBERLAND.

SECTION 1. *Be it enacted by the General Assembly of the State of North Carolina, and it is hereby enacted by the authority of the same,* That Alfred A. McKethan, Col. Thos. W. Devane. Robt. Williams, Jno. Marshall Williams, Hector McAllister, Joseph B. Underwood, William J. McPhail, James McAllister, Daniel Blue Murphy, Niven Culbreath and Jas. Gay, and their associates and assigns, be and they are hereby created a corporation and body politic, by the name and style of the "Flat Swamp, Lock's Creek and Evans' Creek Canal Company," and by that name and style may sue and be sued, plead and be impleaded in any Court of Record; contract and be contracted with, have succession and a common seal, acquire, own and possess real and personal estate, and shall so continue thirty (30) years. Corporators

Powers, &c

SEC. 2. *Be it further enacted,* That said corporation is hereby authorized and empowered to drain the waters of Flat Swamp, Lock's Creek, Evans' Creek and the tributaries of said Swamp and Creeks, by cutting a Canal from some point on the Cape Fear River near Bachelor's Branch, or such other point on the East side of the Cape Fear River in the county of Cumberland as they may select, and said Purposes.

corporation is hereby invested with all the power necessary to carry out the same.

Capital.

SEC. 3. *Be it further enacted,* That the capital stock of said corporation shall not exceed the sum of fifty thousand dollars, divided into shares of one hundred dollars each, but said corporation may borrow money to an amount not exceeding one hundred thousand dollars, and issue therefor such bonds or other evidences of debt, and at such a rate of interest, as said corporation may direct, and, to secure the payment thereof, may mortgage any or all of its property or effects under such regulations as may be prescribed.

Personal and real property, to what amount?

SEC. 4. *Be it further enacted,* That said corporation may acquire real and personal property to an amount not exceeding two hundred thousand dollars, by purchase or otherwise, and hold and dispose of the same.

Officers and Agents

SEC. 5. *Be it further enacted,* That said corporation shall have the power to make all necessary by-laws and regulations for its government, not inconsistent with the laws of the State, and shall have power to appoint its officers and agents to transact its business and conduct its operations.

Annual meetings

SEC. 6. *Be it further enacted,* That annual meetings of the Stockholders, in person or by proxy, shall be held at such a time and place in the county of Cumberland as may be designated, at which meetings proper officers of said corporation shall be appointed, who shall hold their office for one year, or until their successors are chosen, but nothing herein shall be so construed as to prevent general meetings whenever the interest of the corporation may require.

General meeting.

SEC. 7. *Be it further enacted,* That the Stockholders in general meeting shall have the power to adopt rules and regulations with regard to certificates or evidences of stock, and transfers and assignments of the same. In general meeting Stockholders shall have one vote for each share held or represented.

Drainage of lands

SEC. 8. *Be it further enacted,* That said corporation may agree with the owners of any lands that it may become necessary for them to drain in the prosecution of their work, or over which it may be necessary for them to construct said Canal, for the amount that the owner of said land should pay, or may be benefitted by said drainage, which amount may be paid by a conveyance to the corporation of any portion of the Canal itself, in money, or secured by note, payable at such reasonable time as may be agreed upon; and if, from any cause, the value of said drainage, to the owner of the land, cannot be fixed and agreed upon by the parties, said corporation may require the Sheriff of Cumberland county to summon five (5) disinterested freeholders to view the land, and assess the value of said drainage without reference to the cost thereof, but confining themselves strictly to the increased value of the land to the owner for sale and cultivation; and said freeholders shall make a report to the Sheriff, in writing, setting forth the value of said land to the owner before drainage, and the value of the same after drainage, and the increase in the value shall be the amount due and payable to said corporation. In case either party are dissatisfied with the award of the freeholders, they may appeal to the Superior Court.

SEC. 9. *Be it further enacted,* That said corporation shall keep a full record of all its proceedings, and produce said record in any Court of justice, when so required by said Court; and that this Act shall be in force from and after its ratification.

Ratified the 4th day of March, A. D., 1867.

Record of proceedings

CHAPTER LXXIX.

AN ACT TO INCORPORATE THE AMERICAN MINING AND MANUFACTURING COMPANY.

SECTION 1. *Be it enacted by the General Assembly of the State of North Carolina, and it is hereby enacted by the authority of the same,* That a Company, to be entitled the American Mining and Manufacturing Company, shall be, and the same is hereby, created and established with a

Capital.

capital stock of not less than fifty thousand dollars, which may be increased from time to time to such sums as the Board of Directors may determine, not to exceed the sum of one million of dollars, which capital stock shall be divided into shares of fifty dollrs each.

Directors.

SEC. 2. *Be it further enacted,* That the affairs of said Company shall be managed by a Board of Directors, to be chosen from the stockholders of said Company, consisting of not less than five nor more than twenty-five Directors, who shall hold their respective offices for one year, or until their successors shall be elected; said election shall be held on the first Monday of June of each year, at which election each stockholder, by himself or by his properly appointed proxy, shall be entitled to one vote for each share of stock held by him at the date of said election: *Provided,* That the transfer books of stock shall be closed at least ten days prior to such election. Said Directors, when elected as aforesaid, shall choose one of their number as President, and shall select such other officers and agents as they may deem necessary.

Powers, privileges and objects.

SEC. 7. *Be it further enacted,* That said Company shall have power, and are hereby authorized, to purchase or lease coal, oil, mineral, or other lands; to erect buildings and machinery for the purpose of smelting, refining and purifying minerals and oil, and for the manufacturing of fabrics of wool, cotton, hemp, flax, paper, cooperage, and machinery of all kinds, and other articles of commerce; to receive all or any of the foregoing raw or crude materials, smelt, refine or manufacture on the shares, or otherwise; to borrow money when the interest of the Company shall require, and to give their acknowledgments for the same in such form as the Directors of said Company may deem best suited for the mutual protection and convenience of the parties and the Company.

Location of offices

SEC. 4. *Be it further enacted,* That said Company are hereby authorized to open offices for the transaction of business, in each of the cities of Asheville, Salisbury, Raleigh, and at such other points as the interest of the Company may require, under separate issues of stock, which issue shall be liable only for contracts of such office, and said Company may extend said mining, manufacturing and other business to any portion of this State, whenever the Directors may deem advantageous.

SEC. 5. *Be it further enacted,* That Walter Lenoir, Isaac T. Lenoir, Israel P. Lenoir, Geo. H. Lenoir, N. S. Jarrell, Edwin D. Payne, Buckner H. Payne, James W. Ferrell and Dillard L. Love, and their successors and associates, are hereby appointed Commissioners to open books for subscription to the capital stock of said Company, and as soon as the sum of fifty thousand dollars of said stock shall have been subscribed and paid in, or secured to be so paid to the satisfaction of said Commissioners, the Stockholders shall proceed to the election of Directors, and are authorized to commence business as herein provided. Commissioners to open books.

SEC. 6. *Be it further enacted,* That the Board of Directors shall make all by-laws, rules and regulations for the transaction of business, and managing the affairs of the Company, as may be necessary and proper: *Provided,* such by-laws are not in conflict with the Public Laws of this State and the United States.

SEC. 7. *Be it further enacted,* That this Act shall take effect and be in force from and after its passage, and remain in force for sixty years.

Ratified the 18th day of February, A. D., 1867.

CHAPTER LXXX.

AN ACT TO AMEND THE CHARTER OF THE WASHINGTON TOLL BRIDGE COMPANY.

SECTION 1. *Be it enacted by the General Assembly of the State of North Carolina, and it is hereby enacted by the authority of the same,* That the charter of the President and Directors of the Washington Toll Bridge Company be so amended as to reduce the tolls and charges upon the inhabitants of Beaufort county, residing on the south side of Reduction of tolls.

Palmico River, between Blount's Creek on the east, including Buck's, Burney's, Haddock's and Taft's Districts, in Pitt county, extending to the Craven county line on the south, to one-half of the rates and charges specified in the charter and amendments thereto, heretofore granted.

Restrictions. SEC. 2. *Be it further enacted*, That no Bridge or Ferry shall be kept or established upon said River for the purpose of transporting any person or his effects across the same, either for pay or without pay, within the distance of three miles from said Bridge, under the penalties prescribed in section thirtieth of the one hundred and first (101) chapter of the Revised Code.

SEC. 3. *Be it further enacted*, That this Act shall have effect from the time the President and Directors of the Washington Toll Bridge Company accept the same—and that it shall be their duty to signify their acceptance to the Secretary of State.

Ratified the 11th day of December, A. D., 1866.

CHAPTER LXXXI.

AN ACT TO INCORPORATE CENTRE HILL LODGE, NO. 260, FREE AND ACCEPTED MASONS, IN THE COUNTY OF CHOWAN.

Corporators. SECTION 1. *Be it enacted by the General Assembly of the State of North Carolina, and it is hereby enacted by the authority of the same*, That D. Barclift, W. M., Thos. Cochran, S. W., R. D. Simpson, J. W., and other officers and members, who are at present, or in future may be, of Centre Hill Lodge, number two hundred and sixty, of Free and Accepted Masons, at Centre Hill, in Chowan county, be, and they are hereby, incorporated into a body politic and corporate, under the name and style of "Centre Hill Lodge, No. two hundred and sixty, of Free and Accepted Masons,"
Powers, &c. and by that name may have succession and a common seal, sue and be sued, plead and be impleaded, in any Court of Record, or before any Justice of the Peace in this State,

contract and be contracted with, acquire, hold and dispose of personal property for the benefit of said Lodge, and also such real estate as may be necessary for the transacting and carrying on the business of said Lodge.

SEC. 2. *Be it further enacted,* That the said corporation shall have power to pass all necessary by-laws and regulations for its own government, which may not be inconsistent with the Constitution of the United States, nor with the Constitution of North Carolina.

SEC. 3. *Be it further enacted,* That this Act shall be in force from and after its ratification.

Ratified the 27th day of February, A. D., 1867.

CHAPTER LXXXII.

AN ACT TO INCORPORATE THE OLIVIA QUICK SILVER MINING COMPANY OF MACON COUNTY, N. C.

SECTION 1. *Be it enacted by the General Assembly of the State of North Carolina, and it is hereby enacted by the authority of the same,* That J. S. Bonham, Hugh M. Bonham, Ben. Cunningham and N. B. Hamer, and their successors, with perpetual succession, by the name and title of the Olivia Quick Silver Mining Company, by that name may sue and be sued, plea and be impleaded in all Courts and places, contract and be contracted with in all matters pertaining to the business and object of the corporation, and any and all acts which a corporation may or can do in fulfilment of its charter and the object and ends of its organization, may a have a common seal which may be changed or altered at the pleasure of the Company. *Corporators. Powers, &c.*

SEC. 2. *Be it further enacted,* That the object and purpose of the corporation shall be the mining for Quick Silver and other substances of value, the direct product of the earth, and the manufacturing of any precious metals or refining the same and the transportation of the same to market or refineries. *Objects.*

SEC. 3. *Be it further enacted,* That the capital stock of the Company shall be one hundred thousand dollars, to be increased by a majority vote of said Company to any sum not exceeding one million dollars, to be divided into shares of one hundred dollars each, which will be personal property and assignable on the books of said Company, in such manner as may be prescribed by its by-laws. Lands and other real estate, mines, mining rights, may be subscribed as a part or the whole of said stock; all of the above to be in accordance with the laws of the State of North Carolina and of the United States, in reference to real estate.

Capital.

SEC. 4. *Be it further enacted,* That the stock, property and general prudential affairs of the said Company, shall be managed by a Board of not less than three, nor more seven Directors, to be chosen by the Stockholders for one year, a majority in interest being necessary to a change and each share of stock shall count one vote : *Provided,* the Directors first chosen shall hold their offices until their successors are elected, and until a President shall be chosen and appointed by the Board of Directors. The officers shall all be stockholders in said Company.

Directors.

SEC. 5. *Be it further enacted,* That the Company shall keep a book which shall be always kept open to the inspection of each Stockholder; in it shall be kept a registry of the name of each Stockholder, with the respective number of shares owned by each. A majority of the Directors shall constitute a quorum to transact business.

Books and records.

SEC. 6. *Be it further enacted,* That the President and Directors may make such by-laws and regulations as shall enable the Company to prosect to its financial business, not inconsistent with the laws of this State or this charter.

SEC. 7. *Be it further enacted,* That the Company shall have power to purchase or lease such lands as may be necessary for the use of said Company, not to exceed fifty thousand acres, and also to contract for the right of way for roads necessary for the conveyance of the freights of the Company, and to carry the same to any navigable stream or Rail Road, and have such buildings, yards, wharves, boats or floats as may be necessary for all transportation which

Lands right of way, &c.

may give the Company ingress and egress, for bringing in machinery, &c., for the use of said Company, and for carrying the products of said Company to the markets of the country.

SEC. 8. *Be it further enacted*, That this Act shall be in force from and after its passage.

Ratified the 26th day of February, A. D., 1867.

CHAPTER LXXXIII.

AN ACT TO INCORPORATE PASQUOTANK LODGE, NO. 103, ANCIENT FREE AND ACCEPTED MASONS, AT ELIZABETH CITY, NORTH CAROLINA.

SECTION 1. *Be it enacted by the General Assembly of the State of North Carolina, and it is hereby enacted by the authority of the same,* That the Master, Wardens and members of Pasquotank Lodge, (No. 103,) number one hundred and three, of Free and Accepted Masons, at Elizabeth City, Pasquotank county, North Carolina, be, and they are hereby, constituted a body corporate and politic, by the name and style of "Pasquotank Lodge, number one hundred and three, (103,) of Free and Accepted Masons," and by that name shall have perpetual succession and a common seal, may sue and be sued, plead and be impleaded, and may generally exercise and enjoy all such rights, franchises and privileges as usually appertain to corporate bodies of like nature. *Powers, &c*

SEC. 2. *Be it further enacted*, That this Act shall be in force from and after its ratification.

Ratified the 19th day of February, A. D., 1867.

CHAPTER LXXXIV.

AN ACT TO INCORPORATE THE NEW MARKET FOUNDRY AND MANUFACTURING COMPANY IN RANDOLPH COUNTY.

Corporators. SECTION 1. *Be it enacted by the General Assembly of the State of North Carolina, and it is hereby enacted by the authority of the same,* That Riley Miller, Franklin Gardner, Enoch Faston, Thomas Jones, Jonathan Worth and their associates, successors and assigns, be and they are hereby created and constituted a body corporate and politic, by the name and style of the "New Market Foundry and Manufacturing Company," for the purpose of casting, smelting

Powers, &c and moulding castings of all kinds and shapes, pots, ovens, ploughs and machinery of every kind and description whatsoever, and may enjoy all the privileges, rights, powers and immunities incident to manufacturing the same; and, for the purpose of carrying on the same, may also purchase, have, hold, possess and enjoy and sell real and personal estate, that may be necessary for the purposes aforesaid.

SEC. 2. *Be it further enacted,* That said corporation may make all such rules, by-laws and regulations as may be necessary for the successful management of the same; that *Further* they may elect all such officers, either President or Mana-
powers. ger or Agent, under the direction of three or five Directors; and the Stockholders or corporation shall have power to fill all such vacancies as may occur in any office created by their rules and by-laws, and may alter, change or modify the same from time to time as circumstances may require or they may consider best for their interest.

SEC. 3. *Be it further enacted,* That this corporation shall exist for thirty years, and shall be in force and take effect from and after its ratification.

Ratified the 18th day of February, A. D., 1867.

CHAPTER LXXXV.

AN ACT TO INCORPORATE JERUSALEM LODGE, NO. 95, OF FREE AND ACCEPTED MASONS.

SECTION 1. *Be it enacted by the General Assembly of the State of North Carolina, and it is hereby enacted by the authority of the same,* That H. F. Granger, John Patrick, William Coward and J. Q. Jackson, and their associates of the Masonic Fraternity, of the town of Hookerton, and their successors, are hereby incorporated as such, in the name and style of "Jerusalem Lodge, number 95," and by that name may have succession, and a common seal, sue and be sued, plead and be impleaded in any Court of Record, or before any Justice of the Peace in this State, contract and be contracted with, acquire, hold and dispose of personal property for the benefit of said Lodge, and also such real estate as may be required for the convenient transaction of its business. *Corporators*

SEC. 2. *Be it further enacted,* That the said corporation shall have power to pass all necessary by-laws and regulations for its own government, which may not be inconsistent with the Constitution and laws of the State, or of the United States. *Powers.*

SEC. 3. *Be it further enacted,* That this Act shall be in force from and after its ratification.

Ratified the 18th day of February, A. D., 1867.

CHAPTER LXXXVI.

AN ACT TO INCORPORATE MONROE LODGE, NO. 244, OF FREE AND ACCEPTED MASONS, IN THE TOWN OF MONROE, COUNTY OF UNION.

Corporators. SECTION 1. *Be it enacted by the General Assembly of the State of North Carolina, and it is hereby enacted by the authority of the same,* That W. H. Fitzgerald, A. N. Lawson, Samuel H. Walkup and their associates, of the Masonic fraternity, of the town of Monroe, and their successors, are hereby incorporated as such, in the name and style of "Monroe Lodge, No. 244," and by that name may have succession and a common seal, sue and be sued, plead and *Powers and privileges.* be impleaded in any Court of Record, or before any Justice of the Peace in this State, contract and be contracted with, acquire, hold and dispose of personal property for the benefit of said Lodge, and also such real estate as may be required for the convenient transaction of its business.

SEC. 2. *Be it further enacted.* That the said corporation shall have power to pass all necessary by-laws and regulations for its own government, which may not be inconsistent with the Constitution and laws of this State or of the United States.

SEC. 3. *Be it further enacted,* That this Act shall be in force from and after its ratification.

Ratified the 18th day of February, A. D., 1867.

CHAPTER LXXXVII.

AN ACT TO INCORPORATE THE BOARD OF TRADE OF THE CITY OF NEW BERNE, NORTH CAROLINA.

SECTION 1. *Be it enacted by the General Assembly of the State of North Carolina, and it is hereby enacted by the authority of the same,* That Alonzo T. Jerkins, Samuel Blagge, Charles H. Taylor, Wm. C. Whitford, P. A. Leland, Thos. P. Mitchell, J. D. Hanner, Alexander Walker and William S. Walker, and their associates and successors, be, and they are hereby, made a body politic and corporate, by the name and style of the "Board of Trade of the City of New Berne," and by that name may sue and be sued, plead and be impleaded in all the Courts of this State. Corporators.

SEC. 2. *Be it further enacted,* That said corporation shall have power to make all necessary by-laws, rules and regulations for its government, not inconsistent with the Constitution and laws of this State or of the United States. Powers and privileges.

SEC. 3. *Be it further enacted,* That this Act shall be in force from and after its ratification.

Ratified the 18th day of February, A. D., 1867.

CHAPTER LXXXVIII.

AN ACT TO INCORPORATE LEXINGTON MINING COMPANY.

SECTION 1. *Be it enacted by the General Assembly of the State of North Carolina, and it is hereby enacted by the authority of the same,* That Cyrus P. Mendenhall, E. P. Jones, F. P. Cavanagh, George Kinsey, Z. B. Vance, Peter Adams, J. A. Gilmer, Daniel McCann and James E. Purvis, and their associates, successors and assigns, are hereby created and constituted a body politic and corporate, by the name Corporators.

Objects.	and style and title of "The Lexington Mining Company," for the purpose of exploring for coal, copper, lead, gold, iron and other minerals, metals and valuable substances, and for refining, mining, vending and smelting the same, and by that name may sue and be sued, plead and be impleaded, appear, prosecute and defend in any Courts of Law and Equity whatsoever, in all suits and actions, may have
Powers.	a common seal, and the same alter at pleasure, and may enjoy all privileges incident to mining operations, and may purchase, hold and convey real and personal estate to an amount not exceeding one million of dollars.

Sec. 2. *Be it further enacted,* That the first meeting of said corporation may be called by the persons named in this Act, or any of them, at such time and place as they may agree upon, and, at such meeting, and at all other meetings legally held, such corporation may make, alter and repeal such by-laws and regulations for the management of the business of said corporation as a majority of the Stockholders may direct, not repugnant to the laws of this State or of the United States.

<small>General meeting.</small>

Sec. 3. *Be it further enacted,* That said corporation may divide their stock in such number of shares, and provide for the sale and transfer thereof in such manner and form, as they shall from time to time deem expedient, and may levy and collect assessments, forfeit and sell delinquent shares, declare and pay dividends on the shares in such manner as the by-laws shall direct.

<small>Stock</small>

Sec. 4. *Be it further enacted,* That it shall be the duty of the Directors of said Company to have regular books of record and transfer, at all times open to the inspection of the Stockholders.

<small>Books of Record.</small>

Sec. 5. *Be it further enacted,* That the corporation shall be in force and continue for sixty years, and that this Act shall take effect from and after its ratification.

Ratified the 12th day of February, A. D., 1867.

CHAPTER LXXXIX.

AN ACT TO INCORPORATE THE DUPLIN MANUFACTURING COMPANY.

SECTION 1. *Be it enacted by the General Assembly of the State of North Carolina, and it is hereby enacted by the authority of the same,* That Edward K. Hines, George A Newell, Wm. A. Allen, Benjamin F. Cobb, Isaac B. Kelly, Louis Froelick, Edward L. Watson, Jno. N. Stallings, Jonathan Chesnutt, Thomas J. Carr, Sam'l. Gwin, Jesse Lanier, William J. Southerland, and their associates, successors and assigns, are hereby created and constituted a body politic and corporate, by the name, style and title of the "Duplin Manufacturing Company," for the purpose of manufacturing wooden, hollow-ware, working wood, sawing lumber of every description and grinding grain, and may also purchase, hold, sell, mortgage, lease or convey real or personal property or estate, with a capital not to exceed twenty-five thousand dollars. [*Corporators. Objects.*]

SEC. 2. *Be it further enacted,* That said corporation may divide their stock into shares of not less than ten dollars, issue certificates therefor, elect a President, Directors and all necessary officers, and make and adopt rules, regulations and by-laws for the government of said Company, and be entitled to all rights, privileges and immunities, and subject to all restrictions, contained in chapter twenty-six of the Revised Code, entitled "Corporations." [*Powers and privileges.*]

SEC. 3. *Be it further enacted,* That this corporation shall exist for thirty years, and this Act shall be in force from and after its ratification.

Ratified the 18th day February, A. D., 1867.

CHAPTER XC.

AN ACT TO INCORPORATE THE TOWN OF HOOKERTON IN THE COUNTY OF GREENE.

SECTION 1. *Be it enacted by the General Assembly of the State of North Carolina, and it is hereby enacted by the authority of the same,* That a Town is hereby established in the county of Greene, by the name of Hookerton, and the corporate limits of said Town are hereby declared to be as Boundaries. follows, to-wit: Beginning at a chinquepin on the south side of Big Contentnea Creek and running south forty-two poles to a stake in Mr. Edward's field, thence with a cross fence, the dividing line between J. M. Patrick, Julia Jones, Female Institute and F. M. Pittman, to the Kinston Road, thence in the same direction across the plantation of Mrs. Powell to the Mill Pond, thence down said pond to the Mill, thence down the Mill Run to the Creek, thence with the various meanderings of said Creek to the beginning.

SEC. 2. *Be it further enacted,* That the government of Commissioners. said Town of Hookerton shall be vested in the following named persons and their successors in office, to-wit: John M. Patrick, H. F. Grainger, Irvin Jones, F. M. Rountree, John Grizard.

SEC. 3. *Be it further enacted,* That the Commissioners and their successors in office, appointed agreeably to the Powers and directions of this Act, shall be and they are hereby incorporated into a body corporate by the name of the Commissioners of the Town of Hookerton, and by that name shall have succession and a common seal, with all the rights, powers and privileges granted to or invested in Corporations by virtue of chapter 111, of the Revised Code of North Carolina.

SEC. 4. *Be it further enacted,* That an election shall be Elections. held in each and every year, on the first Monday of March, by the inhabitants of said Town, qualified to vote for members of the House of Commons, for five Commissioners, who shall hold their office for one year, or until their successors are appointed.

SEC. 5. *Be it further enacted*, That the Commissioners under this Act shall be and continue to act as such until their successors are appointed.

SEC. 6. *Be it further enacted*, That this Act shall be in force from and after its ratification.

Ratified the 20th day of February, A. D., 1867.

CHAPTER XCI.

AN ACT TO INCORPORATE THE PERQUIMANS STEAM NAVIGATION COMPANY.

SECTION 1. *Be it enacted by the General Assembly of the State of North Carolina, and it is hereby enacted by the authority of the same*, That W. R. Blanchard, James M. Sumner, Elihu A. White, James Gatling, James F. Newby, E. C. Lindsey, J. W. Albertson and James C. Skinner, and their associates, with such other persons as they may hereafter associate with them, their successors and assigns, are hereby constituted a body politic and corporate, by the name of the "Perquimans Steam Navigation Company," and as such, and by said name, may sue and be sued, plead and be impleaded, shall have succession and a common seal, and may acquire, hold, possess and transfer real and personal property for the necessary purposes of the Company, and may make and adopt all rules, regulations and by-laws for the government of said Company, not inconsistent with the laws of this State or of the United States. *Corporators.* *Powers, &c.*

SEC. 2. *Be it further enacted*, That the said Company shall have all the rights and powers which may be necessary to build, construct or purchase steamboats, and other necessary craft for the transportation of persons, goods, wares and merchandise, or any description of property *Objects.*

whatsoever, to and from any place situated on **Albemarle Sound, Pamlico Sound,** and **Croatan Sound,** and their tributaries, to and from the city of **Norfolk, Virginia,** and the ports on **Chesapeake Bay.**

Capital.

SEC. 3. *Be it further enacted,* That the capital stock of said Company shall be ten thousand dollars, distributed in shares of such amount as shall be most convenient and necessary for the purposes of the Company, and that the Stockholders in said Company shall have power, in general meeting of the same, to raise the capital stock of the Company to a sum, not exceeding one hundred thousand dollars.

Elections, &c.

SEC. 4. *B it further enacted,* That the Stockholders, in general meeting, shall have the privilege of voting by proxy in all elections of officers of said Company, and in other matters relating to the business of the Company, and that each share shall be entitled to one vote.

Directors.

SEC. 5. *Be it further enacted,* That there shall be annually elected six Directors, to be called the Board of Directors of the Perquimans Steam Navigation Company, who shall hold their position for one year, or until their successors shall be elected and accept the duties thereof. It shall be the duty of the Board of Directors to appoint, by a majority vote, the President and officers and agents which the Stockholders may deem necessary to appoint, the time and place of the annual meeting of the Stockholders, and to notify the Stockholders thereof, in the interval between the annual meetings of the Stockholders, to conduct the business of the Company.

SEC. 6. *Be it further enacted,* That this Act shall take effect and be in force from and after its ratification.

Ratified the 21st day of February, A. D., 1867.

CHAPTER XCII.

AN ACT TO INCORPORATE UNION CAMP GROUND IN THE COUNTY OF CLEVELAND.

SECTION 1. *Be it enacted by the General Assembly of the State of North Carolina, and it is hereby enacted by the authority of the same,* That John R. Wills, A. J. Elliott, D. H. Peeler, David Whisnant, William Elliott, Dr. D. V. Palmer, Henry Schenck, and their successors, be, and they are hereby, constituted a body politic and corporate, by the name of the "Trustees of Union Camp Ground," and by that name shall have perpetual succession, and a common seal, may sue and be sued, acquire and transfer property, have jurisdiction over all the lands heretofore conveyed, or which may hereafter be conveyed, to the Trustees for the use of the Church or Camp Ground, and pass all such by-laws and regulations for the government of said Camp Ground as shall not be inconsistent with the Constitution and laws of this State and of the United States; and in case of vacancy by death, resignation or otherwise, the remainder, or a majority of them, or the Conference of the Methodist Episcopal Church in that circuit, and according to the discipline and rules of said church, may appoint successors, who shall have the same power and authority as are conferred on the Trustees created by this Act. *[Corporators. Powers, &c.]*

SEC. 2. *Be it further enacted,* That the aforesaid corporation shall possess no more real estate than is necessary and proper for its declared purpose, and the transaction of its business, and in all other respects shall enjoy the privileges of, and be subject to the restrictions of, chapter 26, Revised Code. *[Restrictions]*

SEC. 3. *Be it further enacted,* That this Act shall be in force from and immediately after its ratification, and may continue in force for the term of sixty years.

Ratified the 30th day of January, A. D., 1867.

CHAPTER XCIII.

AN ACT TO AMEND AN ACT, ENTITLED AN ACT TO CONSOLIDATE AND AMEND THE SEVERAL ACTS HERETOFORE PASSED FOR THE BETTER REGULATION OF THE TOWN OF JACKSONVILLE, IN ONSLOW COUNTY.

Amendment.

SECTION 1. *Be it enacted by the General Assembly of the State of North Carolina, and it is hereby enacted by the authority of the same,* That chapter ten (10) section third (3) of the Acts of the Legislature of North Carolina, ratified the twenty-seventh (27) day of February, 1866, be and the same is hereby amended so as to read the third Monday of February of each and every year, instead of the first Monday of April of each and every year.

SEC. 2. *Be it further enacted,* That this Act shall be in force from and after its ratification.

Ratified the 30th day of January, A. D., 1867.

CHAPER XCIV.

AN ACT TO INCORPORATE THE BLADEN LAND COMPANY.

Corporators.

Objects.

SECTION 1. *Be it enacted by the General Assembly of the State of North Carolina, and it is hereby enacted by the authority of the same,* That Joseph C. Abbott, Alfred M. Waddell, George Z. French, L. G. Estes, Daniel Clark, John L. Kelly and George S. Hanson, and their associates and successors, be and they are hereby created a corporation and body politic, in law and in fact, by the name and style of the Bladen Land Company, for the purpose of clearing and draining land, cutting canals, erecting and running mills manufacturing lumber and other articles, and mining for salt and other substances, and by that name and style may sue and be sued, plead and be impleaded in any Court of Record, contract and be contracted with, have perpetual succession, and a common seal, and acquire and retain real personal estate; and shall so continue for thirty years, during which period, and at the expiration thereof, said Company may sell or otherwise dispose of any and all real and personal estate acquired in their corporate character.

<small>Powers, &c.</small>

SEC. 2. *Be it further enacted*, That the capital stock of said Company shall be fifty thousand dollars, in shares of one hundred dollars each, and the same [may] be increased to an amount not exceeding three hundred thousand dollars, according to the discretion of the Stockholders.

<small>Capital.</small>

SEC. 3. *Be it further enacted*, That the Stockholders of the said Company, a majority being present, either in person or by proxy, shall have power to pass all by-laws and regulations necessary for the management of the affairs of the Company, and to elect all such officers as may be deemed proper for the same, said officers to hold their offices for terms to be prescribed in the by-laws, unless sooner removed by the Stockholders.

<small>Elections.</small>

SEC. 4. *Be it further enacted*, That this act shall be in force from and after its ratification.

Ratified the 26th day of January, A. D., 1867.

CHAPTER XCV.

AN ACT TO INCORPORATE THE TOWN OF ROCKY MOUNT IN THE COUNTY OF EDGECOMBE.

SECTION 1. *Be it enacted by the General Assembly of the State of North Carolina, and it is hereby enacted by the authority of the same,* That the Town of Rocky Mount, in Edgecombe county, be, and is hereby, incorporated; and, until Commissioners shall be elected, as hereinafter provided, the government of said Town shall be vested in the following named Commissioners, to-wit: Dr. R. C. Tilley,

<small>Commissioners.</small>

W. W. Parker, T. H. Griffin, A. J. Grey, Robert Ricks and G. W. Hammond.

Elections. Sec. 2. *Be it further enacted,* That an election shall be held on the 1st Monday in April, 1867, and of each successive year, for five Commissioners of said Town, and all persons living within the corporate limits of said Town, and qualified to vote for members of the General Assembly, shall be entitled to vote at said elections; in every other respect said elections shall be held as provided in chapter 3, of the Revised Code.

Boundaries. Sec. 3. *Be it further enacted,* That the boundaries and lines of said Town shall be as follows: Commencing at a Black Gum on Gray Armstrong's land, then running south seventy-three degrees east one mile to a maple on William W. Parker's land, then north seventeen degrees east one mile, to a stake in Spicers' land, then north seventy-three degrees west one mile, to a pine in Brice's land, then south seventeen west one mile to first station.

Corporate powers and privileges. Sec. 4. *Be it further enacted,* That for the good government of the said Town, the said Commissioners and their successors shall have all the rights, powers and privileges, and be governed by the rules, regulations and restrictions conferred upon, and to which Commissioners of incorporated towns are subject, by chapter 3, Revised Code.

Sec. 5. *Be it further enacted,* That this Act shall be in force from and after its ratification.

Ratified the 19th day of February, A. D., 1867.

CHAPTER XCVI

AN ACT TO INCORPORATE THE NEUSE RIVER FERRY COMPANY.

Corporators. Section 1. *Be it enacted by the General Assembly of the State of North Carolina, and it is hereby enacted by the authority of the same,* That S. G. Barrington, Adam Barrington, A. C. Latham and S. W. Chadwick, their associates, their successors and assigns, be, and they are hereby, created and constituted a body politic and corporate, for the space of ten years, by the name and style of the Neuse Ferry Company; and as such shall have succession, and may sue and be sued, plead and be impleaded in any Court of Law and Equity, shall have power to make all such by-laws and regulations, not inconsistent with the laws and constitution of the State, as may be deemed necessary for the government of such company, which shall be binding thereon, and shall have, exercise and enjoy all the privileges of a body corporate. *Powers and privileges.*

SEC. 2. *Be it further enacted,* That the said Company is hereby authorized to construct and establish a Ferry across Neuse River, from the said S. G. Barrington's Ferry to New Berne, in the County of Craven, and shall have power to acquire, hold and transfer such real or personal estate as may be necessary and appropriate to carry this object into effect. *Objects.*

SEC. 3. *Be it further enacted,* That the County Court of Craven County shall have power and authority to fix the rates of tolls for crossing said Ferry as they may see proper. *Tolls.*

SEC. 4. *Be it further enacted,* That after the organization of said Corporation, it shall not be lawful to build, construct or establish any other Ferry on said Neuse River, within three miles of said Neuse Ferry, for public use : *Provided,* That if the said Company shall neglect or refuse to keep suitable accommodation for the travelling public, then and in that case they shall forfeit their charter. *No other Ferry to be established.* *Proviso.*

SEC. 5. *Be it further enacted,* That this Act shall be in force from its ratification.

Ratified the 4th day of March, A. D., 1867.

CHAPTER XCVII.

AN ACT TO INCORPORATE CRANE'S CREEK LODGE, NO. 213, OF FREE AND ACCEPTED MASONS.

Powers, &c.

SECTION 1. *Be it enacted by the General Assembly of the State of North Carolina, and it is hereby enacted by the authority of the same,* That the officers and members who are at present, or in future may be, of Crane's Creek Lodge, number two hundred and thirteen, of Free and Accepted Masons, in Moore county, be and they are hereby incorporated into a body politic and corporate, under the name and style of Crane's Creek Lodge, number two hundred and thirteen, of Free and Accepted Masons; and by that name may have succession and a common seal, sue and be sued, plead and be impleaded in any Court of Record, or before any Justice of the Peace in this State; contract and be contracted with, acquire, hold and dispose of personal property for the benefit of said Lodge, and also such real estate as may be necessary for the transacting and carrying on the business of said Lodge.

Further powers.

SEC. 2. *Be it further enacted,* That the said corporation shall have power to pass all necessary by-laws and regulations for its own government, which may not be inconsistent with the Constitution of the United States, nor with the Constitution and laws of North Carolina.

SEC. 3. *Be it further enacted,* That this Act shall be in force from and after its ratification.

Ratified the 4th day of March, A. D., 1867.

CHAPTER XCVIII.

AN ACT TO AMEND AN ACT PASSED AT THE SESSION OF 1846 AND 1847, RATIFIED THE 7TH JANUARY, 1847, CHAPTER 203, TO INCORPORATE THE TOWN OF HENDERSONVILLE, IN THE COUNTY OF HENDERSON.

SECTION 1. *Be it enacted by the General Assembly of the State of North Carolina, and it is hereby enacted by the authority of the same,* That said Act be so amended as to authorize and require the Sheriff, or other officer holding election for town Commissioners, at their next annual election, and every annual election thereafter, to hold an election in the usual way by ballot, for or against the sale of spirituous liquors within the corporate limits of said Town, in a less quantity than five gallons, except for medicinal purposes, under the certificate of a regular physician advising such sale; all persons residing within the limits of said Town, who are now allowed to vote for members to the Legislature, shall be allowed to vote for or against said license, and those voting in favor of allowing the license shall have the word "license" written or printed on their tickets, whilst those who vote against it shall have the words "no license" written or printed on their tickets.

Sheriff to as certain the sense of the voters as to retailing spirituous liquors

SEC. 2. *Be it further enacted,* That whenever the majority of the votes so cast shall be "no license," the same shall be certified by the officer holding such election, to the Clerk of the County Court, and entered on the journals of the Court, and the Magistrates of the county shall have no power to grant licenses for the sale of spirituous liquors of any kind within said corporation, for the next twelve months after said election, nor shall any person sell any intoxicating liquors of any description within said corporate limits in less quantity than five gallons during the next twelve months after said election, without a written recommendation of a regular physician for medicinal purposes only.

Penalty for violation this Act.

SEC. 3. *Be it further enacted,* That any person violating the provisions of this Act shall be guilty of a misdemeanor, of indictable in the County or Superior Courts of the county, and shall be further subject to a fine of not more than fifty dollars by the town authorities, for each and every offense, one-half to the informer and the other half to the treasury of the corporation.

SEC. 4. *Be it further enacted,* That this Act shall take effect from and after its ratification, and all clauses of laws in conflict with it are hereby repealed, so far as this Act is concerned.

Ratified the 21st day of February, A. D., 1867.

CHAPTER XCIX.

AN ACT CONCERNING THE TOWN OF WARRENTON.

Election of Commissioners.

SECTION 1. *Be it enacted by the General Assembly of the State of North Carolina, and it is hereby enacted by the authority of the same,* That it shall be the duty of the Sheriff of Warren county, on any day which he may appoint within thirty days after the ratification of this Act, to hold an election, at the Court House in Warrenton, for seven Commissioners of said Town, he having previously advertised the same for ten days at the Court House aforesaid, and at two or more public places in said Town: and it shall be also his duty to appoint two freeholders as inspectors of the polls, who are to be duly sworn to conduct the election fairly and impartially according to law and in default of acting, the said inspectors shall be deemed to be guilty of a misdemeanor.

SEC. 2. *Be it further enacted,* That the said election is in every respect to be governed by the provisions of the one hundred and eleventh chapter of the Revised Code, except when the same may conflict with this Act.

SEC. 3. *Be it further enacted,* That the Commissioners, who may be elected at the time aforesaid, are to continue in office until an election shall be held for as many Commissioners as the County Court of Warren may name, and on such day in the year 1868 as the said Court may designate; and an election shall take place annually afterwards on the last mentioned day.

Annual elections.

SEC. 4. *Be it further enacted,* That all of the provisions now contained in the one hundred and eleventh chapter of the Revised Code, entitled "Towns," and all laws of the State concerning towns generally, shall be applicable to the Town of Warrenton and govern the same, any act exclusively relating to said Town to the contrary notwithstanding.

Chap. 111, Rev. Code.

SEC. 5. *Be it further enacted,* That this Act shall be in force from and after its ratification.

Ratified the 29th day of January, A. D., 1867.

CHAPTER C.

AN ACT TO CHARTER WICCACON LODGE, NO. 240, ANCIENT YORK MASONS.

SECTION 1. *Be it enacted by the General Assembly of the State of North Carolina and it is hereby enacted by the authority of the same,* That the Worshipful Master, Wardens and members of Wiccacon Lodge, No. 240, A. Y. M., of Harrelsville, Hertford county, North Carolina, be, and they are hereby, constituted a body corporate and politic, by the name and style of Wiccacon Lodge, No. 240, A. Y. M., and by that name and style shall have perpetual succession and a common seal, and may sue and be sued, plead and be impleaded before any Court of Record or Justice of the Peace in this State, may contract and be contracted with, acquire, hold and dispose of personal property for the benefit of said Lodge, and also such real estate as may be required for the convenient transaction of its business.

Powers, &c.

SEC. 2. *Be it further enacted,* That said corporation shall have power to make all necessary by-laws and regulations for its government : *Provided,* the same be not inconsistent with the Constitution and laws of this State or of the United States.

SEC. 3. *Be it further enacted,* That this Act shall be in force from and after its ratification.

Ratified the 2nd day of March, A. D., 1867.

CHAPTER Cl.

AN ACT TO INCORPORATE THE KEY-STONE PUBLISHING COMPANY, IN THE CITY OF RALEIGH.

<small>Corporators.</small>
SECTION 1. *Be it enacted by the General Assembly of the State of North Carolina, and it is hereby enacted by the authority of the same,* That Wm. B. Smith, J. G. Hester and their associates, be, and they are hereby, constituted a body corporate and politic, for the publishing and diffusion of Masonic books and literature, in the city of Raleigh, under the name and style of "The Key-Stone Publishing Company," and by and under said name shall be known, and shall have common succession and a common seal, and by said name may sue and be sued, plead and be impleaded in any and all Courts of Law and Equity in this State, and shall enjoy all the rights, privileges and incidents usually enjoyed by like corporations, for the space of twenty years, and no longer.

<small>Powers and privileges.</small>

<small>Capital, &c</small>
SEC. 2. *Be it further enacted,* That the capital stock of said Company shall not exceed the sum of twenty-five thousand dollars, to be divided into shares of ten dollars each. Books of subscription shall be at once opened in the city of Raleigh, and at such other points in the State as may be designated by an advertisement inserted in any paper in the city of Raleigh, ten days preceding the opening of the books. As soon as five hundred dollars shall be subscribed, and the half thereof paid in, the Company shall

have authority to proceed to the exercise of the functions and rights hereby conferred.

SEC. 3. *Be it further enacted*, That the said Company shall be governed by a President and Board of Directors, to be elected by the Stockholders annually, who shall have power to elect and appoint such officers as may be necessary for the management of the Company affairs. President and Directors.

SEC. 4. *Be it further enacted*, That the President and Board of Directors shall have power to make such by-laws for the government of the Company as are not inconsistent with the Constitution and laws of the United States and the Constitution and laws of North Carolina.

SEC. 5. *Be it further enacted*, That this Act shall be in force from and after its ratification.

Ratified the 2nd day of March, A. D., 1867.

CHAPTER CII.

AN ACT TO INCORPORATE THE NORTH CAROLINA LAND AND IMMIGRATION AID COMPANY.

SECTION 1. *Be it enacted by the General Assembly of the State of North Carolina, and it is hereby enacted by the authority of the same*, That S. McD. Tate, J. F. Foard, William Johnston, Z. B. Vance, William H. Thomas, Rufus Y. McAden, Geo. W. Swepson, A. C. Avery, R. W. Pulliam and John D. Whitford, their associates, successors and assigns, be, and they are hereby, created a body politic and corporate, under the name and style of the "North Carolina Land and Immigration Aid Company," with powers of perpetual succession, and a common seal, to sue and be sued, plead and be impleaded in Courts of Law and Equity, to hold, enjoy and convey real estate, to make, alter and repeal all rules and regulations and by-laws, necessary for their own government, according to the objects and purposes herein expressed, and generally to do any and all things necessary to the ends of their organization, and to enjoy all the rights and privileges ensured to corporations by the laws of this State, not inconsistent with the Constitution of North Carolina, or of the United States.

Capital.

Sec. 2. *Be it further enacted,* That the capital stock of said Company shall not exceed one million of dollars, in shares of twenty dollars each, and that the amount of real estate to be owned by them, at any one time, shall not exceed the number of five hundred thousand acres, within the bounds of this State.

Directors.

Sec. 3. *Be it further enacted,* That the business of said Company shall be directed and controlled by ten (10) Directors, to be chosen annually by the Stockholders thereof, which Directors shall choose a President from one of their number, to hold their office for one year, or until their successors are chosen ; and the said President and Directors shall appoint and reserve, at their pleasure, all other necessary and subordinate officers of said Company, but the fundamental rules and by-laws hereof shall be adopted by Stockholders alone in full meeting.

Stock may be subscribed in money or lands.

Sec. 4. *Be it further enacted,* That shares in said Company may be subscribed for either in money or lands; and when in lands the value thereof shall be assessed in the manner directed by the by-laws, and certificates of stock shall issue therefor, and be transferable and assignable in such manner as may be prescribed by the Company, which shall also have the power, if necessary, when receiving title to lands subscribed for stock, to require an affidavit, upon oath, that the said property is unencumbered.

Records of the Company. &c.

Sec. 5. *Be it further enacted,* That the said Company shall cause to be kept, at their principal office, by the proper officer, books showing an accurate statement of the assets and liabilities of said Company, the amount, description and title deeds of their lands, the amount of stock subscribed, the per centum paid in, &c., which shall be at all times open to the inspection of the Stockholders, and of persons applying to buy stock or land; and all shares shall be deemed personal estate; and the said Company shall have power to issue and sue [sell?] their corporate bonds to the amount of fifty per centum on the whole amount of their assets and no more, to deal in gold and silver coin and uncurrent money, foreign and domestic exchange, to receive on deposit and for collection all bonds, obligations, notes and other securities, and buy and sell the same: *Provided*, said bonds shall not be issued for less sums than one hundred dollars.

SEC. 6. *Be it further enacted*, That for the purpose of encouraging the immigration of settlers, farmers, mechanics, artizans, shepherds, herdsmen, vine dressers and all manner of laborers, from Europe and elsewhere, into the State of North Carolina, the said Company shall have power to purchase and hold houses and lots in any city or town in the United States, subject to the laws of the same, establish offices and agents therein, and in Europe, charter and purchase ships, and to do any and all other necessary and lawful acts. Immigration.

SEC. 7. *Be it further enacted*, That the corporators named in the first section, or a majority of them, shall have power to organize the said Company and open books for stock subscriptions, call the first regular meeting of the Stockholders, and assess such a er cent. upon the capital stock as may be necessary to the proper organization of said Company, whenever five hundred shares shall have been subscribed.

SEC. 8. *Be it further enacted*, That the corporate privileges herein granted shall continue for sixty years.

Ratified the 2nd day of March, A. D., 1867.

CHAPTER CIII.

AN ACT TO EXTEND THE LIMITS OF THE TOWN OF LUMBERTON, IN ROBESON COUNTY.

SECTION 1. *Be it enacted by the General Assembly of the State of North Carolina, and it is hereby enacted by the authority of the same*, That the boundaries of the Town of Lumberton, in the county of Robeson, shall be extended Extension of limits.

so as to make Lumber river the Western boundary of said Town, and extend the Northern boundary in a straight direction from the Northern course of said Town to Lumber river, so as to include the residences of Dr. William A. Dick and Mrs. Caldwell, and all others included within said boundary. And that all the persons and property included within said boundary shall be subject to the same laws, by-laws, rules and regulations as are or may be imposed by the Mayor and Commissioners of the Town of Lumberton upon other citizens of said Town.

SEC. 2. *Be it further enacted,* That this Act shall be in force from and after its ratification.

Ratified the 4th day of March, A. D., 1867.

CHAPTER CIV.

AN ACT TO INCORPORATE THE CHARLOTTE WATER WORKS.

Corporators.

SECTION 1. *Be it enacted by the General Assembly of the State of North Carolina, and it is hereby enacted by the authority of the same,* That John L. Morehead, John R. Tate, William Johnston, Joseph H. Wilson, James M. Hutchison, John A. Young, Samuel A. Hanes, Robt. M. Oates, Thos. H. Brem, Solomon A. Cohen, Alexander Sinclair, John Wilkes, Thomas W. Dewey, John Y. Bryce and William R. Myers, James P. Irwin and W. J. Yates, and their associates, successors and assigns, be and they are hereby created a body corporate, in law and in fact, by the name and style of the Charlotte Water Works Company, for the purpose of transportation or conveying water by pipe or otherwise, into and through the corporate limits of the City of Charlotte and vicinity, and sell the same to the citizens thereof, and for other purposes; and by that name may sue and be sued, plead and be impleaded in any Court of Law or Equity, may have and use a common seal, and change the same at pleasure, have power to make all such rules and by-laws and regulations, not inconsistent with

Objects.

Powers, &c.

the Constitution of this State or of the United States, which may be deemed necessary for the government of said Company, which shall be binding thereon; and shall possess and enjoy all rights and privileges and immunities of a corporation, a body politic in law, necessary to carry on said business.

SEC. 2. *Be it further enacted,* That the said Company may employ such an amount of capital, not exceeding two hundred and fifty thousand dollars, as may be deemed necessary to carry on the business aforesaid, which may be divided into shares of one hundred dollars each, or such other amount as the Stockholders, in general meeting, may determine, for obtaining which books of subscription may be opened by the corporators aforesaid, and the sum paid in in such manner and at such times as the Board of Directors may require; and if any subscriber shall fail to pay any instalment at the time required, he shall pay interest thereon at the rate of eight per cent. per annum, and his stock shall be forfeited and may be sold by the Directors, and the proceeds be applied to the payment of the aforesaid deficient instalment; certificates of stock may be issued and the same made transferable and assignable as the by-laws of the Company shall prescribe.

Capital.

Delinquents

SEC. 3. *Be it further enacted,* That the affairs of the said Company shall be managed by a Board of Directors, chosen from among the Stockholders, the Mayor of the City of Charlotte, *ex officio*, being one of the number, and shall be composed of such number, and elected in such manner, as the by-laws may prescribe, and shall elect one of their number President of the Company; three of the Board shall be a quorum to transact business, one of whom shall be the President. The President may, by reason of protracted sickness or a necessary absence from the City, appoint, by writing, one of this number to fill his place. They shall have power to fill vacancies in said Board until a regular meeting of the Stockholders, and appoint all such officers as may be necessary, and fix their salaries, and take bonds in such sums as they may think necessary, for the faithful performance of their duties; shall fix the amount

President and Directors.

of compensation to be given to the President for his services.

SEC. 4. *Be it further enacted,* That as soon after the ratification of this Act as they may think proper, said corporators, or a majority of them, may call a general meeting of the subscribers to the stock in said Company, for the purpose of adopting by-laws for and electing Directors of said Company, which Directors shall continue in office until their successors shall be duly elected by a succeeding meeting.

General meeting.

SEC. 5. *Be it further enacted,* That the general meetings of Stockholders may be called and held as the by-laws may prescribe; to constitute a meeting, there must be present in person or by proxy, the proxy being a Stockholder, those who hold a majority of the stock, each share entitling the holder to one vote, and in all cases a majority of the votes cast shall be necessary.

Concerning quorum.

Sec. 6. *Be it further enacted,* That the said corporation shall have full power and authority to build or lay down piping, build aqueducts, reservoirs, culverts, dams and drains for the conveyance and transportation of water in such quantities through, upon, over or under the streets and lots of the City of Charlotte, and lands adjacent thereto, as may be required or necessary to supply the inhabitants thereof and vicinity with water, as aforesaid, and sell the same in such quantities as may meet the requirements of said City of Charlotte and vicinity; to purchase and hold such lots and parcels of land in said City or its vicinity, and erect thereon such buildings and improvements, as may be necessary or convenient for the purposes set forth, and when necessary to sell or exchange the same: *Provided, always,* That in the erection of dams, drains, reservoirs, laying down pipes, the Company shall be required to leave all streets, side-walks, alleys and private property in as good condition as they were in before said structures, pipe, &c., were erected or laid down; also to hold such personal property as may be necessary for successfully carrying on said business; also to erect, and, when necessary, to repair all said works, machinery and engines or other property held

Further powers of the Corporation.

by them, and to dispose of the same when to the interest of said Company

SEC. 7. *Be it further enacted,* That if any person or persons shall negligently or wilfully, by any means whatsoever, injure, impair or destroy conduit, pipes, culvert, reservoir, dam, machine, working implements or buildings, or any thing or property appertaining to the works of said Company, the person or persons so offending shall forfeit and pay to said Company double the amount of damages sustained by said injury, and the same may be recovered in the name of the Company, with cost of suit, in any Court of Record in the County of Mecklenburg; and moreover, they shall be subject to indictments in either the County or Superior Court of said County, as for a misdemeanor, and, upon conviction, shall be fined or imprisoned, or both, at the discretion of the Court. Penalty for injury, &c., to the works.

SEC. 8. *Be it further enacted,* That the Board of Aldermen, of the City of Charlotte, is hereby authorized to subscribe to the stock of said Company an amount not exceeding ten thousand dollars, and, to raise said amount, the said Board of Aldermen is authorized to issue bonds on the faith and credit of the City in such amounts, at such time, and at such rate as they may deem right and proper. Board of Aldermen of Charlotte may subscribe $10,000 to the Company

SEC. 9. *Be it further enacted,* That this Act shall be in force from and after its ratification, and continue in perpetuity.

Ratified the 4th day of March, A. D., 1867.

CHAPTER CV.

AN ACT TO INCORPORATE THE TOWN OF ROCKINGHAM, IN THE COUNTY OF RICHMOND.

SECTION 1. *Be it enacted by the General Assembly of the State of North Carolina, and it is hereby enacted by the authority of the same,* That it shall be the duty of the Sheriff of Richmond county, either by himself or his lawful dep-

<small>Election of Commissioners.</small>

uty, on the first Monday in April in each and every year, to open polls in the Court House, in the town of Rockingham, for the election of five Commissioners, in and for said town of Rockingham, to continue in office for the term of one year, and until others, duly chosen and qualified, have entered upon the duties of their office: *Provided,* That no one shall be eligible as Commissioner, who has not resided, six months preceding his election, within the limits of said town of Rockingham, and is an actual resident at the time of such election.

<small>Qualification of voters.</small>

SEC. 2. *Be it further enacted,* That every inhabitant of said town, who has resided six months therein, and who is qualified according to the Constitution to vote for members of the House of Commons, shall be entitled to vote in said elections, and said election shall be by ballot, and should there be a tie at any election, the inspectors of the same shall determine by lot.

<small>Notice of election.</small>

SEC. 3. *Be it further enacted,* That the Sheriff shall appoint the inspectors of said election from among the voters, and he shall give ten days previous notice of the first election, at some public place in said town.

<small>Mayor.</small>

SEC. 4. *Be it further enacted,* That a Mayor shall also be chosen at said elections, with the same qualifications, powers and duties as prescribed in chapter one hundred and eleven of the Revised Code, entitled "Towns," and that the said charter be in full force and effect as to the said town of Rockingham, except wherever it may be inconsistent with the provisions of this Act.

<small>Powers, &c., of Commissioners.</small>

SEC. 5. *Be it further enacted,* That the said Commissioners shall be styled "The Commissioners of the Town of Rockingham," and constitute a body politic and corporate, and by that name they shall be invested with a succession and a common seal, and shall have power to hold real and personal property, to sue and be sued, and to pass and ordain such by-laws and ordinances, not inconsistent with the Constitution of this State, or of the United States, as a majority of them may deem expedient and proper for the good government of said town; and their jurisdiction,

powers and duties shall extend to all persons and matters within the limits of said town as herein specified.

SEC. 6. *Be it further enacted*, That the corporate limits of said town shall be as follows: that is to say, the said town shall be in the form of an oblong square, as much as may be, extending in length due east and west, and in width due south and north. The eastern side of said town shall be one-half mile in extent, due north and south, and at its centre shall be three-fourths of a mile due east from the Court House door in said town of Rockingham; the north side of said town shall run due west from the most northern point of the eastern side already specified, until it intersects the stream of Hitchcock Creek, so that it will be one-fourth of a mile from the Court House door at the nearest point; the southern side of said town shall extend due west from the most southern point of the east side already specified, until it intersects the stream of Falling Creek, so that it be one-fourth of a mile from the Court House door, at the nearest point; thence down said stream to its junction with Hitchcock Creek; thence the boundary of said town shall extend up Hitchcock Creek to the point where the northern side, already specified, intersects said Creek.

Corporate limits.

SEC. 7. *Be it further enacted*, That the Sheriff or other officer, to whom is intrusted any part of the execution of this Act, on neglecting to perform the duties herein named, and on conviction thereof according to law, shall pay a fine of five hundred dollars, one-half to the State and the other half to the person suing for the same, and this in addition to the penalties now prescribed by law.

Penalty for Sheriffs' or other officers' neglect.

SEC. 8. *Be it further enacted*, That if, from any cause, this Act should not be carried into effect as herein specified, then the Court of Pleas and Quarter Sessions for the county of Richmond may, at any regular term during the year 1867, proceed to elect and organize Commissioners and other officers for the said town of Rockingham, as provided for in chapter one hundred and eleven of the Revised Code, entitled "Towns."

SEC. 9. *Be it further enacted,* That this Act shall be in full force and effect from and after its ratification.
Ratified the 4th day of March, A. D., 1867.

CHAPTER CVI.

AN ACT TO INCORPORATE CAROLINA LODGE, NO. 141, OF FREE AND ACCEPTED MASONS, IN THE COUNTY OF ANSON.

SECTION 1. *Be it enacted by the General Assembly of the State of North Carolina, and it is hereby enacted by the authority of the same,* That the Master, Wardens and members of the Carolina Lodge, No. 141, of Free and Accepted Masons, in the county of Anson, at Ansonville, be, and are hereby, constituted a body politic and corporate, by the name and style of Carolina Lodge, No. 141, of Free and Accepted Masons, and by that name shall have perpetual succession, may sue and be sued, plead and be impleaded, have a common seal, and in general exercise and enjoy all such rights and privileges as are usually incident to corporate bodies of like nature.

Powers, &c.

SEC. 2. *Be it further enacted,* That this Act shall be in force from and after its ratification.
Ratified the 26th day of February, A. D., 1867.

CHAPTER CVII.

AN ACT TO INCORPORATE THE WILMINGTON HOOK AND LADDER COMPANY.

SECTION 1. *Be it enacted by the General Assembly of the State of North Carolina, and it is hereby enacted by the authority of the same,* That George Rappler, P. H. N. Cornehlsen, J. C. DeRosset, Roger Moore, C. D. Myers, H. C. Brock, J. C. Banner, A. Adrian, Sol. Haas, S. Polley, John S. Dudley,

Corporators.

G. Copes, Alex. Anderson, Geo. Anderson, S. Bear, S. R. Bell, S. Boon, R. W. Brown, Benj. Copes, A. David, G. A. Gade, W. Goerkin, C. Hussell, Jacob Haas, J. J. King, J. Herrigan, Jos. Myer, S. Piner, W. H. N. Shorpstein, H. Sherman, Jas. Rasberry, John Rudge, Jas. Wilson, S. Levy and W. M. Monroe, and their associates, in number not more than forty, be, and they are hereby, created and declared to be a body politic and corporate, by the name and style of the Wilmington Hook and Ladder Company, and by that name shall, and may, sue and be sued, plead and be impleaded, in any and all Courts of law and equity, and shall have perpetual succession and a common seal, and may purchase, hold and transfer all such real and personal estate as may be necessary and convenient for the purposes of their association; and for their better government may make all necessary and proper by-laws, rules and regulations, not inconsistent with the laws of the United States and of this State; and shall have and enjoy all other rights, privileges and franchises, which of right belong to bodies politic and corporate. *Powers, &c.*

SEC. 2. *Be it further enacted,* That the officers of said corporation shall consist of a President, a Vice President, and Secretary and Treasurer, who shall be annually elected, and shall hold their offices until their successors are appointed. The President and Vice President shall be *ex officio* Foreman and Assistant Foreman of the Company, and they and the Secretary and Treasurer shall discharge all such duties as may be required of them by the by-laws, rules and regulations of the corporation. *Officers of the Corporation*

SEC. 3. *Be it further enacted,* That to secure a prompt and efficient discharge of duty, on the part of its members, the said corporation is hereby empowered, by its by-laws, rules and regulations, to impose reasonable fines and penalties for any neglect of duty and to provide for the collection of the same.

SEC. 4. *Be it further enacted,* That the members of the said corporation shall be exempt from duty in the militia and from serving on juries. *Exemptions*

Sec. 5. *Be it jurther enacted*, That this Act shall be in force from and after its ratification.

Ratified the 26th day of February, A. D., 1867.

CHAPTER CVIII.

AN ACT TO INCORPORATE THE PYTHAGORAS LODGE, NO. 249, IN THE TOWN OF SMITHVILLE, BRUNSWICK COUNTY.

Corporators.

Section 1. *Be it enacted by the General Assembly of the State of North Carolina, and it is hereby enacted by the authority of the same,* That W. D. Thurston, W. G. Curtis and A. M. Guthrie, and their associates of the masonic fraternity, of the Town of Smithville, Brunswick county, and their successors, are hereby incorporated as such in the name and style of Pythagoras Lodge, number two hundred and forty-nine, (249) and by that name may have succession and a common seal, sue and be sued, plead and be impleaded in any Court of Record or before any Justice of the Peace in this State, contract and be contracted with,

Powers, &c. acquire, hold and dispose of personal property for the benefit of said Lodge, and also such real estate as may be required for the convenient transaction of its business, and in general exercise and enjoy all such rights and privileges as are usually incident to corporate bodies of the like nature.

Sec. 11. *Be it furt'er enacted* That this Act shall be in force from and after its ratification.

Ratified the 26th day of February, A. D., 1867.

CHAPTER CIX.

AN ACT TO INCORPORATE THE TOWN FORK COAL AND PETROLEUM COMPANY.

SECTION 1. *Be it enacted by the General Assembly of the State of North Carolina, and it is hereby enacted by the authority of the same,* That Silas Westmoreland, P. A. Wilson, D. N. Dalton, B. F. Bynum, and such other persons as they may associate with them, be and the same are hereby incorporated and created a body politic and corporate by the name and style of the Directors of Town Fork Coal and Petroleum Company, and by that name may sue and be sued, plead and be impleaded, have a common seal, and, for the purposes hereinafter expressed, shall have all the rights, powers and privileges, and be subject to the rules, regulations and restrictions, contained in chapter twenty-six, Revised Code. *Corporators.* *Powers, &c*

SEC. 2. *Be it further enacted,* That the corporate privileges of said Company shall exist and continue for thirty (30) years, and said Company shall have power to open mines and mills for coal and petroleum on such lands as they may hold or purchase for that purpose, and to build and erect manufactories as may be necessary to carry on their operations and render the same profitable. *Duration.*

SEC. 3. *Be it further enacted,* That the capital stock of said Company shall not exceed three hundred thousand dollars, and shall be divided into shares of fifty dollars each, and the said Company shall commence operations at such time and with such an amount of subscription stock as the said Directors shall direct. *Capital.*

SEC. 4. *Be it further enacted,* That this Act shall go into effect from and after its ratification.

Ratified the 26th day of February, A. D., 1867.

CHAPTER CX.

AN ACT TO AMEND AN ACT ENTITLED AN ACT TO INCORPORATE THE CHEOIH TURNPIKE COMPANY, PASSED AT THE SESSION OF 1856-'57.

New Commissioners.

SECTION 1. *Be it enacted by the General Assembly of the State of North Carolina, and it is hereby enacted by the authority of the same,* That instead of Commissioners named in said Act, the following Commissioners are appointed: Thomas Rhea, Samuel P. Sherril, Calvin A. Colonid, Stephen Whitaker, William Deaver and William Sumpters, are hereby appointed Commissioners, a majority of whom, at such times and places and under the direction of such agents as they may select, are hereby authorized and empowered to open books for the subscription of stock in shares of twenty dollars each, to establish a Ferry or construct a Bridge across the Tennessee River, in the county of Macon, and to open the Turnpike oad from that point to the Tennessee line, and keep the same in good repair.

Objects.

Officers elected, &c., when?

SEC. 2. *Be it further enacted,* That as soon as the sum of one thousand dollars shall have been subscribed, in the manner and form aforesaid, the Company shall be incorporated by the election of the officers for the Road Company, mentioned in said Act, to be entitled to all the rights and privileges conferred on the Turnpike Company, by the recited and subsequent Act, for the period of sixty years from and after the date of the ratification of this Act.

SEC. 3. *Be it further enacted,* That the said Company shall, without any unnecessary delay, proceed to establish a Ferry across the Tennessee River at Negolih, and at any subsequent period, within the period of their charter, may establish a Bridge to separate the Ferry across the Tennessee River, at Negolih, for the passage of passengers, vehicles, &c., as hereinafter mentioned.

Sec. 4. *Be it further enacted*, That as soon as a good, sufficient Ferry shall have been established by the Company, they shall be permitted to appoint toll gatherers, who are hereby empowered to demand and receive the following tolls for crossing said Ferry or Bridge, and to refuse a passage until the tolls are paid for crossing the Bridge, alone, disconnected from the other tolls for travelling the Road: For one-horse gigs and sulkeys, twenty five cents each; for two-horse pleasure carriages, thirty-seven and a half cents; for four-horse carriages of pleasure, seventy-five cents; for six-horse road waggons, fifty cents; for five-horse road waggons, thirty-seven and a half cents; for four-horse road waggons, twenty-five cents; for three-horse road waggons, twenty cents; for two-horse road waggons, for the transportation of produce, fifteen cents; for one-horse carts or waggons, used in the transportation of produce, ten cents; for pedlars' waggons, one dollar each; for each horse or mule, with a rider, ten cents; for every head of cattle, two cents; for every head of hogs or sheep, one cent each; for all animals, intended for public exhibition, fifty cents each. Tolls.

Sec. 5. *Be it further enacted*, That as soon as the Company shall have repaired the waggon road leading from Negolih northward to the Tennessee line, and afterwards while they shall keep it in good repair, they shall be entitled to demand and receive, for travelling the said road, one half of the tolls allowed for crossing the Ferry or Bridge in each case, as specified in the 4th section. Further concerning tolls.

Sec. 6. *Be it further enacted*, That the Company shall have the right to reduce but shall not increase said tolls without the consent of the Legislature. Tolls shall not be increased.

Sec. 7. *Be it further enacted*, That the Company, as provided for in this Act, may increase the capital stock of the Company to three thousand dollars, or to an amount sufficient to complete the Bridge and Road. Capital may be increased.

Sec. 8. *Be it further enacted*, That nothing in this Act, or the recited Acts, shall be so construed as to authorize the Agent of the State, for the collection of Cherokee Bonds, to subscribe any bonds or moneys to said Ferry, Bridge or Road, and that all laws coming in conflict with this section be and the same are hereby repealed.

SEC. 9. *Be it further enacted,* That this Act shall be in force from and after its ratification and continue in force sixty years.

Ratified the 26th day of February, A. D., 1867.

CHAPTER CXI.

AN ACT TO AMEND THE THIRD SECTION OF THE 97TH CHAPTER OF THE REVISED CODE, ENTITLED "RELIGIOUS SOCIETIES."

Amendment. SEC. 1. *Be it enacted by the General Assembly of the State of North Carolina, and it is hereby enacted by the authority of the same,* That the 3rd section of the Act referred to in the title hereto, be amended, by inserting after the word "to," at the end of the 8th line, the words "take by devise."

Repeal of proviso. SEC. 2. *Be it further enacted,* That the proviso in said section contained be and the same is hereby repealed:

St. James' Parish. *Provided,* That the provisions of this Act shall extend and apply to St. James Parish, in the city of Wilmington, and to no other religious Society whatever.

Ratified the 22nd day of December, A. D., 1866.

CHATER CXII.

AN ACT TO REPEAL ALL ACTS HERETOFORE PASSED IN RELATION TO THE INCORPORATION OF THE TOWN OF MORGANTON, AND TO PROVIDE A SUBSTITUTE THEREFOR.

SECTION 1. *Be it enacted by the General Assembly of the State of North Carolina, and it is hereby enacted by the authority of the same,* That all acts heretofore passed in relation to the incorporation of the Town of Morganton be, and same are hereby, repealed. *Repeal.*

SEC. 2. *Be it further enacted,* That the Town of Morganton, in Burke county, be, and the same is hereby, created a body politic, with full authority to use and exercise all the corporate powers and privileges granted to incorporated towns by the 111th chapter Revised Code, entitled "Towns," and may elect such officers, and manage the affairs of the corporation in such manner, as the law prescribes for the better government of said Town : *Provided,* that the Commissioners of said Town shall not be empowered to require any person to perform the duty of patrol or Town-watch, except those who may be employed by contract and duly compensated for their services. *Corporate powers.*

SEC. 3. *Be it further enacted,* That the Commissioners of said Town shall be authorized and empowered to collect all arrearages of taxes due said Town, and to demand of, and receive from, the former tax collector, all moneys due said corporation by reason of the tax heretofore collected and not paid over to said corporation. *Arrearages of taxes.*

SEC. 4. *Be it further enacted,* That the Commissioners of the said Town shall have power to sue for and receive all moneys in the hands of all defaulting officers, due the said corporation under the former acts of incorporation. *Defaulting officers.*

SEC. 5. *Be it further enacted,* That this Act shall be in force from and after its ratification.

Ratified the 18th day of December, A. D., 1866.

MISCELLANEOUS.

CHAPTER CXIII.

AN ACT FOR THE RELIEF OF WM. A. PHILPOT, SHERIFF OF GRANVILLE.

WHEREAS, William A. Philpot, Sheriff of the county of Granville, by reason of protracted illness, has been unable to collect his taxes in full: *And whereas*, the said Wm. A. Philpot has paid into the Treasury of the State the sum of $660 00, and there remains the sum of $822 38 yet to be paid:

SECTION 1. *Be it enacted by the General Assembly of the State of North Carolina, and it is hereby enacted by the authority of the same,* That the said Wm. A. Philpot be allowed until the 15th day of March, 1867, to collect and pay the said balance into the Treasury of the State.

Allowed until March 15 to collect and pay over taxes

Ratified the 22nd day of December, A. D., 1866.

CHAPTER CXIV.

AN ACT TO ALLOW THE LEGAL REPRESENTATIVES OF W. E. MANN, LATE SHERIFF OF PASQUOTANK, TO COLLECT ARREARS OF TAXES.

SECTION 1. *Be it enacted by the General Assembly of the State of North Carolina, and it is hereby enacted by the authority of the same,* That the legal representative of the late W. E. Mann, late Sheriff of Pasquotank county, be and is hereby authorized and empowered to collect any taxes levied and unpaid for the years 1859 and 1860: *Pro-*

Authorized to collect taxes for 1859-'60

vided, That no person who will say upon oath, that the taxes appearing upon the list against him are not due and have been paid, [shall be required to pay the same]: *And, provided,* That this Act shall not apply to any executor or administrator or to persons who have removed from the county.

Provisos.

SEC. 2. *Be it further enacted,* That this Act shall be in force from and after its ratification.

Ratified the 2nd day of March, A. D., 1867.

CHAPTER CXV.

AN ACT IN FAVOR OF THE SHERIFF OF GASTON COUNTY.

WHEREAS, The General Assembly of North Carolina has shown a magnanimous spirit of liberality to the distressed and impoverished people of the State, in extending to the people of a portion of the State time to pay their taxes now due; *and, whereas,* the people of the county of Gaston were greatly injured by Stoneman's raiders, who were quartered upon the people of said county for a considerable time, and who committed immense devastation upon the people: Therefore,

SECTION 1. *Be it enacted by the General Assembly of the State of North Carolina, and it is hereby enacted by the authority of the same,* That the Sheriff of Gaston county be allowed until the first day of February, A. D., 1867, to make return of the public taxes due the State.

Allowed to Feb. 1, to make returns of taxes.

Ratified the — day of December, A. D., 1866.

CHAPTER CXVI.

AN ACT FOR THE RELIEF OF JAMES S. SNOW, SHERIFF OF HALIFAX COUNTY.

SECTION 1. *Be it enacted by the General Assembly of the State of North Carolina, and it is hereby enacted by the authority of the same,* That indulgence be granted to James

Allowed to March 1, to make returns. S. Snow, Sheriff of Halifax county, until the 1st March, 1867, to make his returns and settle his accounts with the Public Treasurer, for all taxes due the State by the people of aforesaid county.

SEC. 3. *Be it further enacted,* That this Act shall be in force from and after its ratification.

Ratified the 20th day of December, A. D., 1866.

CHAPTER CXVII.

AN ACT TO AUTHORIZE "THE MAYOR AND COMMISSIONERS OF FAYETTEVILLE," TO FUND THE INTEREST DUE ON THEIR BONDS ISSUED IN PAYMENT FOR STOCK IN THE WESTERN RAILROAD COMPANY.

SECTION 1. *Be it enacted by the General Assembly of the State of North Carolina, and it is hereby enacted by the authority of the same,* That the Mayor and Commissioners of the Town of Fayetteville be, and they are hereby, authorized, at their discretion, to issue the Bonds of their corporation, in such form and at such rate of interest as to them may seem most expedient, *provided* the issue shall not be of a less denomination than thirty dollars, to the full amount of the coupons due on their Bonds issued under an Act of the General Assembly, ratified 3rd February, 1857, chapter 71, due and to become due, up to and inclusive of 1st July, 1867, which said bonds, so issued, shall be binding upon the corporation of said Mayor and Commissioners, to all intents and purposes, and the faith and credit of said corporation shall be pledged for the payment of such Bonds and the interest which may accrue thereon.

May issue bonds, under certain restrictions, to full amount of coupons on existing bonds.

SEC. 2. *Be it further enacted,* That this Act shall be in force from and after its ratification.

Ratified the 9th day of February, A. D., 1867.

CHAPTER CXVIII.

AN ACT TO AUTHORIZE THE COUNTY OF CUMBERLAND AND THE TOWN OF FAYETTEVILLE TO ISSUE BONDS FOR THEIR INDEBTEDNESS.

SECTION 1. *Be it enacted by the General Assembly of the State of North Carolina, and it is hereby enacted by the authority of the same,* That the Justices of the county of Cumberland, at a regular or called term of the Court of Pleas and Quarter Sessions of said county, a majority (or a lawful quorum for the transaction of public business) being present, be, and they are hereby, authorized and empowered to issue, or cause to be issued, Bonds, in such form, at such rate of interest, and payable at such time and place, as they may designate, to the full amount of the present indebtedness of said county, say not exceeding $50,000, and to such extent may waive the immediate collection of taxes to meet such indebtedness. Justices may issue bonds to amount of present indebtedness.

SEC. 2. *Be it further enacted,* That the Mayor and Commissioners of the Town of Fayetteville may and shall have power to issue Bonds, at such rate of interest and payable at such time and place as they may designate, to the full amount of their indebtedness, the purpose being to waive the immediate collection of taxes to meet such indebtedness. Same powers to Commissioners of Fayetteville.

SEC. 3. *Be it further enacted,* That this Act shall be in force from and after its ratification.

Ratified the 2nd day of March, A. D., 1867.

CHAPTER CXIX.

AN ACT TO AUTHORIZE THE JUSTICES OF CUMBERLAND COUNTY TO FUND THE INTEREST DUE ON ITS BONDS GIVEN IN PAYMENT FOR STOCK IN THE WESTERN RAIL ROAD COMPANY.

SECTION 1. *Be it enacted by the General Assembly of the State of North Carolina, and it is hereby enacted by the authority of the same,* That the Justices of the County Court of Cumberland, a majority being present, may at their discretion issue bonds, to be signed by the Chairman of said Court, and countersigned by the Clerk, and attested by the seal of said Court, to an amount sufficient to pay and take up the Coupons due and to become due up to and inclusive of the 1st June, 1867, upon the bonds of said county issued under an Act of the General Assembly, ratified the 3d day of February, 1857, chapter 7, which said bonds, to be issued under this Act, shall bear interest, at such rate not exceeding ten per cent. per annum, as the said Justices may agree upon and establish; said bonds to run for such time and the interest thereon to be payable at such period and in such form as the said Justices may prescribe: *Provided,* the issues shall not be of less denominations than thirty dollars.

May issue bonds sufficient to pay Coupons due and to become due.

SEC. 2. *Be it further enacted,* That upon the determination of the said Justices to issue bonds under the authority hereby given, and when an order to issue may be made, either at a regular term of the Court, or at a meeting of said Justices called for that purpose, to be held at any time after twenty days' notice, the Chairman of said Court and the Clerk thereof shall prepare proper forms, under the order of said Justices, passed as aforesaid, either in regular term session, or at a meeting called for that purpose, and shall give notice to the holders of the Coupons for interest due on the said bonds issued under the Act of 3rd Febru-

Forms, &c

ary, 1857, that they are ready to fund the interest so due; and upon surrender of such Coupons, the said Chairman and Clerk shall deliver to the party presenting such Coupons, a bond or bonds to the full amount thereof, running for such time and bearing such rate of interest, not exceeding ten per cent., as the Justices of said Court may have prescribed.

SEC. 3. *Be it further enacted,* That the Clerk of said Court shall prepare a book for the purpose, and keep a complete and full register of all bonds so issued, and shall exhibit to the Committee of Finance for said county, the Coupons for which said bonds are issued, who shall compare the same with the register, and cause them to be cancelled or destroyed.

Clerk of the Court to keep a register of bonds.

SEC. 4. *Be it further enacted,* That the bonds issued under the provisions of this Act shall be binding to all intents and purposes, and the faith and credit of the said county of Cumberland is hereby pledged for their payment.

Faith of the County pledged to their payment.

SEC. 5. *Be it further enacted,* That this Act shall be in force from and after its ratification.

Ratified the 9th day of January, A. D., 1867.

CHAPER CXX.

AN ACT AUTHORIZING THE JUSTICES OF THE COURT OF PLEAS AND QUARTER SESSIONS OF WARREN COUNTY TO SELL CERTAIN PROPERTY BELONGING TO SAID COUNTY.

SECTION 1. *Be it enacted by the General Assembly of the State of North Carolina, and it is hereby enacted by the authority of the same,* That it shall be lawful for the Justices of the Court of Pleas and Quarter Sessions of Warren county, at least one-third of them being on the bench, to order a sale of such portion of the public square in the town of Warrenton, on which the jail now stands, as they may think proper, at such time and on such terms as they

Public Square in Warrenton.

may deem reasonable, and also to direct by whom the title thereto is to be made.

Proceeds. SEC. 2. *Be it further enacted.* That the proceeds of the sale are to be applied in the same manner as other funds belonging to said county.

SEC. 3. *Be it further enacted,* That this Act shall be in force from and after its ratification.

Ratified the 29th day of January, A. D., 1867.

CHAPTER CXXI.

AN ACT FOR THE BENEFIT OF DANIEL JOHNSON, SENIOR, OF BLADEN COUNTY.

Preamble. WHEREAS, On the 24th day of June, A. D., 1824, a grant of land lying in Bladen county, on and in Indian Creek, joining land formerly owned by David Davis and William Richardson, was, by Gabriel Holmes, Esq., then Governor of our State, issued to Joshua Tatum for one hundred and fifty acres, (which said grant is numbered 3904,) and, of the land therein granted, it appears Daniel Johnson, Senior, of Bladen county, is now the owner : *And whereas,* it has been made to appear to this General Assembly that by reason of a want of particularity on the part of the surveyor, who surveyed and plotted said land, the first line of said survey is described as running north sixty-five west, when by the plot and directions it should have been north sixty-five east, and the fifth line, though marked out and defined in the plot as running north thirty, east twenty chains, is neither set forth nor alluded to in the survey, by reason of which omissions the grant is imperfect: Therefore,

Correction of grant. SECTION 1. *Be it enacted by the General Assembly of the State of North Carolina, and it is hereby enacted by the authority of the same,* That the aforesaid grant be, and the same is hereby, reformed and corrected, as follows: The first line thereof is declared to run north sixty-five degrees east, instead of west, and the fifth line running north thirty degrees east twenty chains, is hereby declared established and incorporated in said grant.

SEC. 2. *Be it further enacted,* That the Secretary of State be, and he is hereby, directed to issue a new grant to date and take effect, as of the year 1824, to said Daniel Johnson, Senior, in which the corrections made by virtue of section first of this Act in the lines and courses shall be incorporated. Issue of new grant.

SEC. 3. *Be it further enacted,* That this Act shall be in force from and after its ratification.

Ratified the 18th day of February, A. D., 1867.

CHAPTER CXXII.

AN ACT TO SECURE A BETTER DRAINAGE OF THE LOW LANDS ON LOWER CREEK, IN THE COUNTIES OF BURKE AND CALDWELL.

SECTION 1. *Be it enacted by the General Assembly of the State of North Carolina, and it is hereby enacted by the authority of the same,* That R. G. Tuttle, A. S. Kent, R. C. Miller, Alfred Dula, Jos. E. Norwood, M. A. Boonhardt, P. C. Halyburton and T. S. Hoover, be appointed Commissioners, whose duty it shall be, as soon as practicable, to lay off the main Lower Creek, in the counties of Burke and Caldwell, from Johnson's Bridge to E. M. Shuford's Mill, into seven sections of convenient length, and for each section shall appoint one overseer, who shall be a land owner in the section for which he is appointed, and shall hold his office for the term of two years. Commissioners.

SEC. 2. *Be it further enacted,* That a majority of said Commissioners shall have power to elect one of their own number Chairman, and may fill vacancies in their own number or that of overseers, and in case they shall fail or neglect to fill vacancies occasioned by death or otherwise, the Courts of Pleas and Quarter Sessions of said counties, Powers, &c., of Commissioners.

seven Justices being present, shall, on application being made, appoint Commissioners and overseers for the purposes herein mentioned.

Duties of Commissioners.

SEC. 3. *Be it further enacted*, That said Commissioners shall estimate the number of acres of bottom land belonging to each land owner, and shall furnish each overseer with a copy of the estimate for his section, and said land owners, when required, after five days notice by the overseer, shall furnish one hand, with appropriate tools, for each twenty-five acres of bottom land so estimated, and on failing to do so shall forfeit and pay two dollars for each failure, which may be recovered by said overseer by warrant as in cases of failure to work on public roads; and it shall be the duty of each overseer, with the hands so provided, to work not less than two nor more than ten days, at the discretion of the Commissioners, in each and every year, on the channel of said Creek, within the bounds of their respective sections, in removing obstructions and improving the banks thereof, under such directions as said Commissioners may prescribe.

Penalty for obstructions.

SEC. 4. *Be it further enacted*, That any person or persons who shall wilfully and knowingly fell timber, or otherwise obstruct the waters in the channel of said Creek, between Johnson's Bridge and M. Shuford's Mill, in said counties, and shall permit the same to remain therein for the space of twenty days, shall be deemed guilty of a misdemeanor, and, on conviction thereof, before any Court of competent jurisdiction, shall be fined not less than ten, and not more than twenty, dollars: *Provided*, That if any person or persons so offending shall pay the penalty herein mentioned, to the overseer of the section wherein the offence was committed, before a presentment is made of the same, he or they shall not be liable to indictment for said offence.

How fines, &c., may be appropriated.

SEC. 5. *Be it further enacted*, That all monies arising from failure to work on said Creek, and all penalties collected under the provisions of this Act, shall be paid over to the overseer of the section in which it may arise, and by him shall be expended in improving the channel of said Creek; and any overseer failing or neglecting to perform the duties required by this Act, shall be deemed guilty of a misdemeanor, and, on conviction thereof, shall be fined not less than ten, and not more than twenty, dollars *Provided*, That no person shall be required, without his consent, to serve as an overseer more than one term of two years at any one time.

SEC. 7. *Be it further enacted*, That nothing in this Act contained shall prevent the building of public bridges on public roads across said stream, or private bridges and water gates by the land owners for their own convenience. Proviso

SEC. 8. *Be it further enacted*, That nothing herein contained shall be so construed as to exempt persons therein mentioned from work on the public roads. Further proviso.

SEC. 9. *Be it further enacted*, That this Act shall be in force and take effect from and after the 1st day of April, 1867.

Ratified the 1st day of March, A. D., 1867.

CHAPTER CXXIII.

AN ACT TO AMEND AN ACT TO AUTHORIZE THE LAYING OUT AND ESTABLISHING A TURNPIKE ROAD FROM THE SOUTH CAROLINA LINE AT SOME POINT NEAR THE BLOCK HOUSE, IN RUTHERFORD COUNTY, TO CAIN CREEK BRIDGE, IN BUNCOMBE COUNTY, PASSED AT THE SESSION OF 1855, CHAPTER 53.

SECTION 1. *Be it enacted by the General Assembly of the State of North Carolina, and it is hereby enacted by the authority of the same*, That the said Act be, and is hereby, amended as follows, to-wit: That the said Turnpike Company, at their next annual meeting, or any meetings thereafter, a majority of the stock being represented in said meeting, may, by a majority vote, and said vote entered on their books, surrender their chartered privileges to all that portion of said Road extending west from the Cross Road near Pennel Gilbreath's, and also to all that portion of the Road extending east from Hezekiah Collins', and retain all Amendment.

their rights and privileges over said Road lying between said designated points.

Extent of Company's responsibility.
SEC. 2. *Be it further enacted,* That the said Turnpike Company shall only be held responsible for that portion of the Road retained by them from Hezekiah Collins', to the Cross Roads west of P. Gilbreath's, and that they shall be released from all liabilities on that portion of Road west of said Cross Road and east of Hezekiah Collins'. And that

Duration of privileges.
the chartered privileges to said Company be extended to a term of thirty years from the ratification of this Act.

Ratified the 27th day of February, A. D., 1867.

CHAPTER CXXIV.

AN ACT TO REPEAL AN ACT FOR THE BETTER REGULATION OF THE WESTERN TURNPIKE ROAD AND FOR OTHER PURPOSES.

Repeal of Act of May 28, 1864.
SECTION 1. *Be it enacted by the General Assembly of the State of North Carolina, and it is hereby enacted by the authority of the same,* That an Act passed at the adjourned session of the General Assembly of 1864, and ratified on 28th day of May, 1864, entitled "An Act for the better regulation of the Western Turnpike Road," be and the same is hereby repealed.

Tolls.
SEC. 2. *Be it further enacted,* That the payment of tolls upon said road shall be regulated by the laws in force previous to the passage of said Act, and that the same shall extend to the citizens of Clay county.

Compensation of Agents
SEC. 3. *Be it further enacted,* That the Agents on the road aforesaid, appointed by the Governor of the State, shall each receive for their services two (2) dollars for every day necessarily employed in superintending the same, and shall report under oath to the Agent of the State for the collection of Cherokee bonds, (Mr. Siler,) the number of days thus employed, together with the amounts of money expended in repairing said road, and the amount of money

collected from the different Toll-gate Keepers on the end of the road of which he has charge, and such report shall be made quarterly, as required under existing laws.

SEC. 2. *Be it further enacted*, That the different Toll-Gate Keepers, appointed by the Agents aforesaid, shall be required to make their quarterly returns under oath, of the amount of money collected at the gate kept by them, and pay the same over to the Agent, deducting twenty per centum as commission for their services.

<small>Toll-Gate Keepers.</small>

SEC. 2. *Be it further enacted*, That all laws and clauses of laws coming in conflict with this Act, be and the same are hereby repealed, and this act shall be in force from and after its ratification.

Ratified the 26th day of February, A. D., 1867.

CHAPTER CXXV.

AN ACT TO GIVE TWO WEEKS TO THE COURTS OF PLEAS AND QUARTER SESSIONS OF ANSON COUNTY, AT THEIR SEVERAL TERMS OF JANUARY, APRIL, JULY AND OCTOBER.

SECTION 1. *Be it enacted by the General Assembly of the State of North Carolina, and it is hereby enacted by the authority of the same*, That the Justices of the Courts of Pleas and Quarter Sessions of the county of Anson shall have full power and authority to hold their several Courts in January, April, July and October, for two weeks instead of one, if they, in their discretion, deem that the business of their said several Courts requires it.

SEC. 2. *Be it further enacted*, That this Act shall be in force and effect from and after its ratification.

Ratified the 28th day of February, A. D., 1867.

CHAPTER CXXVI.

AN ACT EMPOWERING THE CHAIRMAN OF THE COUNTY COURT OF ANSON COUNTY TO SELL AND CONVEY TITLE TO CERTAIN TOWN LOTS IN THE TOWN OF WADESBORO.

Three town lots in Wadesboro'.

SECTION 1. *Be it enacted by the General Assembly of the State of North Carolina, and it is hereby enacted by the authority of the same,* That the Chairman of the County Court of Anson county, or his successors in office, be, and they are hereby, fully authorized and empowered to sell and convey, either publicly or privately, upon a credit or for cash, three Town lots in the Town of Wadesboro', known as a part of the lot adjoining the jail, and a lot adjoining the Bank of Wadesboro', all of which lots belong to the county of Anson; and the said Chairman, or his successors in office, shall be fully authorized and empowered to make all proper deeds and assurances, for the same.

SEC. 2. *Be it further enacted,* That this Act shall be in full force and effect from and after its ratification.

Ratified the 28th day of February, A. D., 1867.

CHAPTER CXXVII.

AN ACT TO ENABLE THE COMMISSIONERS OF JONES COUNTY TO SELL A LOT BELONGING TO SAID COUNTY.

SECTION 1. *Be it enacted by the General Assembly of the State of North Carolina, and it is hereby enacted by the authority of the same,* That F. G. Simmons, Thomas J. Whitaker, A. McDaniel, James T. Dillahurst and Benjamin Askew, Commissioners appointed by the County Court of the County of Jones, be and they are hereby authorized and empowered to make sale of the lot of land in the Town of Trenton, which had formerly been improved by said County, as a common jail, and make title to the purchaser.

SEC. 2. *Be it further enacted,* That this Act shall take effect from and after its ratification.

Ratified the 26th day of January, A. D., 1867.

CHAPTER CXXVIII.

AN ACT IN FAVOR OF K. P. HARRIS.

SECTION 1. *Be it enacted by the General Assembly of the State of North Carolina, and it is hereby enacted by the authority of the same,* That John O. Wallace, Clerk of the Court of Pleas and Quarter Sessions, for Cabarrus county, is hereby authorized and fully empowered to make a deed to Kiah P. Harris, for the old jail lot, in the town of Concord, purchased by Kiah P. Harris, under an order from the County Court, made at January session, 1844, which report was confirmed at April session, 1844.

Clerk of the County Court to make K. P. Harris a deed for the old jail lot in Concord.

SEC. 2. *Be it further enacted,* That this Act shall be in force from and after its ratification.

Ratified the 14th day of December, A. D., 1866.

CHAPTER CXXIX.

AN ACT AUTHORIZING THE CHAIRMAN OF THE COUNTY COURT OF LENOIR COUNTY TO SELL THE OLD JAIL LOT IN THE TOWN OF KINSTON.

SECTION 1. *Be it enacted by the General Assembly of the State of North Carolina, and it is hereby enacted by the authority of the same,* That the Chairman of the County Court of Lenoir county, be, and is hereby, fully authorized and empowered to sell, at public sale, the old jail lot, in the town of Kinston, and, upon the payment of the purchase money for the same, to make the necessary deeds and assurances of title to the purchaser for the same.

SEC. 2. *Be it further enacted,* That this Act shall be in full force and effect from and after its ratification.

Ratified the 4th day of March, A. D., 1867.

CHAPTER CXXX.

AN ACT TO AMEND AN ACT, ENTITLED AN ACT FOR THE CONSTRUCTION OF A BRIDGE ACROSS THE NOTLA RIVER, AND FOR OTHER PURPOSES, RATIFED 21st DECEMBER, A. D., 1866.

Construction of the Act of December 21, 1866.

SECTION 1. *Be it enacted by the General Assembly of the State of North Carolina, and it is hereby enacted by the authority of the same,* That the recited Act shall not be construed as applying to the Tuckaseegee Turnpike, intended to connect the Tuckaseegee and Keowee Turnpike with the line of the Blue Ridge Rail Road, so far as the same may have been authorized by the Acts of 1856-'57, and Acts of 1858-'59; also the Oconalufta and Qualla Town Turnpike, from Qualla Town to the Tennessee line, so far as the same may have been authorized by the Acts of 1856-'57 and 1858-'59, and bonds remain due to contractors for work already done on the roads; but the Agents of Cherokee bonds shall receive the certificates, which have been issued or which may be issued for work already done under said Acts for the construction of the said roads and bridge, in payment for bonds or lands pledged for the use of the Western Turnpike by the Acts of 1848, and subsequent Act: *Provided,* this Act shall not deprive the Jonathan Creek and Tennessee Mountain Turnpike Company from receiving the bonds set apart for said road under the recited Act of 21st December, 1866.

Ratified the 4th day of March, A. D., 1867.

CHAPTER CXXXI.

AN ACT FOR THE BENEFIT OF THE COUNTY COURT CLERK OF BEAUFORT COUNTY.

SECTION 1. *Be it enacted by the General Assembly of the State of North Carolina, and it is hereby enacted by the authority of the same,* That the Clerk of the County Court of said county of Beaufort, for all transcripts of records made out by him transferring suits from said County Court to the Superior Court, under Act of Assembly, passed the 11th of September, 1861, entitled "An Act to change the rules of pleading, &c.," shall be allowed the same fees, for such transcripts, as are now allowed by law in case of appeal from the County to the Superior Courts of the State.

Fees for certain transscripts.

SEC. 2. *Be it further enacted,* That this Act shall take effect from and after its ratification.

Ratified the 2nd day of March, A. D., 1867.

CHAPTER CXXXII.

AN ACT TO ELECT ALL THE COUNTY OFFICERS OF PERQUIMANS, PASQUOTANK, WASHINGTON AND TYRRELL COUNTIES AT THE SAME COURT.

SECTION 1. *Be it enacted by the General Assembly of the State of North Carolina, and it is hereby enacted by the authority of the same,* That the Courts of Pleas and Quarter Sessions of Perquimans, Pasquotank, Washington and Tyrrell counties, at the first Court held after the first day of January, A. D., 1868, a majority of the Justices being present, shall elect all their county officers, to hold their said offices under the same rules and regulations as they now do, according to the existing laws of this State : *Provided,* That the provisions of this Act shall not apply to Clerks and Sheriffs.

Ratified the 4th day of March, A. D., 1867.

CHAPTER CXXXIII.

AN ACT FOR THE RELIEF OF HENRY WILLIAMS.

Preamble.

WHEREAS, Henry Williams, of the County of Edgecombe, is charged upon the tax list of the said county, by a mistake of the list taker, with tax on the amount of eight thousand four hundred and sixty dollars, instead of eighty-four dollars and sixty cents, which was the true amount given in by him; *and, whereas,* the term of the County Court has passed, at which the same could have been commuted, the said Henry Williams not having any knowledge of said error : Now, therefore,

Release from payment of tax.

SECTION 1. *Be it enacted by the General Assembly of the State of North Carolina, and it is hereby enacted by the authority of the same,* That the said Henry Williams be, and he is hereby, released from the payment of tax on the above amount, in excess of the said sum of eighty-four dollars and sixty cents.

SEC. 2. *Be it further enacted,* That this Act shall be in force from and after its ratification.

Ratified the 11th day of February, A. D., 1867.

CHAPTER CXXXIV.

AN ACT FOR THE RELIEF OF THE ESTATE OF LAWRENCE O'B. BRANCH, DECEASED.

Description of Bonds.

WHEREAS, The late Lawrence O'B. Branch was possessed, at the time of his death, in September, 1862, of the following described Bonds, issued by the State of North Carolina, for the sum of One Thousand Dollars each, with coupons attached, payably semi-annually, at the rate of six per cent., viz:

1. One Bond, No. 2853, dated April 1st, 1855, payable April 1st, 1885, coupons due before April 1st, 1865, cut off, issued under Act of 1854, chapter 32, entitled "an Act for the completion of the North Carolina Rail Road."

2. One Bond, No. 324, dated January 1st, 1856, payable January 1st, 1886, coupons due before 1st January, 1865, cut off, issued under Act of 1854, chapter 232, entitled "an Act to amend an Act entitled an Act to incorporate the Atlantic and North Carolina Rail Road Company and the North Carolina and Western Rail Road Company."

3. One Bond, No. 325, dated January 1st, 1856, payable January 1st, 1886, coupons due before 1st January, 1865, cut off, issued under Act of 1854, chapter 232, entitled as next above.

4. One Bond, No. 408, dated October 1st, 1858, payable October 1st, 1888, coupons due before 1st April, 1865, cut off, issued under Act of 1854, chapter 223, entitled "an Act to incorporate the Western North Carolina Rail Road Company."

5. One Bond, No. 384, dated July 1st, 1858, payable July 1st, 1888, (coupons due before January 1st, 1865, cut off,) issued under Act of 1854, chapter 223, entitled as next above.

6. One Bond, No. 810, dated October 1st, 1859, payable October 1st, 1889, coupons due before April 1st, 1865, cut off, issued under Act of 1854, chapter 223, entitled as next above.

7. One Bond, 817, dated October 1st, 1859, payable October 1st, 1889, coupons due before April 1st, 1865, cut off, issued under Act of 1854, chapter 223, entitled as next above.

8. One Bond, No. 153, dated January 1st, 1860, payable January 1st, 1890, issued under an Act of 1858, chapter 168, entitled "an Act to amend the charter of the Wilmington, Charlotte and Rutherford Rail Road Company."

9. One Bond, No. 580, dated January 1st, 1860, payable January 1st, 1890, coupons due before January 1st, 1865,

cut off, issued under Act of 1858, chapter 43, entitled "an Act to authorize the Public Treasurer to sell the Bonds of the State for certain purposes."

10. One Bond, No. 581, dated January 1st, 1860, payable January 1st, 1890, coupons due before 1st January, 1865, cut off, issued under Act of 1858, chapter 43, entitled as next above.

And, whereas, It appears to this General Assembly that each of said Bonds was duly registered in the office of the Treasurer of the State, according to the provisions of the Act of the General Assembly, ratified on the 8th day of January, 1857, chapter 16, entitled "an Act to secure the holders of the Coupon Bonds of the State against losses by accident to said Bonds," whereby the said owner, L. O'B. Branch, by the endorsement made on each of said Bonds, by the Public Treasurer, appeared to be the legal owner thereof, and they ceased to be transferable from him, except at the office of the Public Treasurer, by written endorsement on said Bonds, witnessed by the Treasurer: *And whereas,* It appears that said Bonds, about the month of April, 1865, while still the property of the said L. O'B. Branch's estate, (they nor any of them having been transferred by him or his representatives,) were obtained by fraud and violence, and against the will of the representatives of the estate of the deceased, and are either destroyed or concealed from such representatives, so that the estate cannot have the benefit thereof: And William A. Blount, the administrator, hath applied to the General Assembly for relief in the premises, having duly made public, for the space of thirty days, his intention to make application for such relief: Now, therefore,

Pub. Treas. forbidden to pay the foregoing except to certain persons.

SECTION 1. *Be it enacted by the General Assembly of the State of North Carolina, and it is hereby enacted by the authority of the same,* That the Public Treasurer be, and he is hereby, instructed not to pay the principal money of any of the aforesaid Bonds, to any person whatever, except to the representative of the said Lawrence O'B. Branch, or to such other person to whom they may be duly transferred at the Treasury, in the manner specified in said Act.

SEC. 2. *Be it further enacted,* That the said representative is now entitled to Bonds of the State for like sum of principal money, without interest, as those stolen as aforesaid, and payable at the Treasury of the State, at the times when said stolen Bonds are payable.

SEC. 3. *Be it further enacted,* That the Public Treasurer be, and he is hereby, instructed to issue ten Bonds, of $1000 each, without coupons, payable at the times respectively when the said registered Bonds are payable, and deliver the same to the representative of the said Lawrence O'B. Branch, which Bonds, thus issued, shall be in all respects, other than having Coupons attached, duplicates and copies of the said stolen Bonds, with the registry endorsed, and it shall be stated, in each of said Bonds, that it is a duplicate and copy of one that is lost, stolen or destroyed.

Pub. Treas. instructed to issue new bonds.

SEC. 4. *Be it further enacted,* That the expense of issuing duplicates of Bonds shall be paid by the representative of said Lawrence O'B. Branch.

Expense of issue.

Ratified the 19th day of February, A. D., 1867.

CHAPTER CXXXV.

AN ACT TO MAKE VALID THE SALE OF THE OLD JAIL LOT BY THE COUNTY COURT OF EDGECOMBE, AND TO SECURE THE TITLE TO THE PURCHASER, AND TO SELL AND PURCHASE OTHER LANDS FOR CERTAIN PURPOSES.

WHEREAS, Joseph H. Baker, Wm. S. Battle and W. P. Lloyd, by virtue of an order of the Court of Pleas and Quarter Sessions of the county of Edgecombe to them directed, did, on the first day of October last, expose to public sale Lot No. 61, in the Town of Tarboro, further known as the Jail Lot, belonging to said county: And, whereas, further, Henry Bryan, upon said sale, became the purchaser

Preamble.

of said lot; in order therefore that the said sale may be made valid and title to be made to the said purchaser, and for other purposes :

<small>Confirmation of sale.</small>

SECTION 1. *Be it enacted by the General Assembly of the State of North Carolina, and it is hereby enacted by the authority of the same,* That the said sale be, and is hereby, confirmed and made valid to all intents and purposes, as if the same had been made and conducted under a special Act of this General Assembly, enacted therefor, and the Chairman of said Court is hereby fully authorized and empowered to make and convey title to the said lot in *fee simple* unto the said Bryan, by a deed executed and delivered under the hand and private seal of the said Chairman.

<small>Justices may purchase other lands for Jail site</small>

SEC. 2. *Be it further enacted,* That the said Court, a majority of the Justices being present, is hereby authorized and empowered to purchase other lands, not exceeding one acre, the title whereof to be made to said County for the purpose of erecting a Jail, Post and Stocks, for the use of said County.

<small>Court empowered to sell certain lots.</small>

SEC. 3. *Be it further enacted,* That the said Court, a majority of the Justices being present, is further empowered to sell lots one hundred and eleven, and one hundred and twelve, in the plan of said Town, title to be made in *fee simple,* as aforesaid, to the purchaser by the Chairman of said Court, the proceeds of said sales to be applied to the payment of the ordinary expenses of said County, and to such other County and public uses as the said Court may direct.

<small>Poor-House Tract.</small>

SEC. 4. *Be it further enacted,* That the said Court, as aforesaid, is further empowered to sell and dispose of the lands now known as the Poor-house tract, of said County, as they may direct, and to apply the proceeds thereof to the purchase of other lands, (the number of acres to be determined by them,) which purchase they are hereby empowered to make and take the title to the County of Edgecombe, for the purpose of building houses thereon for the maintenance and support of the poor of said County.

SEC. 5. *Be it further enacted*, That all laws conflicting with this Act are hereby repealed, and that this Act shall be in force from and after its ratification.

Ratified the 11th day of December, A. D., 1866.

RESOLUTIONS

OF A PRIVATE NATURE,

PASSED BY THE

GENERAL ASSEMBLY

OF

NORTH CAROLINA,

1866–'67.

RESOLUTION IN FAVOR OF R. H. S. BOND, SHERIFF OF GATES.

Resolved, by the General Assembly of the State of North Carolina, That R. H. S. Bond, Sheriff of the county of Gates, be, and he is hereby, allowed until Wednesday of the Court of Pleas and Quarter Sessions, to be holden for the said county of Gates, on the third Monday in May next, to settle his account with the Trustees of said county of Gates. Allowed until Wednesday of May Court to settle tax account.

Ratified the 31st day of January, A. D., 1867.

RESOLUTION IN FAVOR OF JACOB SILER, AGENT OF THE STATE FOR THE COLLECTION OF CHEROKEE BONDS.

Resolved, That Wm. Angel, John Ingram and D. C. Harden, of Macon County, be appointed Commissioners to examine the books and papers, kept by Jacob Siler as Agent of the State for the collection of Cherokee bonds, and ascertain the amount of extra services the said Agent has been required to perform in compliance with the various acts of the General Assembly, in relation to Cherokee bonds and Western Turnpikes, for which no compensation has heretofore been allowed; and such a sum, as a majority of said Commisioners may agree upon, shall be paid in bonds in the hands of said Agent and retained by him in payment of said extra service, and that his commissions of three per centum be paid in a like manner, to be selected by the Agent: *Provided,* That the Agent of the State be authorized to pay the amount of bonds in bulk set apart by an Act passed at the present Legislature, to build the Notla Bridge and for other purposes, to the President of the Company. and issue the certificate for insolvent bonds in blank, to be filled up by the President or Treasurer of the Company by inserting the name of the person paying the same.

Be it further resolved, That this resolution be in force from and after its ratification.

Ratified the 18th day of February, A. D., 1867.

Commissioners to examine Agent's books and ascertain, &c.

Allowance for said services.

Proviso.

RESOLUTION IN FAVOR OF JAMES M. NEAL, SHERIFF OF THE COUNTY OF McDOWELL.

WHEREAS, James M. Neal, being Sheriff of the county of McDowell, in the year 1860, did in the fall of said year fully pay and discharge, to the proper officer, the taxes due from the citizens of said county, leaving due him individually, as arrearages of taxes, the sum of —— dollars: *And whereas, further,* The said Neal did, in the Spring of the year 1861, enter the army of the Confederate States, where he remained until the surrender, being thereby precluded from collecting the said arrearages, which he could have done by the Fall of 1861: Therefore, be it

Preamble.

Resolved, That the said Neal be, and he is hereby, authorized to collect the said arrearages of taxes due him: *Provided*, This resolution shall not apply to any person who will swear they have paid the same, or to the estate of any deceased person in the hands of an executor or administrator.

Be it further resolved, That the provisions of the foregoing resolution be extended to the securities of W. T. J. Vann, late Sheriff of New Hanover county, to enable them to collect the uncollected taxes due upon the tax list for the years 1862–'63: *Provided*, The claim of the county against them, and the taxes to be collected, be subject to the scale of depreciated currency.

Be it further resolved, That this resolution shall be in force from its ratification.

Ratified the 2nd day of March, A. D., 1867.

RESOLUTION IN FAVOR OF J. L. WITHERS AND JAMES H. WHITE.

Resolved, That J. L. Withers and James H. White be released from the penalties of a bond given to the State for the maintenance of E. D. Lineberger, in the Insane Asylum, as a pay patient, and from the judgment and execution obtained in Wake Superior Court thereon; the said E. D. Lineberger having become indigent before the forfeiture of said bond and the county of Gaston having assumed to pay the State charges against said lunatic, as an indigent insane person from the 29th Oct., 1864, the date from which the said Withers and White's liability on said bond commenced.

Ratified the 27th day of February, A. D., 1867.

RESOLUTION IN FAVOR OF MARY M. TRANSON.

Preamble. WHEREAS, Mary M. Transon did, in April, 1862, surrender to the Public Treasurer a registered six per cent. bond of the State, for $1,000, which was dated March 22nd, 1852, and became due March 22nd, 1862, and received therefor an eight per cent. coupon bond of the State, dated March 1st, 1862, for $1,000:

Public Treasurer to issue a new bond. *Resolved,* That the Public Treasurer be authorized, on the surrender of said eight per cent. bond to him, to issue to said Mary M. Transon, for the principal and interest from date of maturity, of said registered bond, a new bond or bonds under the provisions of the Act of the General Assembly, ratified March 10th, 1866, entitled "An Act to provide for the payment of the State debt contracted before the war."

Resolved, That this resolution shall be in force from and after its ratification.

Ratified the 27th day of February, A. D., 1867.

RESOLUTION IN FAVOR OF THE ATTORNEY GENERAL.

Compensation for extra services. *Resolved,* That the Public Treasurer pay to Sion H. Rogers, Attorney General, the sum of three hundred ($300) dollars for his services in the investigations of the affairs of the Cape Fear Navigation Company, and of the contracts between certain Rail Road and Express Companies, in accordance with former resolutions of the General Assembly.

Ratified the 1st day of March, A. D., 1867.

RESOLUTION IN FAVOR OF THE REPRESENTATIVES OF D. F. BAGLEY, LATE SHERIFF OF PERQUIMANS COUNTY.

WHEREAS, D. F. Bagley, the late Sheriff of Perquimans county, was confined to a sick bed during the greater part of the year 1866, from which sickness he died in January, 1867: *And, whereas,* There is a balance of unlisted taxes and a balance of the merchants' tax for said county still due, for which his securities are liable : *And, whereas,* the said D. F. Bagley was unable to make his report to the Clerk of the County Court, on account of which the Clerk was unable to transmit to the Public Treasurer the transcript of the taxes for said county : Therefore, {Preamble.}

Be it resolved by the General Assembly, That the personal representatives of D. F. Bagley, late Sheriff of the county aforesaid, be and they are hereby authorized and empowered to collect all arrearages of taxes for said county during the years 1865 and 1866, and that they be invested with all the authority vested by law in the Sheriff, to enable them to carry out the provisions of this Act in collecting and receipting for the same. {Allowed to collect arrears of taxes.}

Be it further resolved, That the said representatives be, and they are hereby, authorized and empowered to make all such returns as are required by law to the County Court of said county, and to make settlement with the Treasurer and Comptroller of State ; and, to facilitate an early settlement, the Clerk is hereby required to forward the transcript required by law to the Comptroller so soon as the report is made to him by the representatives. {Further privileges.}

Ratified the 4th day of March, A. D., 1867.

RESOLUTION IN FAVOR OF WILLIAM GORDON.

WHEREAS, By the will of the late John C. Gordon, of Gates county, North Carolina, he bequeathed to his son,

Preamble.

William Gordon, now and for many years an inmate of the "Insane Asylum," the annual interest upon seven thousand dollars of North Carolina six per cent. coupon bonds; and the aforesaid annual interest upon the aforesaid coupon bonds being the only estate of the aforesaid William Gordon, or means by which he can support himself in the Asylum, the aforesaid John C. Gordon having devised the aforesaid State bonds to other parties, after the death of the said William Gordon; and, *whereas,* the State of North Carolina has not, for some time, by reason of the impoverished condition of her Treasury, paid the interest upon her bonds, and is not likely to do so in full for some time to come; *and, whereas,* the aforesaid William Gordon is only unable to pay for his support in the "Insane Asylum," by reason of the State's inability to meet her obligations, the interest upon seven thousand dollars being ample for that purpose:

Public Treasurer to receive certain coupons in payment of the maintenance of Wm. Gordon in the Insane Asylum.

Be it therefore, resolved by the General Assembly of the State of North Carolina, That the State Treasurer be, and he is hereby, authorized and required to receive the coupons upon the aforesaid seven thousand dollars of State bonds, as they may fall due, in full payment for the maintenance and support of the aforesaid William Gordon, in the "Insane Asylum;" and the Supervisors and Superintendent of the Insane Asylum are hereby authorized, empowered and required to keep and provide for the aforesaid William Gordon in the Asylum, upon the payment to the State Treasurer of the coupons of the aforesaid State bonds, from time to time, as they shall fall due, until the State shall resume the payment in full of the interest upon her liabilities.

Ratified the 9th day of February, A. D., 1867.

RESOLUTION IN FAVOR OF HON. A. S. MERRIMON.

Resolved, That the Public Treasurer be authorized and directed to pay to the Hon. A. S. Merrimon the sum of seventy-five dollars for loss of time and expenses incurred by him in travelling as far as Raleigh, on his way to hold a special term of Chowan Superior Court, which has been postponed by this General Assembly to the 1st Monday in February next. Appropriation for traveling expenses.

Ratified the 11th day of February, A. D., 1867.

RESOLUTION IN FAVOR OF THE MEMORIAL ASSOCIATION OF THE CITY OF RALEIGH.

Resolved, That the Public Treasurer be, and he is hereby, directed to pay to the President of the Memorial Association, of the city of Raleigh, the sum of fifteen hundred dollars, out of any moneys in the Treasury, not otherwise appropriated, to be applied by said Association in removing and protecting the remains of Confederate soldiers buried in the vicinity of Raleigh. Appropriates $1,500.

Ratified the 15th day February, A. D., 1867.

RESOLUTION IN FAVOR OF W. B. MARCH AND JOHN PEEBLES.

Resolved, That W. B. March and John Peebles, both of the county of Davie, be respectively released from the payment of a double tax to the State and said county, for the year 1866. Released from double tax.

Ratified the 19th day of February, A. D., 1867.

RESOLUTION IN FAVOR OF MRS. P. P. DICK, EXECUTRIX OF THE LATE JUDGE JOHN M. DICK.

Preamble.

WHEREAS, The General Assembly, by resolution dated 10th February, 1863, entitled a Resolution in favor of Mrs. P. P. Dick, Executrix of the late Judge John M. Dick, directed the Public Treasurer to pay the said Mrs. Dick three hundred dollars, the residue of salary due the said Judge Dick at the time of his death, on the 15th October, 1860, which sum has not been paid:

Appropriates $300.

Resolved, That the Public Treasurer carry into effect the foregoing Resolution, by paying said sum of three hundred dollars in accordance with the tenor thereof.

Ratified the 18th day of February, A. D., 1867.

RESOLUTION FOR THE RELIEF OF CULPEPPER AUSTIN, SHERIFF OF UNION COUNTY.

Refunds over-payment of taxes.

Resolved, That the Public Treasurer pay unto Culpepper Austin, Sheriff of the county of Union, two hundred and seventy-five dollars and fifty-nine cents, being the amount over-paid by him, by mistake, into the Public Treasury, for taxes.

Resolved, That this Resolution shall be in force from its ratification.

Ratified the 4th day of February, A. D., 1867.

RESOLUTION IN FAVOR OF J. J. KITCHUM, ELISHA DAVIS, OF WILKES COUNTY, AND OTHERS.

Resolved, That J. J. Kitchum, Elisha Davis, of Wilkes county, James Hall, Archer Robeson and S. J. Roe, who lost legs in the war, and Green Alderman, who lost an arm, and who ordered limbs from the limb factory, but who find that they are not able to use them, be allowed to return them to the factory, and that they be allowed to draw from the Treasury the amount in cash, instead of taking the limbs, as they are of no use to them, the stumps being too short to apply the limb to them.   *Commutation for artificial limbs.*

Ratified the 11th day of February, A. D., 1867.

RESOLUTION IN FAVOR OF WM. H. PERKINS, TAX COLLECTOR OF PITT COUNTY.

Resolved by the General Assembly of North Carolina, That William H. Perkins, Tax Collector for the county of Pitt, be allowed until the first day of March, A. D., 1867, to collect and pay over the State and County Taxes of said county, for the year 1866.   *Allowed to Mar 1st, to collect and pay over taxes*

Ratified the 22nd day of February, A. D., 1867.

RESOLUTION FOR THE RELIEF OF WILLIAM S. MASON.

Resolved, That the Public Treasurer be, and he is hereby, authorized to pay, upon the warrant of the Governor, the sum of two hundred dollars to William S. Mason, for services rendered and expenses incurred in executing a commission from His Excellency, the Governor, to investigate certain matters in the Western part of the State.   *Appropriates $200 for services rendered*

Ratified the 14th day of February, A. D., 1867.

RESOLUTION IN FAVOR OF THE TRUSTEES OF THE REX HOSPITAL FUND.

Preamble.

WHEREAS, The Trustees of the Rex Hospital Fund did, on the 20th day of January, 1865, surrender to the Public Treasurer a Bond of the State for one thousand dollars, ($1,000) numbered 62, which fell due on the 1st of January, 1865, and took from the Public Treasurer a certificate promising to deliver to said Trustees a Bond of the State for one thousand (1,000) dollars, in lieu of said surrendered Bond, which Bond was not delivered:

Pub. Treas. to issue to the Trustees certain Bonds.

Resolved, That the Public Treasurer issue to the said Trustees of the Rex Hospital Fund, Coupon Bonds, for the principal of said surrendered Bond and interest from date of maturity, under the provisions of an Act of the General Assembly, entitled "an Act to provide for the payment of the State debt, contracted before the war," ratified March 10th, 1866.

Ratified the 18th day of February, A. D., 1867.

RESOLUTION IN FAVOR OF HORTON S. REEVES.

Appropriates $122

Resolved, That the Public Treasurer pay to Horton S. Reeves, of Alleghany county, the sum of one hundred and twenty-two dollars, out of any monies not otherwise appropriated in the Public Treasury

Ratified the 26th day of February, A. D., 1867.

RESOLUTION FOR THE RELIEF OF SETH JONES' ESTATE.

WHEREAS, The late Seth Jones, of the county of Wake, on or about the first day of May, 1865, was possessed in his own right of nine bonds, issued by the State of North Carolina, and made payable to him or bearer, each for the sum of one thousand dollars, dated on the first day of July, 1854, and payable on the first day of July, 1864, numbered, respectively, one, two, three, four, five, seven, eight, nine, ten, signed by David S. Reid, Governor, and countersigned by D. W. Courts, Public Treasurer, each of which said bonds had been duly registered by the Public Treasurer on June 12th, 1860, as provided by the Act of the General Assembly, entitled an Act "to secure the holders of the coupon bonds of the State, against losses by accident to said bonds," ratified the eighth (8th) January, 1857, and thereby became transferable only at the Treasury of the State ; and, *whereas,* said bonds were stolen from the possession of said Seth Jones, about the first day of May, 1865, and it appears that they are utterly lost to the owner; *and, whereas,* since that time, the said Seth Jones hath died, leaving a last will and testament, which has been duly admitted to probate, and Edward A. Crudup and Henry W. Montague, the Executors therein named, have been duly qualified, and have applied to this General Assembly for relief, and it further appears that due notice of this application hath been published : Now, therefore, Preamble.

Be it resolved by the General Assembly, That the Public Treasurer is hereby instructed to allow the principal money due on said bonds, and the interest accruing since the first day of July, 1864, [to] be funded under the provisions of an Act of the General Assembly, entitled, "An Act to provide for the payment of the State debt contracted before the war," ratified 10th day of March, 1866. Public Treasurer instructed to allow the principal and part interest to be funded.

Be it further resolved, That the representatives of the said Seth Jones give a bond of indemnity, payable to the State, to be approved by the Treasurer, prior to issuing the bonds herein provided for. Bond of indemnity.

RESOLUTION IN FAVOR OF DAVID OUTLAW, SENATOR FROM 7th SENATORIAL DISTRICT.

Allowance of per diem

Resolved, That the Senator from the 7th Senatorial District, composed of the county of Bertie, be allowed his per diem from the time he arrived at Raleigh and not from the time when he qualified, he having been prevented from qualifying sooner, from extreme illness.

Ratified the 21st day of December, A. D., 1866.

A RESOLUTION IN FAVOR OF THE SHERIFFS OF CUMBERLAND, NORTHAMPTON, WAYNE, ONSLOW, MOORE AND CASWELL COUNTIES.

Allowed until March 1 to pay balance of taxes.

Resolved, That the Sheriffs of Cumberland, Northampton, Wayne, Moore and Caswell be allowed until 1st day of March, 1867, to pay into the Treasury the balance of taxes due from those counties.

Ratified the 21st day of December, A. D., 1866.

RESOLUTION IN FAVOR OF THE SHERIFFS OF UNION, ORANGE AND BRUNSWICK, AND THE TAX COLLECTORS OF WAYNE AND JOHNSTON COUNTIES.

Allowed until March 1 to settle their accounts.

Resolved, That John L. Banks, Tax Collector of Johnston county, the Sheriff of Orange county, the Sheriff of Brunswick county, the Sheriff of Union county, and the Tax Collector of Wayne county, be allowed until the first day of March next, to settle with the Public Treasurer the unpaid arrears of taxes due from citizens of those counties,

due for the year 1866, and all penalties for failing to settle prior to that time be and the same are hereby remitted.
Ratified the 26th day of January, A. D., 1867.

RESOLUTION IN FAVOR OF RUFUS H. JONES, EXECUTOR OF ALFRED JONES.

Resolved, That the Public Treasurer be, and he is hereby, instructed to issue to Rufus H. Jones, Executor of Alfred Jones, deceased, of the county of Wake, a duplicate of Bond No. 29, issued on account of Fayetteville and Western Plank Road Company, for the sum of $1,000, dated September 18, 1850, running twenty years, signed by Charles Manly, Governor, and C. L. Hinton, Public Treasurer, which Bond has been lost, and to fund the interest due on the same, since the first (1st) July, 1864, according to the provisions of the funding Act. *(Pub. Treas. to issue duplicate Bonds.)*

Be it further resolved, That the Executor of Alfred Jones be required to give a Bond of indemnity to the State, to be approved by the Public Treasurer, upon the issuance of the Bonds as herein provided for. *(Bond of indemnity.)*

Ratified the 22nd day of December, A. D., 1866.

RESOLUTION IN FAVOR OF MRS. T. J. JUDKINS.

Resolved, That the Public Treasurer pay to Mrs. T. J. Judkins, the mileage and per diem to which her late husband is entitled, up to the 24th December.
Ratified the 22nd day of December, A. D., 1866.

RESOLUTION IN FAVOR OF A. J. ADKINS AND OTHERS.

Reward of $250 for apprehension of a fugitive.

Resolved, That the sum of two hundred and fifty dollars be, and the same is hereby, appropriated out of any moneys in the treasury not otherwise appropriated, to be equally distributed and paid to A. J. Adkins, Bennet Furguson, David Byers and James Grayson, for pursuing and arresting, in the State of Tennessee, one Thomas Dula, who was subsequently convicted of the murder of Laura Foster, in the county of Wilkes, in May last.

Ratified the 22nd day of December, A. D., 1866.

RESOLUTION IN FAVOR OF JESSE B. LEE, LATE SHERIFF OF CURRITUCK COUNTY.

Preamble.

WHEREAS, The people of Currituck county are indebted to Jesse B. Lee, late Sheriff of said county, for taxes due for the years 1860 and '61 : *And whereas,* The said Sheriff could not collect said taxes, by reason of the fall of Roanoke Island, and the evacuation of Norfolk, within two months after the tax list for said years were put into his hands for collection : *And whereas, further,* The said Jesse B. Lee, after that, entered into the army of the so-called Confederacy, and was thereby prevented from collecting said taxes : Therefore, for the relief of said Sheriff, be it

Allowed two months longer time to collect Taxes.

Resolved, That Jesse B. Lee, late Sheriff of Currituck county, be allowed two months from and after the ratification of this Resolution, to collect the taxes due him, by the people of Currituck, for the years 1860 and 1861, under the same rules and regulations as are now prescribed for the collection of taxes.

Exemption.

Resolved, That all Administrators, Executors, Guardians, and all other persons who will make oath that they have paid their taxes, be exempt from paying.

Ratified the 4th day of March, A. D., 1867.

RESOLUTION IN FAVOR OF HON. DAVID OUTLAW

Resolved, That the Hon. David Outlaw, the Senator from Bertie, who has been detained from the Senate a portion of the time during the session by indisposition, shall be entitled to draw full pay and mileage for the session. [Per diem and mileage.]

Ratified the 2nd day of March, A. D., 1867.

RESOLUTION IN FAVOR OF WILLIAM PATTERSON, LATE SHERIFF OF ALAMANCE COUNTY.

Resolved, That the Treasurer be, and he is hereby, authorized to pay William Patterson, late Sheriff of Alamance county, thirty-nine dollars and twenty-four cents, it being taxes paid to the Treasurer by mistake, in the settlement of his State taxes as Sheriff. [Overpaid taxes.]

Ratified the 1st day of March, A. D., 1867.

RESOLUTION IN FAVOR OF JAMES H. WHITE.

Resolved, That James H. White be released from the payment of $175, due the State on account of board and maintenance of Mary Shelby, at the Lunatic Asylum, ten and a half months during the years 1864 and 1865. [Release from payment of $175.]

Ratified the 28th day of February, A. D., 1867.

RESOLUTION IN FAVOR OF MRS. TERISSA BELL.

Appropriates $66.
Resolved, That the Public Treasurer be authorized to pay over to Mrs. Terissa Bell, widow of S. R. Bell, sixty-six dollars, that being the amount claimed by the said widow for eleven days due S. R. Bell, after he was taken sick, before the Convention adjourned, for which he has never received any compensation.

Ratified the 15th day of February, A. D., 1867.

STATE OF NORTH CAROLINA,

OFFICE SECRETARY OF STATE,
Raleigh, April 4th, 1867.

I, Robert W. Best, Secretary of State, do hereby certify that the foregoing are true copies of the original Acts and Resolutions on file in this office, as passed by the General Assembly, at its session in 1866-'67.

R. W. BEST,
Secretary of State

INDICES

TO THE

PUBLIC AND PRIVATE LAWS

AND

RESOLUTIONS.

1866-'67.

INDEX
TO
PUBLIC LAWS
1866-'67.

AGRICULTURE—
    An act to secure advances for agricultural purposes,   3
    An act to transfer the Land Scrip given by the United States to the State of North Carolina,   5

AMNESTY—
    An act granting a General Amnesty and Pardon to all officers and soldiers of North Carolina, or of the C. S. A., or of the U. S., for offences committed against the criminal laws of the State,   6
    An act to grant Amnesty and Pardon to females,   8

APPEALS—
    An act concerning appeals in criminal cases,   9

APPRENTICES—
    An act to amend chapter 5, Revised Code,   10

ASYLUMS—
    An act providing for the support of the Insane Asylum,   11

ATTACHMENTS—
    An act to amend an act ratified December 23, 1864, to authorize attachments against corporations,   12

AUCTIONEERS—
    An act to change the mode of appointing
        Auctioneers,   13
BASTARDS—
    An act to construe "An Act more effectually
    to secure the maintenance of Bastard Children," &c., ratified March 2, 1866,   14
BURKE SQUARE—
    An act in regard to Burke Square and other
    public property in Raleigh,   15
CAPITOL—
    An act for the assignment of certain rooms in
    the Capitol,   16
CITIES AND TOWNS—
    An act to authorize the Mayor, &c., of any
    incorporated town or city in this State to
    enforce the collection of fines and penalties,   17
    An act to authorize incorporated towns and
    cities to establish systems of public schools,   17
COMMON SCHOOLS—
    An act to protect certain interests of the
    Common Schools, and for other purposes,   21
COSTS—
    An act to provide for including the value of
    stamps in the taxation of costs,   23
COURTS—
    An act to change the jurisdiction of the Courts
    and the rules of pleading therein,   23
    An act explanatory of "An Act to change the
    jurisdiction of the Courts and the rules of
    pleading therein."   26
    An act amendatory of "An Act to change the
    jurisdiction of the Courts," &c.,   27
    An act to extend the term of Chowan Superior Court,   28
    An act to change the time of holding the
    summer and winter terms of the County
    Courts of Buncombe and Mitchell,   29

COURTS—

An act to repeal an Ordinance of the Convention ratified May 20, 1866, to alter the time of holding the Courts of Pleas and Quarter Sessions of Stanly,	30
An act to authorize a Special Court for Wilson county,	30
An act to change the time of holding the Courts in the 7th Judicial District,	31
An act to extend the regular terms of the County Courts of Granville,	33
An act to abolish Jury trials in the County Courts of Macon,	34
An act to establish a Criminal Court in the county of Craven,	35
An act to establish a Criminal Court in the county of New Hanover,	41
An act to extend the session of the County Court of Wake,	47
An act giving to the County and Superior Courts authority to sentence criminals to work the public roads,	47
An act authorizing the Justices of Robeson County Court to appoint a Special Magistrate,	50
An act to authorize the County Court of Wake to borrow money and issue bonds,	51
An act to authorize County Courts of Wake to reform their financial system,	51
An act to authorize County Court of Cumberland to appoint Inspectors of crude turpentine,	53
An act to postpone the Special Term appointed for Chowan on the 2nd Monday of December, 1866,	55
An act in relation to the County Courts of Hyde,	56
An act to enable County Courts of Craven and Cumberland to extend their sessions,	56

COURTS—
An act to extend present term of the Court
of Pleas and Quarter Sessions of Wake, 57
An act to empower Court Court of Mecklenburg to hold extra tems, 58
An act supplemental to the foregoing, 59
An act to change the time of holding the County Courts of Alexander. 59
An act to change the time of holding the County Court of Yadkin, 60
An act to extend the time for the return to the County Courts of the lands to be sold for taxes, 61

CONFEDERATE CURRENCY—
An act to construe "An Act to establish a scale of depreciation of Confederate Currency," ratified March 12th, 1866, 62

COUNTIES—
An act to extend the time for the collection and return of taxes in certain counties, 63
An act to protect the people of Chatham county, 63
An act to allow fees to Justices of the Peace in Mecklenburg, &c., 64
An act for relief of purchasers of vacant lands in Macon 65

CURRITUCK SOUND—
An act to prohibit citizens of other States from fishing in Currituck Sound, 66

DEBTS CONTRACTED DURING THE WAR—
An act relating to debts contracted during the war, 67

DESTRUCTION OF RECORDS—
An act to amend "An Act for the relief of such persons as may suffer from the destruction of the records and other papers of the several counties of the State, and for other purposes," ratified February 3rd, 1866, 68

DISABLED SOLDIERS—
　An act for the relief of disabled soldiers, ... 69
　An act to supply artificial limbs to disabled
　　soldiers, and for other purposes, ... 70
DOWER—
　An act restoring to married women the common law right of Dower, ... 71
ELECTIONS—
　An act to repeal an Ordinance of the Convention, "To change the time of elections in North Carolina, and for other purposes," 73
EXCHANGE OF BONDS—
　An act to authorize the exchange of certain bonds, issued during the war for Internal Improvement purposes, for new bonds, ... 74
EXECUTIONS—
　An act to protect property sold under execution from sacrifice, ... 76
　An act to stay executions in Courts of Record, ... 78
EXECUTORS, ADMINISTRATORS, &c.,
　An act for the relief of Executors, Administrators, &c., ... 78
GINSENG—
　An act to prevent the destruction of Ginseng in the mountains of North Carolina, ... 81
HOMESTEADS—
　An act to establish Freehold Homesteads for the citizens of the State, and also to exempt certain personal property 81
HORSE-STEALING—
　An act for the better suppression of the crime of stealing horses and mules, ... 84
IMPRISONMENT FOR DEBT—
　An act to abolish the same, ... 85
　An act supplemental and explanatory of the above, ... 86
JURORS—
　An act to pay jurors in capital cases, ... 87

LANDLORDS—
    An act to amend "An act for the relief of Landlords," ratified January 26th, 1863, and "An act amendatory of the same," ratified May 28th, 1864,   87
    An act to protect Landlords against insolvent tenants,   89

LITERARY BOARD—
    An act to authorize the consolidation of the curities of the State, held by the Literary Board, and for other purposes,   90

MARRIAGE LICENSE—
    An act to amend chapter sixty-eight, Revised Code, prescribing the duties of Clerks in issuing marriage license,   92
    An act to amend section 6, chapter 40, Act of March 10, 1866,   93

PUBLIC LAWS—
    An act to secure proper Indexes to the Laws and Journals,   94

REVENUE—
    An act to raise Revenue,   95
    An act to regulate taxation by the County Court,   116
    An act to revise and consolidate the various acts relating to the collection and return of taxes for support of the indigent insane,   117
    An act to empower Secretary of State and Public Treasurer to administer oaths in matters pertaining to Revenue,   120
    An act to provide for the collection and payment into the Treasury of moneys due by paying patients in the Insane Asylum,   120
    An act to amend the Act for collecting Revenue, of March 12, 1866,   121

REVISED CODE—
    An act to repeal part of section 14, chapter 26,   122
    An act to amend section 3, chapter 7, entitled "Attachments,"   123

RIVERS—

	Ses. 1866-'67.
An act to amend section 6, chapter 48, Revised Code, entitled "Fences,"	124
An act to prevent the cutting and felling timber in Pigeon River,	124
An act to declare Roanoke a lawful fence,	125
An act to declare Tar River a sufficient fence,	125

RAIL ROADS—

An act to convert the debt due the State from the Atlantic and North Carolina Rail Road Company, into capital stock,	126
An act to amend charter of Plaster Bank and Salt Works Rail Road Company,	127
An act to amend charter of Wilmington and Weldon Rail Road Company,	127
An act to amend act of 1833, to incorporate Wilmington and Raleigh Rail Road Company,	128
An act to incorporate Rockingham and Henry Rail Road Company,	129
An act to authorize the subscription of lands, bonds and stock to the Cheraw and Coalfields Rail Road,	132
An act to charter Oxford Branch of Raleigh and Gaston Rail Road Company,	133
An act to incorporate the Greensboro' and Dan River Rail Road,	137
An act to authorize certain counties to subscribe to the capital stock of the Cheraw and Coalfields Rail Road,	149
An act to amend the charter of the Western Rail Road Company,	151
An act to amend the charter of the Western North Carolina Rail Road Company,	152
An act to enable the Western Rail Road to extend its road to the Virginia line, near Mt. Airy, &c.,	152

RAIL ROADS—

An act to authorize the Commissioners of Halifax to grant the right of way through said town, to the Wilmington and Weldon Rail Road,	154
An act to aid the Williamston and Tarboro' Rail Road Company,	155
An act to authorize President and Directors of Western North Carolina Rail Road Company to put said Road under contract,	156
Act act to enable Western North Carolina Rail Road Company to discharge its debt,	158
An act to incorporate the North Western Rail Road Company	159
An act supplemental to the foregoing,	164
An act to incorporate the Fayetteville Street Railway Company,	164
An act to incorporate the Yanceyville and Milton Rail Road Company,	167
An act to amend the charter of the Fayetteville and Florence Rail Road Company,	174
An act to harmonize and give through freight and travel, without the expense of transfer, on the different Rail Road lines in the State,	176
An act to enhance the value of the bonds to be issued for the completion of the Western North Carolina Rail Road, and for other purposes,	177
An act to enable the Western Rail Road Company to complete its road from the Coalfields to some point on the North Carolina Rail Road,	178
An act to enable the Wilmington, Charlotte and Rutherford Rail Road Company, to complete its road, pay its debts to the State, &c.,	181

RAIL ROADS—

An act to amend the charter of the Raleigh
and Gaston Rail Road Company 183

An act to re-enact and confirm the charter of
the Williamston and Tarboro' Rail Road
Company, &c., 184

ROADS, FERRIES AND BRIDGES—

An act to amend section one, chapter twenty-
ninth, Laws of North Carolina, of 1865 '66,
relative to Roads, Ferries and Bridges, 185

An act to appoint Commissioners to improve
the road from John Allen's to the top of
Blue Ridge, in Surry county, 186

An act to amend the charter of the Wilmington Railway Bridge Company, 187

An act to enable the Buncombe Turnpike
Company to subscribe the stock in their
road to the Western North Carolina Rail
Road, 188

An act to provide for keeping up the public
road, near Sampson Mountain, 189

An act to amend an "Act to lay off, locate,
&c., a road from Statesville to Wilkes-
boro'," 190

An act to amend an "Act to improve the public road from Taylorsville to Boone," &c., 190

An act for the construction of a bridge across
Notla river, in Cherokee county, 191

An act to authorize a public road from Shelby
to the South Carolina line, and the construction of a toll bridge and dam across
Broad River, 193

An act to repeal an "Act to provide hands to
work on the public roads," ratified August
4th, 1861, 194

An act to establish a Free Ferry across Pamlico River, opposite Washington, 195

SALARIES AND FEES—
 An act to amend an Act of February 27th, 1866, "to regulate Salaries and Fees,"   196
SECRETARY OF STATE—
 An act to amend an Act of February 1st, 1865, "to authorize the Secretary of State to employ a Clerk,"   197
SERVANTS, &c.—
 An act to amend an Act of 1866, (chapter fifty-eight) "to prevent enticing servants from fulfilling their contracts, or harboring them,"   197
WEIGHTS AND MEASURES—
 An act to repeal an Act of 1856-7, chapter thirty-eight,   198
 An act in relation to Weights and Measures,   199
WILLS, &c.—
 An act relating to Wills, Deeds, and other papers destroyed in the late war,   200
WILMINGTON—
 An act to enable the city of Wilmington to provide for the payment of the debt of said city, contracted prior to 1866,   201
WRECKS—
 An act to permit the people of Currituck county to elect Commissioners of Wrecks,   203
WORK-HOUSES, &c.—
 An act to amend an "Act to establish Work-houses and houses of correction," ratified March 2, 1866,   204
MISCELLANEOUS—
 An act to authorize the appointment of special magistrates for incorporated towns in Carteret county,   206
 An act to establish the dividing line between the towns of Salem and Winston,   207
 An act to repeal an act of 1865-'66, to establish a Board of Commissioners for the port of Ocracoke, &c.,   207

MISCELLANEOUS—

An act for the benefit of the poor of Bladen county, &c., 208

An act to amend an "Act to encourage the raising of sheep in the counties of Watauga and Ashe," ratified January 28, 1861, 209

An act to amend section 12, chapter 52, Revised Code, 210

RESOLUTIONS—

For the benefit of the Sheriffs of Randolph, Yadkin and Bertie counties, 211

In favor of the people of Lincoln county, 211

In favor of the Sheriff of Richmond county, 212

In favor of Stanly county, 212

In regard to Sheriffs and Tax Collectors, 213

To extend the time for the collection of taxes in Halifax county, 213

Rejecting the proposed amendment as Art. XIV of the Constitution of the U. S., 213

Providing for the printing of certain Ordinances, 214

In regard to the tax on Cotton, 214

In regard to Confederate Soldiers detained in Northern prisons, 214

In favor of Oakwood Cemetery, in Virginia, 215

Providing for commutation to soldiers, who have lost arms in the military service, 215

In favor of soldiers maimed in the late war, (commutation,) 216

In reference to disabled soldiers (commutation where arm or leg is rendered useless, though not amputated,) 216

To ascertain the names and number of wounded and disabled soldiers; nature of wounds; number of widows, orphans, &c., 217

In regard to the Direct Tax, 218

In regard to the message of the Governor and Report of the Public Treasurer, 219

RESOLUTIONS—

Ses. 1866-'67.
Amendatory of the foregoing, (includes Report of Comptroller,) 219
Declaring the loyalty of the people of North Carolina, 219
For the benefit of the Institution for the Deaf, Dumb and the Blind, 220
Providing for the payment of the Sheriffs holding elections, 221
Authorizing the Governor to extend the provisions of the Act granting Amnesty and Pardon, 221
Authorizing the Governor to accept the aid offered by the United States Government, 222
In regard to printing the Reports of Railroad and other Companies, 222
In regard to repairs on the Executive Mansion, 223
Authorizing the Governor to employ Counsel in certain cases, 223
Proposing the call of a National Convention, 224
Authorizing the publication of Dr. Curtis' Botany, 225
Postponing the valuation of the Land of the State, 226
Concerning printing the Laws and Journals of the General Assembly, 226
In favor of the Public Librarian, 227
Concerning per diem and mileage, 227
Concerning Mileage, (2nd session,) 227
In relation to Weights and Measures, 228
In favor of the city of Raleigh, (subscription to Chatham Rail Road,) 229
Authorizing the Governor to pay freight on donations, 230
Increasing the pay of the Governor's Messenger, 231
Authorizing the Public Treasurer to employ counsel in certain cases, 231

RESOLUTIONS—
 Authorizing the Finance Committee to burn
  Treasury notes and coupons, 231
 Authorizing Commissioners to Washington,
  for certain purposes, 231
 Of thanks to the aforesaid Commissioners, 232
 In regard to the Cape Fear Navigation Company, 232
 In regard to the North Carolina Rail Road
  Company, (authorizes a Committee of Investigation,) 233
 In favor of the aforesaid Committee, 233
 Continuing existence of the aforesaid Committee, 234

INDEX

TO

PRIVATE LAWS

1866–'67.

AGRICULTURAL—
    An act to incorporate the Agricultural and Mineral Land Company,   249
    An act to incorporate the North Carolina Agricultural and Manufacturing Company,   267

AMENDMENT OR REPEAL OF CHARTERS—
    An act to repeal "An act to amend the charter of the Washington Toll Bridge Company,"   266
    An act to amend section 4, act of 1858–'59, to authorize the Roanoke Navigation Company to discontinue the use of their Canal around the grand Falls of Roanoke, &c.,   267
    An act to amend section 2 of an act to incorporate the town of Marshall,   278
    An act to amend the charter of the town of Murfreesboro',   285
    An act to amend an act entitled "The North Carolina Joint Stock Publishing Company,"   295
    An act to amend charter of Greensboro' Female College,   300

AMENDMENTS, &c.—

Ses. 1866-'67.

An act to amend charter of Olin High School,	301
An act to amend charter (change name) of the Carolina Joint Stock and Insurance Company,	304
An act to amend chapter 122, acts of 1858-'59, "to incorporate the Bingham Coal Mining Company,"	307
An act to amend the charter of the town of Jefferson,	307
An act to amend the charter of the town of Wilson,	309
An act to amend charter of Oceanic Hook and Ladder Company, in Beaufort,	317
An act to amend the charter of the Cape Fear Steamboat Company,	317
An act to amend the charter (change the name) of Wayne Female College,	318
An act to amend chapter 42, Private Laws of 1866,	321
An act to amend and re-enact the act of January 25, 1843, to incorporate the Albemarle Swamp Land Company,	322
An act to amend the charter of Hillsboro' Military Academy,	327
An act to amend the charter of the Washington Toll Bridge Company,	337
An act to amend and consolidate the various acts heretofore passed for the better regulation of Jacksonville,	352
An act to amend an act of January 7, 1847, to incorporate the town of Hendersonville,	35
An act to amend the charter of the Cheoih Turnpike Company,	374
An act to amend section 3, chapter 97, Revised Code, entitled "Religious Societies,"	376

INDEX.   437

                                                Ses. 1866-'67.
AMENDMENTS, &c.—
  An act to repeal all acts heretofore passed in
    relation to the incorporation of the town of
    Morganton,   376
  An act to amend act of 1835, to authorize a
    turnpike from the South Carolina line to
    Cane Creek Bridge, in Buncombe county,   387
  An act to repeal an act for the better regula-
    tion of the Western Turnpike,   388
  An act to amend an act of December 21, 1866,
    for the construction of a bridge across Notla
    river,   393
ASYLUMS—
  An act to incorporate the North Carolina Or-
    phan Asylum,   303
BENEVOLENT SOCIETIES—
  An act to incorporate the Hibernian Benevo-
    lent Society, in Wilmington,   314
CANAL COMPANIES, &c.—
  An act to authorize the Dismal Swamp Canal
    Company to issue eight per cent. bonds,   276
  An act to incorporate the Flat Swamp, Lock's
    Creek and Evan's Creek Canal Company,   333
CEMETERIES—
  An act to set apart and make perpetual the
    McIntyre Cemetery, in Cumberland,   330
CHAMBER OF COMMERCE—
  An act to incorporate the Wilmington Cham-
    ber of Commerce,   326
  An act to incorporate the Board of Trade of
    Newberne,   345
FERRIES—
  An act to incorporate the Neuse River Ferry
    Company,   354
FIRE COMPANIES—
  An act to incorporate the Newbern Steam
    Fire Engine Company, No. 1,   305
  An act to incorporate the McLean Fire En-
    gine Company, No. 1,   306

FIRE COMPANIES—
 An act to consolidate the Fire Companies of the city of Newberne,   328
 An act to incorporate the Wilmington Hook and Ladder Company,   370
IMMIGRATION—
 An act to incorporate the North Carolina Land Agency for the encouragement of immigration,   298
LAND COMPANIES—
 An act to incorporate the Bladen Land Company,   352
 An act to incorporate the North Carolina Land and Immigration Aid Company,   361
LOAN AND TRUST COMPANIES—
 An act to incorporate the National Loan and Trust Company,   269
MANUFACTURING & MINING COMPANIES—
 An act to incorporate the Bladen Manufacturing Company,   247
 An act to incorporate the Rocky Point Manufacturing Company,   250
 An act to incorporate the Cranbery Manufacturing and Mining Company,   251
 An act to incorporate the Hoover Hill Mining Company,   252
 An act to incorporate the Durham N. Carolina Industrial Association,   262
 An act to incorporate the Pigeon River Mining and Manufacturing Company,   273
 An act to incorporate the Collins Gold Mining Company,   278
 An act to incorporate the Thomas Gold Mining Company,   279
 An act to incorporate the Sturgis Gold Mining Company,   280
 An act to incorporate the Tuckasegee Gold and Copper Mining Company,   286

MANUFACTURING & MINING COMPANIES—

An act to authorize the formation of the English and American Wool and Vine-Growing, Manufacturing, &c., Association in the United States,	288
An act to incorporate the South Union Manufacturing Company,	290
An act to incorporate the Wilmington Manufacturing Company,	296
An act to authorize Blount's Creek Manufacturing Company to re-build their Factory,	307
An act to incorporate the Rocky Mount Manufacturing Company,	312
An act to incorporate American Industrial Association,	331
An act to incorporate the American Mining and Manufacturing Company,	335
An act to incorporate the Olivia Quick Silver Mining Company,	339
An act to incorporate New Market Foundry and Manufacturing Company,	342
An act to incorporate the Lexington Mining Company,	345
An act to incorporate the Duplin Manufacturing Company,	347
An act to incorporate the Town Fork and Petroleum Company,	373

MASONIC—

An act to incorporate Wilson Lodge, No. 226,	281
An act to incorporate Newbern Lodge, No. 245,	297
An act to incorporate Franklin Lodge, No. 109,	313
An act to incorporate Black Rock Lodge, No. 135,	325
An act to incorporate Centre Hill Lodge, No. 260,	338
An act to incorporate Pasquotank Lodge, No. 103,	341

INDEX.

MASONIC—
    An act to incorporate Jerusalem Lodge, No. 95,   343
    An act to incorporate Monroe Lodge, No. 244,   344
    An act to incorporate Crane's Creek Lodge, No. 213,   356
    An act to incorporate Wiccacon Lodge, No. 240,   359
    An act to incorporate Carolina Lodge, No. 141,   370
    An act to incorporate Pythagoras Lodge, No. 249,   372

MEDICAL COLLEGE—
    An act to incorporate Edinboro Medical College, in the county of Robeson,   319

MEMORIAL ASSOCIATIONS—
    An act to incorporate the Newbern Memorial Association,   246
    An act to incorporate the Raleigh Memorial Association,   261

MERCHANTS' AND PLANTERS' ASSOCIATION—
    An act to incorporate the Charlotte Merchants' and Planters' Benevolent Association,   260
    An act to incorporate the Merchants' and Mutual Planters' Benefit Company, (Wilmington,)   283

MISCELLANEOUS—
    An act to incorporate the Wilmington Institute,   284
    An act to regulate the retailing of spirituous liquors in Williamston,   312
    An act to authorize the sale of the Academy lot in Elizabeth city,   314
    An act to authorize a sale of lands of Vine Hill Academy, in Halifax,   316
    An act to increase the capital stock of the Clarendon Bridge Company,   321
    An act to incorporate the Union Camp Ground in Cleveland,   351

MISCELLANEOUS—

An act to authorise the county of Cumberland and the town of Fayetteville, to issue bonds for their indebtedness,	381
An act to authorize the Mayor and Commissioners of Fayetteville to fund the interest due on their bonds issued in payment of stock in the Western Rail Road,	380
An act to authorize the Justices of Cumberland to fund the interest due on its bonds, given in payment of stock in the Western Rail Road,	383
An act to authorize the Justices of Warren to sell certain property,	383
An act for the benefit of Daniel Johnson, Sr., of Bladen,	384
An act to secure a better drainage of the Low Lands on Lower Creek, Caldwell county,	385
An act to give two weeks to the County Court of Anson,	389
An act to empower the Chairman of Anson County Court to sell certain town lots,	390
An act to enable the Commissioners of Jones county to sell a certain lot,	390
An act in favor of K. P. Harriss,	391
An act to authorize the Chairman of Lenoir County Court to sell the old jail lot,	391
An act for the benefit of the County Court Clerk of Beaufort,	393
An act to elect all the county officers of Perquimans, Pasquotank, &c., at the same Court,	393
An act for the relief of Henry Williams,	394
An act for the relief of estate of L. O'B. Branch, deceased,	394
An act to make valid the sale of the old jail lot of Edgecombe,	397

INDEX.

NAVIGATION COMPANY—
   An act to incorporate the Perquimans Steam
     Navigation Company,   349
PUBLISHING COMPANY—
   An act to incorporate the Key Stone Publish-
     ing Company,   360
RELIGIOUS CORPORATIONS—
   An act to incorporate Holston Conference M.
     E. Church (South,)   264
SAVINGS INSTITUTIONS—
   An act to incorporate the Jones County Sa-
     vings Institution,   242
   An act to incorporate the Wadesboro' Savings
     Institution,   256
✓ SCHOOLS AND COLLEGES—
   An act to incorporate the Trustees of the
     Lowell Colored School Society,   254
   An act to incorporate Kittrell's Springs Fe-
     male College,   265
   An act to incorporate the Pequimans Male
     and Female Academy,   272
   An act to incorporate the Mecklenburg Fe-
     male College,   275
   An act to incorporate the Rockford Male and
     Female Seminary,   282
   An act to incorporate the Colored Educational
     Association of North Carolina,   294
   An act to incorporate the Rocky Point Acad-
     emy, in New Hanover county,   315
   An act to incorporate the Waynesville Bap-
     tist College,   318
   An act to incorporate the Table Rock Semin-
     ary, in Burke,   325
SHERIFFS—
   An Act for the relief of W. A. Philpot, Sheriff
     of Granville,   378

SHERIFFS—

An act to allow the representatives of Wm.
E. Mann, late Sheriff, to collect arrears of
taxes, 378
An act in favor of the Sheriff of Gaston, 379
An act for the relief of Jas. S. Snow, Sheriff
of Halifax, 379

SINGING SOCIETY—

An act to incorporate the St. Philip's Singing Society, 281

TOWNS, &c.—

An act to incorporate the town of Franklinsville, 237
An act to incorporate the town of Nahunta, 276
An act to incorporate the town of Durham, 277
An act to incorporate the town of Scotland Neck, 293
An act to incorporate the town of Columbia, 297
An act to incorporate the town of Hookerton, 348
An act to incorporate the town of Rocky Mount, 353
An act concerning the town of Warrenton, 358
An act to extend the limits of the town of Lumberton, 363
An act to incorporate the town of Rockingham, 367

WATER WORKS—

An act to incorporate the Charlotte Water Works. 364

RESOLUTIONS—

In favor of R. H. S. Bond, Sheriff of Gates, 401
In favor of Jacob Siler, Agent of the State for the Collection of Cherokee Bonds, 401
In favor of James M. Neal, Sheriff of the county of McDowell, 402
In favor of J. L. Withers and James H. White, 403
In favor of Mary M. Transon, 404
In favor of the Attorney General, 404

RESOLUTIONS—

In favor of the representatives of D. F Bagley, late Sheriff of Perquimans county,	405
In favor of William Gordon,	405
In favor of Hon. A. S. Merrimon,	407
In favor of the Memorial Association of the city of Raleigh,	407
In favor of W. B. March and John Peebles,	407
In favor of Mrs. P. P. Dick, Executrix of the late Judge John M. Dick,	408
For the relief of Culpepper Austin, Sheriff of Union county.	408
In favor of J. J. Kitchum, Elisha Davis, of Wilkes county, and others,	408
In favor of Wm. H. Perkins, Tax Collector of Pitt county,	409
For the relief of William S. Mason,	409
In favor of the Trustees of the Rex Hospital Fund,	410
In favor of Horton S. Reeves,	410
For the relief of Seth Jones' Estate,	410
In favor of David Outlaw, Senator from 7th Senatorial District,	412
In favor of the Sheriffs of Cumberland, Northampton, Wayne, Onslow, Moore and Caswell counties,	412
In favor of the Sheriffs of Union, Orange and Brunswick, and the Tax Collectors of Wayne and Johnston counties,	412
In favor of Rufus H. Jones, Executor of Alfred Jones,	413
In favor of Mrs. T. J. Judkins,	413
In favor of A. J. Adkins and others,	414
In favor of Jesse B. Lee, late Sheriff of Currituck county,	414
In favor of Hon. David Outlaw,	415

LUTIONS— Ses. 1866-'67

In favor of William Patterson, late Sheriff of
  Alamance county, 415
In favor of James H. White, 415
In favor of Mrs. Terissa Bell, 416

ORDINANCES

PASSED BY THE

NORTH CAROLINA

E CONVENTION,

AT THE

SESSIONS OF 1865–'66.

RALEIGH:
WM. E. PELL, STATE PRINTER,
1867.

ORDINANCES

PASSED BY THE

NORTH CAROLINA STATE CONVENTION.

SESSIONS 1865–'66.

CHAPTER I.

AN ORDINANCE DECLARING NULL AND VOID THE ORDINANCE OF MAY TWENTIETH, EIGHTEEN HUNDRED AND SIXTY-ONE.

Be it declared and ordained *by the delegates of the good people of the State of North Carolina, in Convention assembled, and it is hereby declared and ordained*, That the ordinance of the Convention of the State of North Carolina, ratified on the twenty-first day of November, seventeen hundred and eighty-nine, which adopted and ratified the Constitution of the United States, and also all acts and parts of acts of the General Assembly, ratifying and adopting amendments to the said Constitution, are now, and at all times since the adoption and ratification thereof have been, in full force and effect, notwithstanding the supposed ordinance of the twentieth day of May, eighteen hundred and sixty-one, declaring that the same be repealed, rescinded and abrogated; and the said supposed ordinance is now, and at all times hath been, null and void. [Ordinance of Nov. 21, 1789, declared to have been always in force.]

Ratified in Convention the 7th day of October, 1865.

E. G. READE, *President.*
JAMES H. MOORE, *Secretary of the Convention.*
R. C. BADGER, *Assistant Secretary.*

CHAPTER II.

AN ORDINANCE PROHIBITING SLAVERY IN THE STATE OF NORTH CAROLINA.

Slavery prohibited.
Be it declared and ordained by the delegates of the people of the State of North Carolina, in Convention assembled, and it is hereby declared and ordained, That slavery and involuntary servitude, otherwise than for crimes, whereof the parties shall have been duly convicted, shall be, and is hereby forever prohibited in this State.

Ratified in Convention the 9th day of October, 1865.

EDWIN G. READE, *President.*

JAMES H. MOORE, *Secretary of the Convention.*
R. C. BADGER, *Assistant Secretary.*

CHAPTER III.

AN ORDINANCE IN RELATION TO THE AUTHENTICATION OF ORDINANCES AND OTHER ACTS OF THE CONVENTION.

Mode of authentication.
Be it ordained by this Convention, That ordinances and resolutions of the Convention, having the effect of laws, shall be authenticated by the signature of the President and attestation of the Secretary and Assistant Secretary, and shall have the date of their final passage annexed thereto; from which date each ordinance and resolution shall take effect and go into operation, unless some other time shall be therein appointed.

Ratified in Convention the 7th day of October, 1865.

EDWIN G. READE, *President.*

JAMES H. MOORE, *Secretary of the Convention.*
R. C. BADGER, *Assistant Secretary.*

CHAPTER IV.

AN ORDINANCE TO DIVIDE NORTH CAROLINA INTO SEVEN CONGRESSIONAL DISTRICTS.

SECTION 1. *Be it ordained by the people of North Carolina in Convention assembled, and it is hereby ordained by the authority of the same,* That for the purpose of electing Representatives in the Congress of the United States, the State shall be divided into seven districts, as follows, namely: The first district shall be composed of the counties of Currituck, Camden, Pasquotank, Perquimans, Chowan, Hertford, Gates, Northampton, Halifax, Martin, Bertie, Washington, Tyrrell, Hyde and Beaufort; the second district of the counties of Pitt, Craven, Jones, Lenoir, Wayne, Greene, Edgecombe, Wilson, Onslow, Carteret, Duplin and New Hanover; the third district of the counties of Brunswick, Columbus, Bladen, Sampson, Cumberland, Robeson, Richmond, Harnett, Moore, Montgomery, Anson and Stanly; the fourth district of the counties of Wake, Franklin, Warren, Granville, Orange, Nash, Johnson and Chatham; the fifth district of the counties of Alamance, Randolph, Guilford, Rockingham, Davidson, Forsyth, Stokes, Surry, Person and Caswell; the sixth district of the counties of Rowan, Cabarrus, Union, Mecklenburg, Gaston, Lincoln, Catawba, Iredell, Davie, Yadkin, Wilkes and Alexander; the seventh district of the counties of Ashe, Alleghany, Watauga, Yancey, Mitchell, McDowell, Burke, Caldwell, Rutherford, Cleaveland, Polk, Henderson, Transylvania, Buncombe, Madison, Haywood, Jackson, Macon, Cherokee and Clay; each of which districts shall be entitled to elect one representative in the Congress of the United States.

Districts.

SEC. 2. The election for Representatives in Congress shall be held and conducted in every respect in conformity with the rules, regulations and restrictions as set forth and prescribed in the sixty-ninth chapter Revised Code, except

Manner of conducting elections, &c.

that the polls shall be compared in the first district at the court-house in the county of Chowan; in the second district at the court-house in the county of Lenoir; in the third district, at the court-house in the county of Cumberland; in the fourth district, at the court-house in the county of Wake; in the fifth district, at the court-house in the county of Guilford; in the sixth district, at the court-house in the county of Iredell, and in the seventh district, at the court-house in the county of Buncombe.

Ratified in Convention the 16th day of October, 1865.

EDWIN G. READE, *President.*
JAMES H. MOORE, *Secretary of the Convention.*
R. C. BADGER, *Assistant Secretary.*

CHAPTER V.

AN ORDINANCE PROVIDING FOR THE ELECTION OF THE MEMBERS OF THE GENERAL ASSEMBLY, TO BE CONVENED ON THE FOURTH MONDAY OF NOVEMBER, EIGHTEEN HUNDRED AND SIXTY-FIVE, AND FOR ELECTING REPRESENTATIVES IN CONGRESS, AND GOVERNOR OF THE STATE.

Meeting of Assembly. SECTION 1. *Be it ordained by the delegates of the people of the State of North Carolina, in Convention assembled, and it is hereby ordained by the authority of the same,* That a General Assembly of the State shall be convened on the fourth Monday of November, eighteen hundred and sixty-five, the members whereof shall hold their places till the next election of such members, which shall be held on the first Thursday of August, eighteen hundred and sixty-six.

Provisional Governor to issue writs of election. SEC. 2. *Be it further ordained,* That the Provisional Governor is hereby authorized and requested to issue forthwith, to the Sheriff of each county, a writ, directing that an election be held for the Senators and members of the House of Commons of such General Assembly, on the second Thursday of November next, under the rules, regulations and provisions of chapter fifty-two of the Revised Code.

SEC. 3. *Be it further ordained,* That immediately on the receipt of the writ, each Sheriff shall summon the Justices of the Peace, of the Court of Pleas and Quarter Sessions, to assemble at the Court House on a day appointed by him, which shall be as early as practicable, and they, or so many as may assemble, shall appoint inspectors for each place of election, who shall be forthwith notified of their election and make returns of the polls, in the manner prescribed in said chapter. *Inspectors.*

SEC. 4. *Be it further ordained,* That each member and voter shall be qualified according to the now existing Constitution of the State: *Provided, however,* That no one shall be eligible to a seat, or be capable of voting, who, being free in all respects, shall not, before the twenty-ninth day of May, eighteen hundred and sixty-five, either have voluntarily taken or subscribed the oath of amnesty prescribed in the proclamation of President Lincoln, with the purpose to suppress the insurrection and restore the authority of the United States, and thenceforward shall have observed the same, or shall not have taken and subscribed the oath of amnesty prescribed in the proclamation of President Johnson, bearing date twenty-ninth day of May, eighteen hundred and sixty-five; and who, moreover, shall not in either case be of those who are excepted from the amnesty granted by any of the said proclamations, unless pardoned: *But, provided also,* That all persons who may have preferred petitions for pardons, shall be deemed to have been pardoned, if the fact of being pardoned shall be announced by the Governor, although the pardon may not have been received: *And, provided also,* That the payment of a public tax shall not be required as a qualification of the voter in the elections in November next. *Voters.*

SEC. 5. *Be it further ordained,* That for the purpose of ascertaining the qualifications of persons proposing to vote, the inspectors may, and it shall be their duty, whenever the vote may be challenged, or they shall have cause to suspect *Inspectors may administer oaths.*

that he is not duly qualified, examine him and others, on oath, touching the question.

Election for members of Congress.

SEC. 6. *Be it further ordained,* That at the same time and places, elections shall be held for seven representatives in the Congress of the United States, in pursuance of chapter sixty-nine of the Revised Code, which shall be conducted under the rules and regulations therein prescribed for such elections, and the voters in said elections shall be such only as shall be qualified to vote for members of the House of Commons, and the provisional Governor shall give the certificate required by the ninth section of said chapter.

Election for Governor.

SEC. 7. *Be it further ordained,* That at the same time and places an election shall be held for a Governor of the State, under the same rules and regulations as are prescribed in chapter fifty-three, of the Revised Code, and the persons qualified to vote for members of the House of Commons, under this ordinance, shall be qualified to vote for Governor.

Qualifications for Governor.

SEC. 8. *Be it further ordained,* That no person shall be eligible as Governor, unless he shall be qualified according to the Constitution of the State, and also shall be capable, under the provisions of this ordinance, of voting for members of the General Assembly.

SEC. 9. *Be it further ordained,* That the Governor thus elected shall take his seat as soon as the authority of the Provisional Governor shall cease, either before the first day of January, eighteen hundred and sixty-six, or afterwards, before the first day of January, eighteen hundred and sixty-seven.

Term of office.

SEC. 10. *Be it further ordained,* That the Governor, thus elected, shall continue in office till the first day of January, eighteen hundred and sixty-seven.

SEC. 11. *Be it further ordained,* That it shall be in the power of the General Assembly to modify so much of this ordinance as relates to the provisions for electing a Governor, and his term of office.

Ratified in Convention the 10th day of October, 1865.

EDWIN G. READE, *President.*

JAMES H. MOORE, *Secretary of the Convention.*
R. C. BADGER, *Assistant Secretary.*

CHAPTER VI.

AN ORDINANCE FOR THE ELECTION OF CLERKS AND SHERIFFS.

SECTION 1. *Be it ordained by the good people of North Carolina in Convention assembled, and it is hereby ordained by the authority of the same,* That an election be held for Sheriffs and County and Superior Court Clerks on the same day, and at the same time and places, that the election for members of the General Assembly shall take place, and in the same manner as heretofore prescribed for the election of said officers, and that all persons qualified to vote for members of the House of Commons shall be qualified to vote for these officers. <small>Qualification of voters, &c.</small>

SEC. 2. *Be it further ordained,* That said officers shall have all the qualifications heretofore required.

SEC. 3. *Be it further ordained,* That they shall enter upon the duties of their office as soon as the Provisional Government expires, and hold said offices until further provided for by the General Assembly.

Ratified in Convention the 17th day of October, 1865.

EDWIN G. READE, *President.*

JAMES H. MOORE, *Secretary of the Convention.*
R. C. BADGER, *Assistant Secretary.*

CHAPTER VII.

AN ORDINANCE PROVIDING FOR THE ELECTION OF TWO MEMBERS OF THE HOUSE OF COMMONS FROM THE COUNTY OF CUMBERLAND, AND ONE FROM THE COUNTY OF HARNETT.

Be it ordained by the delegates of the people of North Carolina in Convention assembled, and it is hereby ordained by the authority of the same, That until otherwise provided by law,

Cumberland to have two members and Harnett one. the County of Cumberland shall elect two members to the House of Commons, and the County of Harnett one member, the election to be held in accordance with the rules and regulations prescribed by law for the elections of members to the House of Commons: *Provided*, that nothing in this ordinance shall change the representation of the two counties in the Senate, but they shall vote together for one Senator until the next apportionment of Senatorial Districts.

Ratified in Convention the 17th day of October, 1865.

EDWIN G. READE, *President.*
JAMES H. MOORE, *Secretary of the Convention.*
P. C. BADGER, *Assistant Secretary.*

CHAPTER VIII.

AN ORDINANCE SUBMITTING TO THE QUALIFIED VOTERS OF THE STATE THE RATIFICATION OR REJECTION OF CERTAIN ORDINANCES.

SECTION 1. *Be it ordained by the delegates of the people of North Carolina, and it is hereby ordained by the authority of* *Ordinances concerning secession and slavery.* *the same,* That on the second Thursday of November next, there shall be submitted to the voters of the State, qualified to vote for members of the House of Commons, for their ratification or rejection, the ordinance passed by this Convention, entitled "An ordinance declaring null and void the ordinance of May the twentieth, eighteen hundred and sixty-one," and such persons as shall favor the ratification, shall vote a ticket with the words "Anti-Secession Ordinance ratified," and those opposed shall vote a ticket in the words "Anti-Secession Ordinance rejected." Also at the same time shall be submitted for their ratification or rejection an ordinance passed by the Convention, entitled "An Ordinance prohibiting slavery in the State of North Carolina," and those who favor the ratification of the same shall vote a ticket with the words "Anti-Slavery Ordinance ratified," and those opposed shall vote a ticket with the words "Anti-Slavery ordinance rejected."

SEC. 2. *Be it further ordained*, That the sheriff or other officers, who may ascertain the results of the polls in each county, shall transmit the same to the Provisional Governor, who is hereby empowered and requested to cause the number of votes each way to be ascertained and proclaimed through as many as three newspapers published in different parts of the State. Returns of elections.

SEC. 4. *Be it further ordained*, That, if ratified, thenceforth the said ordinances shall be the laws of the land, and that abolishing slavery shall become a part of the Constitution of the State. If ratified?

Ratified in Convention the 17th day of October, 1865.

EDWIN G. READE, *President.*

JAMES H. MOORE, *Secretary of the Convention.*
R. C. BADGER, *Assistant Secretary.*

CHAPTER IX.

AN ORDINANCE TO PROVIDE REVENUE FOR THE YEAR EIGHTEEN HUNDRED AND SIXTY-FIVE.

SECTION I. *Be it ordained by the delegates of the people of North Carolina in Convention assembled, and it is hereby ordained by the authority of the same,* That the Sheriffs of this State collect in their respective counties in the existing national currency, and pay over to the Public Treasurer, before the first day of February, eighteen hundred and sixty-six, taxes on the subjects and persons, and according to the rates, hereinafter set forth, these taxes applying and operating during the twelve months next preceding the first day of January, eighteen hundred and sixty-six. Sheriffs to collect.

Subjects of taxation.

SEC. 2. On every surgeon, dentist, physician, lawyer, portrait painter, daguerrean artist, or other person taking likenesses of the human face, every commission merchant, factor, broker, owner of a cotton or woolen factory, except when such factory has been destroyed, and auctioneer, whose total receipts and income in the way of practice, fees, commissions or emoluments from his profession or business exceed one thousand dollars, one per cent. on the total amount of his receipts or income.

SEC. 3. On every gallon of whiskey, brandy or other spirituous liquors distilled for his own use, or for sale by, the owner or person using any distillery, twenty-five cents; and a like sum on every gallon distilled for other persons, to be paid by the persons for whom the same was distilled; and on every gallon of whiskey, brandy, or other spirituous liquor distilled out of this State and imported into it for sale, a tax of fifty cents.

SEC. 4. On every company of circus riders, or exhibitors of collections of animals, for every county in which they shall exhibit for reward, fifty dollars.

SEC. 5. On every company of theatrical players or persons performing feats of strength or agility, or exhibiting natural or artificial objects, for each county in which they shall exhibit for reward, fifteen dollars.

SEC. 6. On the gross receipts of every insurance company incorporated out of the State, five per cent.

SEC. 7. Six per cent. on the profits of every bond or note broker, private banker, or agent of a broker or banker in any other State.

SEC. 8. On every public billiard table, one hundred dollars, and on every private billiard table in use, twenty-five dollars.

SEC. 9. On every bowling alley, whether called a nine or ten pin alley, or by any other name, fifty dollars.

SEC. 10. On every livery stable, or place where horses are kept for hire, twenty-five dollars.

SEC. 11. On every retailer by a measure less than a quart of spirituous liquor, wine or cordial, or malt liquors, seventy-five dollars for each place where such retailing may be carried on: *Provided, however,* That in all cases in which a license has been granted to any retailer of spirituous liquors, and he has paid any amount to the Sheriff or Clerk of the County Court of his county for such license, the amount so paid shall be credited to such retailer in the collection of the tax laid by this section: *Provided, however,* That if any such retailer shall, on or before the first day of November next, have altogether ceased to retail as aforesaid, and shall not again so retail during the year, in all such cases, such retailer shall pay a tax of but forty dollars.

SEC. 12. Two per cent. on the amount of all purchases of spirituous liquors, wines or cordials, made in this State or elsewhere, for the purpose of sale in this State, either by wholesale or retail.

SEC. 13. On every pedler, either on land or water, for each county in which he may peddle hereafter any spirituous liquors, goods, wares or merchandise, whether such pedler travels on foot or with a conveyance of any kind whatever, fifty dollars.

SEC. 14. Five per cent. on the gross amount received by any Express Company for the carriage or transportation in this State, of any package, article or thing.

SEC. 15. On each bale of cotton, or hogshead of tobacco, or on every two hundred dollars' worth of manufactured tobacco, of the growth of this State, held or owned in this State, or elsewhere, at any time during the year eighteen hundred and sixty-five, by persons producing the same, a tax of one dollar.

SEC. 16. On each bale of cotton, or hogshead of tobacco, or on every two hundred dollars' worth of manufactured tobacco held or owned in this State at any time during the year eighteen hundred and sixty-five, by any person other than the producer, without regard to the time or place when or where purchased or otherwise required, a tax of two dollars.

SEC. 17. On each barrel of tar, turpentine and rosin held in this State at any time during the year eighteen hundred and sixty-five, by persons producing the same, a tax of five cents.

Sec. 18. On each barrel of tar, turpentine and rosin held in this State at any time during the year eighteen hundred and sixty-five, or by any person other than the producer, without regard to the time when purchased or otherwise acquired, a tax of ten cents.

Sec. 19. One half of one per cent. on the amount of all purchases made in or out of the State, whether for cash or on credit, by any merchant, merchant-tailor, grocer, jeweller, druggist, apothecary, produce-dealer, commission merchant, factor, produce-broker or dealer, and every other trader, who, as principal or agent for another, carries on the business of buying and selling goods, wares or merchandize, of whatever name or description : *Provided, however*, That purchases of cotton, tobacco, turpentine, rosin, tar and spirituous liquors, wine and cordials, shall not be included in the amount of purchases on which the tax laid by this section is to be estimated : *And provided further*, That in all cases in which Treasury notes of the Confederate States, or of this State, or bank notes, constituted the currency in which purchases have been made, the value in specie of such currency at the time of such purchase shall be counted in estimating the amount of any such purchase.

Exemptions. Sec. 20. All cotton, tobacco, rosin, tar, and other articles or things specifically taxed by this ordinance, and all such articles or things which are taxed by this ordinance as part of the amount of purchases made during the year eighteen hundred and sixty-five, which may have been destroyed, or of which the owner or purchaser has been deprived of the possession without his consent, shall be exempt from the operation of this ordinance.

Sheriffs may administer oaths, &c. Sec. 21. To ascertain the amount of taxes due from any person, company, firm or corporation, the sheriff or his deputy is hereby authorized and empowered to examine, on oath, any person or any member of any firm or company, or any president, agent, or other officer of any company or corporation, and in case any such person shall refuse fully to answer, on oath, such person shall be deemed guilty of a misdemeanor, and said sheriff or deputy sheriff shall commit him to prison, unless he shall enter into recognizance with good security, in such sum as shall be required, to appear before the Superior court of law of his county at its next term, to answer the charge, and, on conviction, he shall be fined or imprisoned, at the discretion of the Court.

Sec. 22. It shall be the duty of the Sheriff, or his deputy, to demand payment of the taxes by this ordinance imposed, from the parties ow'ng the same, as promptly as may be practicable; and, if such taxes shall not be paid within twenty days after such demand, it shall be lawful for such Sheriff, by himself or his deputy, to proceed to collect such taxes, with ten per cent. additional thereto, by distraint and sale of goods, chattels, or effects of the delinquent tax payers, and use all other remedies prescribed in the Revised Code against delinquent tax payers. *Duties of Sheriff.*

Sec. 23. The persons now acting in the several counties of this State as Sheriffs, under the existing Provisional Government, shall, as soon as practicable, summon the Justices of the Peace appointed by the Provisional Governor for their respective counties, to meet at the Court House of their several counties on a day certain, and, before a majority, or such number of Justices as shall be so assembled, such Sheriffs shall enter into the bonds as required by chapter one hundred and five of the Revised Code, entitled "Sheriffs," with good security, to be approved by a majority of the Justices so assembled, and deliver such bonds to the Clerks of the County Courts heretofore appointed by the Justices aforesaid, and thereupon such Sheriffs are empowered and directed to collect the taxes imposed or laid by this ordinance, under the provisions, and subject to the pains and penalties, set forth in the chapter of the Revised Code above referred to, except in such particulars as are otherwise provided for in this ordinance: *Provided, however,* That if the persons referred to as acting Sheriffs refuse or decline to enter into the bonds required, then, and in that event, the Justices aforesaid may appoint some other person to qualify and act as Sheriff, under the provisions of this ordinance, who shall enter into bond as aforesaid. *Sheriffs to enter at once into bonds.*

Sec. 24. The several Sheriffs shall file with the Clerks of the County Courts of their respective counties, the names of

Lists of tax-ers, &c. — the persons from whom they shall have collected any tax under this ordinance, annexing to the name of each tax payer the amount collected from him, with careful additions of the whole, showing the aggregate amount collected, which statement he shall subscribe and verify by affidavit before such Clerk in the words following: "I swear that the foregoing statement truly sets forth the name of each indvidiual, firm and corporation from which I have collected taxes, and the amount paid by each of them, under the ordinance of the Convention, entitled an ordinance to provide revenue for the year eighteen hundred and sixty-five, ratified the eighteenth day of October, eighteen hundred and sixty-five." All sums which may have been received by any Sheriff, or Clerk of any Court in the name of the State, as taxes, fines, forfeitures or otherwise, shall, if received by the Clerk, be paid to the Sheriff; and all such sums shall be entered in the statement to be filed by the Sheriff aforesaid, and the Clerk shall furnish to the Sheriff a certificate, verified by his signature and official seal, showing the total amount of such collections, to be filed by said Sheriff with the Public Treasurer when he shall pay over the same to said Treasurer.

Sec. 25. The Clerks of said Courts shall make a copy of the statement returned by the sheriff, and keep the same posted up in some conspicuous and accessible place in the Court House, for one month immediately after the filing of the same, and he shall, at all times, allow any tax payer of his county to inspect the original.

Clerks to make a copy, &c.

Sec. 26. The sheriff shall pay over the money collected as aforesaid by him, less six per cent. where the amount collected is under one thousand dollars; five per cent., where the amount collected is over one thousand dollars, and under two thousand dollars; and four per cent. where the amount is over two thousand dollars, by way of commissions for his services, which he is hereby authorized to retain, to the Public Treasurer, on or before the first day of February, eighteen hunded and sixty-six. Any Sheriff failing to pay to the Public Treasurer, as aforesaid, shall forfeit to the State one thousand dollars, and the Public Treasurer shall report such defaulting Sheriff to the Solicitor for the Judicial

Fees of Sheriffs.

Penalty for delinquency.

District in which such Sheriff resides, and such Solicitor shall, at the next term of the Superior Court of the county in which such Sheriff resides, move for judgment for the amount due from such Sheriff, and also the penalty aforesaid, and the presiding Judge is hereby empowered to render judgment in favor of the State against such defaulting Sheriff, and the sureties on his bond, for the amount so due by him, including said penalty, without other notice to such Sheriff or his sureties than is given by the delinquency of such Sheriff.

Sec. 27. For his settlement with the Treasurer, the Sheriff shall be paid by the Treasurer five dollars for each day he may be necessarily engaged therein, and four dollars for every thirty miles of twice the estimated distance from his home to the seat of government by the most usual way traveled.

Sec. 28. That five hundred copies of this Ordinance be printed for distribution by the Treasurer among the Sheriffs and Clerks of the different counties of this State.

Ratified in Convention the 18th day of October, 1865.

EDWIN G. READE, *President.*
JAMES H. MOORE, *Secretary of the Convention.*
R. C. BADGER, *Assistant Secretary.*

CHAPTER X.

AN ORDINANCE TO PROTECT THE OWNERS OF PROPERTY AND FOR OTHER PURPOSES.

Section I. *Be it ordained by the delegates of the people of North Carolina in Convention assembled, and it is hereby ordained,* That the persons appointed by the Provisional Governor, Judges of the Courts of Oyer and Terminer, are hereby invested with power to exercise severally at their chambers, all such powers and authorities as by the laws

Courts at Chambers.

of the State are conferred on the Judges of the Superior Courts of Law and Equity, at chambers, and may issue writs of injunction, sequestration, *ne exeat* and *capias*, under the rules and regulations prescribed in chapter thirty-two, of the Revised Code, for the purpose of protecting and securing against loss or damage, the owner of any kind of estate, real, personal or mixed, or the creditor of any person whatsoever, and to this end may make all necessary rules, orders, and decrees, for disobedience whereof the party offending may be attached for contempt.

<small>Powers of Provisional Judges.</small> SEC. 2. *Be it further ordained,* That said Judges may depute any person to execute the process issued by them, and may appoint a clerk when necessary. They may prescribe in each case the time within which the process issued by them shall be served, and the defendant shall appear.

SEC. 3. *Be it further ordained,* That when any defendant shall be enjoined or restrained, unless in case of irreparable injury, and such defendant will enter into bond with ample security, payable to the plaintiff in double the amount of the sworn value, if the property or any part thereof should be the property of the plaintiff, the defendant will pay to the plaintiff the value thereof, with twenty-five per cent. added thereto, and interest on the amount and all the costs incurred by him; the property may, in the discretion of the Court, be delivered to said defendant, and the bond to the plaintiff who may bring suit thereon: *Provided always,* if the defendant should not appear and execute such bond, it shall, nevertheless, be in the power of the Court to make all necessary decrees, rules and orders for preserving the property, or its value for the rightful party by sale, and keeping the proceeds or otherwise, to abide the final decree.

<small>Process for arrest, habeas corpus, &c.</small> SEC. 4. *Be it further ordained,* that said Judge may issue process for arrest of persons violating the criminal law, and may grant writs of *habeas corpus* and take bail; and the recognizance shall be returned to the proper Courts; they may also take and certify the probate of deeds and the privy examinations of *femes covert* in the manner prescribed by law,

SEC. 5. *Be it further ordained,* That the General Assembly shall make suitable compensation to said Judges for the services which they may render under this ordinance, and also such persons as may be employed by them in the discharge of the duties hereby imposed on them. <small>Compensation to Judges.</small>

SEC. 6. *Be it further enacted,* That so soon as the Superior Courts shall be restored, the duties herein prescribe for the Judges aforesaid shall cease, and the cases before them shall be transferred by them into the Courts of Equity of the proper counties, and the latter Courts shall proceed with them as if the said proceedings had been authorized and had been begun in said court. <small>Duties prescribed to cease, when?</small>

Ratified in Convention the 18th day of October, 1865.

EDWIN G. READE, *President.*
JAMES H. MOORE, *Secretary of the Convention.*
R. C. BADGER, *Assistant Secretary.*

CHAPTER XI.

AN ORDINANCE DECLARING WHAT LAWS AND ORDINANCES ARE IN FORCE, AND FOR OTHER PURPOSES.

WHEREAS, Doubts may arise from the late attempt of the State of North Carolina to secede from the United States, whether any, and what laws have been and are now in force, and what acts done by officers and individuals are valid and obligatory: Now, for the purpose of preventing such doubts about these and other matters hereinafter mentioned: <small>Preamble.</small>

SECTION 1. *Be it declared and ordained by the delegates of the people of the State of North Carolina, in Convention assembled, and it is hereby declared and ordained, as follows:*

1. All the laws of the State except as hereinafter is excepted, which, on the twentieth day of May, eighteen hundred and sixty-one, were compatible with the allegiance of <small>Laws, &c., in force?</small>

the citizens of the State to the government of the United States, and not since repealed or modified; and all the laws and ordinances passed since that day, except as hereinafter is excepted, compatible with such allegiance, and not since repealed or modified, and which are consistent with the Constitution of the State and the United States, are hereby declared to have been, at all times since their enactment, and now, to be in full force, in like manner and to the same extent, and not otherwise, as if the State had not on that day, nor at any time since, attempted to secede from the government of the United States, and as if no question had been made of the lawful authority of the Convention assembled on that day, or of any General Assembly assembled since that day, to enact such laws and ordinances, and all other of said ordinances and laws are hereby declared to have been and to be null and void: *Provided, however,* That nothing herein contained shall be so construed as to prevent the General Assembly from repealing or modifying any of said laws and ordinances hereby ratified, which shall not form a part of the Constitution of the State.

Proviso.

SEC. 2. All the judicial proceedings had or which may be had in the Courts of Record and before Justices of the Peace, shall be deemed and held valid in like manner and to the same extent, and not otherwise, as if the State had not on the said day, or since, attempted to secede from the United States.

Judicial proceedings valid.

SEC. 3. All contracts, executory and executed, of every nature and kind, made on or since the twentieth day of May, eighteen hundred and sixty-one, and all marriages solemnized on or since that day, under any authority, purporting to be the law of the State, shall be deemed to be valid and binding between the parties in like manner and to the same extent, and not otherwise, as if the State had not on the said day, or afterwards, attempted to secede from the United States; and it shall be the duty of the General Assembly to provide a scale of depreciation of the Confederate currency from the time of its first issue to the end of the war; and all executory contracts, solvable in

Contracts.

money, whether under seal or not, made after the depreciation of said currency before the first day of May, eighteen hundred and sixty-five, and yet unfulfilled, (except official bonds and penal bonds payable to the State,) shall be deemed to have been made with the understanding that they were solvable in money of the value of the said currency; it shall be competent for either of the parties to show, by parol or other relevant testimony, what the understanding was in regard to the kind of currency in which the same are solvable; and in such case, the true understanding shall regulate the value of the contract: *Provided,* That in case the plaintiff, in any suit upon such contracts, will make an affidavit that it was solvable in other currency than that above referred to, then such presumption shall cease, and it shall be presumed to be payable in such currency as shall be mentioned in the affidavit, subject to explanation by evidence as aforesaid.

SEC. 4. All the acts and doings of the civil officers of the State, since the twentieth day of May, eighteen hundred and sixty-one, done or which may be done under and in virtue of any authority purporting to be a law of the State, which is consistent with its allegiance to the United States and with the Constitution of the State, shall be deemed valid, and of the same force and effect as if the State had not on that day, or since, attempted to secede from the United States. Acts and doings of civil officers.

SEC. 5. No person who may have been in the civil or military service of the State, or of the Confederate States, shall be held liable for any act done, or which may be done, in the proper discharge of the duties imposed on him by any authority purporting to be a law of the State or Confederate States government; but such person shall be exempt from all personal liability therefor, in like manner as if such act had been done under lawful authority *Provided, nevertheless,* That nothing herein contained shall be so construed as to bar any citizen of the State from his civil action for the recovery of damages or from indictment on account of any improper or illegal execution of the law or authority imposing such duties: *Provided,* That no order Acts done by military officers.

Proviso.

issued without authority of what purported to be a law of the State or Confederate States shall be any protection to illegal acts done thereunder.

Acts of Provisional Governor.

SEC. 6. All the acts and deeds of the Provisional Governor of the State, appointed by the President of the United States, and likewise all the acts of any officer or agent by him appointed, or under his authority done, or which may be done in pursuance of the authority conferred on such officer or agent, are hereby ratified and declared to be valid to all intents and purposes : *Provided, nevertheless,* That so far as it may be competent for this Convention to declare the same, all appointments made, and all offices and places created, by or under the authority of the Provisional Governor, shall cease at the close of the first session of the next General Assembly, or at such other times as that Assembly shall direct, successors in such appointments or offices to be chosen or to be qualified, subject however, to the provisions of the Revised Code, chapter seventy-seven, section three : *Provided, however,* That in all cases of appointments made by him of directors in any corporation, they shall continue until the regular elections of its officers.

Repeal.

SEC. 7. All provisions for a change in the rates of taxation that were in force upon the twentieth of May, eighteen hundred and sixty-one, and all laws rendering criminal the distillation of grain and other articles, are hereby repealed, and, until otherwise provided by the General Assembly, Sheriffs and other revenue officers shall collect and account for the taxes and other public dues according to the rates that were in force upon the twentieth day of May aforesaid.

Ratified in Convention the 18th day of October, 1865.

EDWIN G. READE, *President.*

JAMES H. MOORE, *Secretary of the Convention.*

R. C. BADGER, *Assistant Secretary.*

CHAPTER XII.

AN ORDINANCE APPOINTING A JUDGE TO DETERMINE STATE CLAIMS TO PROPERTY.

SECTION 1. *Be it ordained by the delegates of the people in Convention assembled, and it is hereby ordained by the same,* That Daniel G. Fowle, Esquire, of the city of Raleigh, be, and he is hereby appointed a Judge of the State, to hold a Court in the city of Raleigh for the purpose of hearing such complaints as may be made by the Public Treasurer, or any person under his direction, against such persons as hold and detain, or may have used, sold, destroyed or otherwise unlawfully converted to their own use, any money or property belonging to the State, and for which, according to law, he ought to account. D. G. Fowle appointed.

SEC. 2. *Be it further ordained,* That the proceedings to recover such property or its value, when converted or wasted, may be by bill, in the nature of a bill in equity, which shall create a lien on such property from the filing of such bill, and the Court, whenever it may be deemed expedient, shall have power to issue writs of injunction, sequestration and attachment in order to protect such money or property, or its value, and secure it to the State; and moreover, shall have power to order the sale of such property at any time pending the controversy, and hold the proceeds to abide the final decree in the cause; and generally, shall have all the powers of a Court of Equity of the State, and shall be a Court of Record. Nature of proceedings.

SEC. 3. *Be it further ordained,* That the Court shall be at all times open, and sit from day to day, and the business shall be conducted under such rules as the Judge may prescribe. He shall appoint a clerk and fix his compensation, and the taxed fees of the clerk and counsel. Court to sit from day to day.

ORDINANCES.

Expenses.

SEC. 4. *Be it further ordained,* That the Treasurer shall furnish the necessary stationery, and pay out of any moneys on hand all such incidental expenses as may be necessary to enable the Court to proceed in its business.

Moneys collected under decree of court

SEC. 5. *Be it further ordained,* That all moneys collected under any decree or order of the Court, shall be paid to the Public Treasurer, and his receipt shall be taken therefor and handed to the Comptroller, and if any moneys shall be paid or delivered into the office of the Court, pending any controversy, to abide the event thereof, the same shall be delivered to the Treasurer as a special deposit for safe keeping, and shall be under the control of the Court.

Compensation of Judge.

SEC. 6. *Be it further ordained,* That the Judge shall be compensated for his service by the General Assembly, and that the services of any Attorney, whom the Public Treasurer shall employ to aid him, shall be compensation in like manner.

Judge to deputize ministerial officers &c.

SEC. 7. *Be it further ordained,* That until other Sheriffs and Coroners shall be in office, the Judge shall deputise any person to execute all such process and precepts as he may cause to issue, and such person shall be entitled to the same fees as Sheriffs are in like case, and if such fees will not, in the opinion of the Court, compensate the services rendered, the Court shall fix them and cause them to be taxed in the costs.

Appeals.

SEC. 8. *Be it further ordained,* That either party may appeal to the Supreme Court in the manner allowed for appeals from the Courts of Equity, and the bond of the defendant, if he appeal and a bond is required, shall be transmitted as part of the record, and be subject to the law relating to appeal bonds in other cases carried by appeal to the said Court.

SEC. 9. *Be it further ordained,* That if the person herein appointed Judge shall decline to accept the office, or at any time it should become vacant for that, or any other cause, the Provisional Governor is hereby empowered and requested to fill the office with some other competent person, and any person who may fill it shall be qualified by taking the oath of office.

SEC. 10. *Be it further ordained,* That nothing in this ordinance contained shall have the effect of disqualifying any person holding said office, from holding at the same time any other office not incompatible with it.

SEC. 11. *Be it further ordained,* That this ordinance may be repealed or modified by the General Assembly.

Ratified in Convention the 18th day of October, 1865.

EDWIN G. READE, *President.*
JAMES H. MOORE, *Secretary of the Convention.*
R. C. BADGER, *Assistant Secretary.*

CHAPTER XIII.

AN ORDINANCE TO ORGANIZE A TEMPORARY FORCE FOR THE PRESERVATION OF LAW AND ORDER.

SECTION 1. *Be it ordained by the delegates of the people in Convention assembled, and it is hereby ordained by the authority of the same,* That the Sheriffs appointed under the Provisional Government shall, as soon as practicable, summon the Justices of the Peace as appointed by the Provisional Governor for their respective counties, to meet at the Court House of their several counties on a day certain, and a majority, or such number of said Justices as shall be assembled, shall have power, and they are hereby authorized, to enrol and organize as many military companies as auxiliaries to the county police, as they in their discretion may deem necessary for the preservation of law and order, under the following rules and regulations: The said Justices shall enroll all or any portion of the free white male residents between the ages of eighteen and thirty-five years, and if necessary extend the enrollment to forty-five years. They shall appoint or direct the election of all necessary officers. They shall prescribe the duties, police or otherwise, to be discharged by said forces. They shall make such ex-

Justices of the various counties to organize military companies.

emptions as they may deem proper. They shall have power to enforce all their orders, by the infliction of such pains and penalties as they may consider just and proper. And in case of any serious disturbance or outbreak, the said forces shall be deemed auxiliary to the county police, and shall be subject to the same orders. And the said Justices, from time to time, shall have power, and they are hereby authorized, to adopt all such measures as they may consider necessary to render said forces efficient for the purposes herein set forth.

SEC. 2. *Be it further ordained,* That this ordinance shall continue in force until the organization of the militia, or until modified or repealed by the General Assembly.

SEC. 3. *Be it further ordained,* That the Clerk of the Convention transmit a copy of this ordinance to each Sheriff and County Court Clerk within the State, immediately after the ratification of the same.

Ratified in Convention the 18th day of October, 1865.

EDWIN G. READE, *President.*

JAMES H. MOORE, *Secretary of the Convention.*

R. C. BADGER, *Assistant Secretary.*

CHAPTER XIV.

AN ORDINANCE DECLARING VACANT ALL THE OFFICES OF THE STATE IN EXISTENCE ON THE TWENTY-SIXTH DAY OF APRIL, EIGHTEEN HUNDRED AND SIXTY-FIVE.

Preamble.

WHEREAS, No person elected or appointed to any office under the State, can rightfully claim any vested interest therein, until he shall have taken the oath to support the Constitution of the United States, as prescribed in that instrument, and also an oath of office; and whereas, those officers who did take such oaths and thereafter took an oath to support the Constitution of the Confederate States, did thereby incur the penalty of forfeiting their offices, and are incapable of resuming the duties thereof, to which they were respectively elected or appointed, without again taking like oaths; and whereas, it is in the power of this Convention to allow or deny to such persons the privilege of again qualifying themselves anew by taking such oaths; and this Convention deems it expedient, after so great a popular convulsion as has happened amongst the people of this State, that all such offices should be filled anew by persons hereafter chosen or appointed:

Be it therefore ordained by the delegates of the people in this Convention assembled, and it is hereby ordained by the authority of the same, That no officer of this State who may have taken an oath of office to support the Constitution of the Confederate States, shall be capable of holding under the State any office or place of trust and profit which he held when he took such oath to support the Constitution of the Confederate States, until he may be re-appointed or re-elected to the same; and all the offices lately held by such persons are hereby declared vacant.

<small>Vacates all offices held by those who took an oath to support the C. S. Constitution.</small>

Ratified in Convention the 19th day of October, 1865.

EDWIN G. READE, *President.*

JAMES H. MOORE, *Secretary of the Convention.*
R. C. BADGER, *Assistant Secretary.*

CHAPTER XV.

AN ORDINANCE IN RELATION TO THE DEPOSIT AND PUBLICATION OF THE ORDINANCES AND RESOLUTIONS OF THE CONVENTION.

Be it ordained by the delegates of the people of the State of North Carolina in Convention assembled, That the Secretary of this Convention deposit in the office of the Secretary of State, for safe keeping, all the Ordinances and Resolutions passed by the Convention having the force and effect of

<small>To be deposited with Secretary of State, &c.</small>

laws; and the Secretary of the Convention shall cause the same to be published in three newspapers published in the city of Raleigh; and he is hereby authorized to contract for such publication at reasonable rates; the expense thereof shall be paid as other public printing; and it shall be sufficient for him to furnish one certified copy only, for which he shall be paid the same fee as is now allowed to the Secretary of State for certifying the Acts of the General Assembly to one of the newspapers, and a printed copy to the others.

Ratified in Convention the 19th day of October, 1865.

E. G. READE, *President.*

JAMES H. MOORE, *Secretary of the Convention.*

R. C. BADGER, *Assistant Secretary.*

CHAPTER XVI.

AN ORDINANCE PROVIDING FOR COMPENSATION TO SHERIFFS FOR HOLDING ELECTIONS FOR DELEGATES TO THIS CONVENTION.

Usual compensation.
Be it ordained by the delegates of the people of the State of North Carolina in Convention assembled, That the Provisional Sheriffs of the several counties in this State are entitled to and are hereby allowed the same compensation for holding the late elections for delegates to this Convention as Sheriffs are now allowed by law for holding elections for members of the General Assembly, and the Treasurer is hereby directed to allow the same to such Sheriffs in the settlement of their accounts.

Ratified in Convention the 19th day of October, 1865.

EDWIN G. READE, *President.*

JAMES H. MOORE, *Secretary of the Convention.*

R. C. BADGER, *Assistant Secretary.*

CHAPTER XVII.

AN ORDINANCE TO GIVE JURISDICTION TO THE PROVISIONAL COURTS OF PLEAS AND QUARTER SESSIONS.

SECTION 1. *Be it ordained by the people of North Carolina, in Convention assembled, and it is hereby ordained by the authority of the same,* That the Provisional Courts of Pleas and Quarter Sessions shall have all the criminal jurisdiction that is now allowed to Courts of Pleas and Quarter Sessions in chapter thirty-one, of the Revised Code, and that appeals shall lie from the judgments of such Courts to the next regular term of the Superior Courts of Law that shall be held for the county in which the case may be pending. *[Jurisdiction of Courts.]*

SEC. 2. *Be it further ordained,* That the Provisional Justices of the Peace shall have and exercise all the criminal powers and jurisdiction that are now allowed to Justices of the Peace by the Revised Code. *[Jurisdiction of Justices.]*

SEC. 3. *Be it further ordained,* That this Ordinance shall continue during the existence of the Provisional Government and no longer.

Ratified in Convention the 19th day of October, 1865.

EDWIN G. READE, *President.*

JAMES H. MOORE, *Secretary of the Convention.*
R. C. BADGER, *Assistant Secretary.*

CHAPTER XVIII.

AN ORDINANCE RECOGNIZING THE JUST DEBTS OF NORTH CAROLINA AND PROHIBITING THE PAYMENT OF ALL DEBTS CREATED OR INCURRED IN AID OF THE LATE REBELLION.

SECTION 1. *Be it declared and ordained by the delegates of the people of the State of North Carolina, in Convention assembled, and it is hereby declared and ordained,* That it shall be the duty of the General Assembly of the State, so soon as is practicable, to provide for the payment of all debts and obligations created or incurred by the State otherwise than in aid of the late rebellion.

Voids debts incurred in aid of the rebellion. SEC. 2. *Be it further declar d and ordained,* That all debts and obligations created or incurred by the State in aid of the late rebellion, directly or indirectly, are void, and no General Assembly of this State shall have power to assume or provide for the payment of the same or any portion thereof: nor shall any General Assembly of this State have power to assume or provide for the payment of any portion of the debts or obligations created or incurred, directly or indirectly, by the late so-called Confederate St tes, or by its agents or under its authority.

Ratified in Convention the 19th day of October, 1865.

EDWIN G. READE, *President.*

JAMES H. MOORE, *Secretary of the Convention.*

I. C. BADGER, *Assistant Secretary.*

CHAPTER XIX.

AN ORDINANCE TO CHANGE THE JURISDICTION OF THE COURTS AND THE RULES OF PLEADING THEREIN.

SECTION 1. *Be it ordained by the people of North Carolina, in Convention assembled, and it is hereby ordained by the authority of the same,* That the jurisdiction of the several Courts of the State, and of Justices of the Peace, except as provided in this ordinance, shall be as in the year 1860. Jurisdiction of Courts and Justices of Peace.

SEC. 2. *Be it further ordained,* That the several Superior Courts of Law, at the Spring Terms thereof only, unless otherwise herein provided, shall have exclusive original jurisdiction to hear, try and determine all actions of debt, covenant, assumpsit or account, where the sum, due or owing, amounts (principal and interest) to sixty dollars or more. Actions of debt, where sum amounts to $60, or more

SEC. 3. *Be it further ordained,* That all writs in debt, covenant, assumpsit or account shall be returnable to Spring Term and be served at least thirty days (Sundays included,) before the return day. Within the first three days of the return term, should the defendant pay to the plaintiff, or into Court to his use, one-tenth of the debt or demand (principal and interest,) and all costs to that time, he shall be allowed until next Spring Term to plead. At the said Spring Term, should the defendant pay to the plaintiff, or into Court to his use, one-fifth of the residue of the debt or demand and cost, he shall be allowed until the succeeding Spring Term to plead. At the said Spring Term, should the defendant pay to the plaintiff, or into Court to his use, one-half of the residue of the debt or demand, he shall be allowed until the succeeding Spring Term to plead. At the said Spring Term the plaintiff shall have judgment for the residue of his debt or demand : *Provided, however,* That Should defend ant pay to plaintiff, within first three days of return term, one-tenth of debt & cost, he shall be allowed until next Spring Term to plead, then one-fifth of residue, succeeding Spring Term one half of residue, &c. Proviso.

the plaintiff, if required, shall file his debt or demand in writing, and if the defendant shall make oath that the whole or any part thereof is not justly due, or that he has a counter claim, all of which shall be particularly set forth by affidavit, then the defendant shall only pay the instalment required, of what he admits to be due, and the Court shall order a jury, at the same or some subsequent term, to try the matters in dispute between the parties, and at the next Spring Term the defendant shall be allowed time to plead only upon payment of one-fifth of the residue of the admitted amount, and whatever the jury may find him indebted over *Proviso.* and above the same : *Provided, further,* That should the defendant fail to pay the first or any subsequent instalment, then and in that case the plaintiff shall be entitled to proceed to judgment and execution according to the course of the Court in 1860.

Sec. 4. *Be it further ordained,* That all writs in actions *All writs in actions of debt* of debt, covenant, assumpsit or account, issued to Fall Term *issued to Fall* of the Superior Courts, shall be returned by the Sheriffs to *Term, made* Spring Term, 1867, and all actions of debt, covenant, *returnable to Spring Term,* assumpsit or account, now pending in the Superior Courts, *1867.* shall be continued to Spring Term, and if the defendant has entered his plea, he shall be allowed to withdraw the same, and take the benefits of section 3, of this ordinance.

Sec. 5. *Be it further ordained,* That dormant judgments *Dormant* shall only be revived by actions of debts, and every *scire judgments. facias* to revive a judgment shall be dismissed on motion : *Proviso. Provided,* That those now issued shall be dismissed at the cost of the debtor.

Sec. 6. *Be it further ordained,* That the Clerks of the several County Courts shall transfer all actions of debt, *Duty of County* covenant, assumpsit or account, now pending in their re- *ty Court Cl'ks* spective Courts, to the Spring Term, 1867, of the Superior Courts, and the said Spring Term shall be deemed the return term thereof, and the said actions shall stand as if originally instituted in that Court.

Sec. 7. *Be it further ordained,* That the Clerks of the several County Courts, if requested to do so by the plaintiffs, sixty days before the Spring Term, 1867, of the Superior

Courts, shall transmit to said Spring Terms certified copies of the judgments in actions of debt, covenant, assumpsit or account entered on the dockets of their Courts, together with the writs of *fieri facias* or *venditioni exponas* issued thereon, and shall issue notices thereof to the defendants, which notices shall be served at least thirty days before said Superior Courts. At the Spring Terms aforesaid, the Courts shall, on motion, order the said judgments to be entered on the minute dockets: *Provided*, The same were not dormant when transmitted from the County Courts; and on such entries being made, the said judgments shall be taken and held to be judgments of the Superior Courts and writs of *fieri facias* and *venditioni exponas* may issue, as provided in section tenth of this ordinance, following the writs transmitted from the County Courts and preserving the liens, as if issued by the same Court. Clerks of County Courts if requested, shall transmit certified copies of actions in debt, &c., to Spring Term of Superior Court.

Proviso.

SEC. 8. *Be it further ordained*, That the Sheriff in each county shall return all writs of *fieri facias* and *venditioni exponas* issued from the County Court on judgments in actions of debt, covenant, assumpsit or account to the next term of said Court, without sale; and shall return all writs of *fi fa* or *venditioni exponas* issued on similar judgments from the Superior Court or decrees of the Court of Equity on money demands to Spring Term, 1867, without sale. Duty of Sheriffs.

SEC. 9. *Be it further ordained*, That no writs of *fi fa* or *venditioni exponas* on judgments in actions of debt, covenant, assumpsit or account shall hereafter issue from the County Courts, nor shall said writs on such judgments issue from or to the Fall Terms of the Superior Courts, except in cases where defendant fails to comply with the provisions of this ordinance, and it is directed that plaintiff may proceed according to the regular course of the Court. No writs of fi fa or venditioni exponas shall issue from County Courts or Fall Term of Superior Courts.

SEC. 10. *Be it further ordained*, That no writs of *fi fa* or *venditioni exponas* on judgments in actions of debt, covenant, assumpsit or account, or decrees for money demands in Equity, shall issue from Spring Term, 1867, without permission of Court, and should the defendant within the first three days pay one-tenth of the judgment or decree Should defendant pay one-tenth, writ shall be credited, issued and returned "indulged."

and costs, then the writ shall be credited one-tenth, issued and immediately returned "Indulged :" *Provided,* No plaintiff shall be allowed to take the said one-tenth without first entering his assent to said return : *And, provided further,* That such assent and return shall not prejudice any lien the plaintiff may then have by virtue of said *fi fa* or *venditioni exponas : Provided further,* That at Spring Term, 1868, the defendant, upon paying one-fifth of the residue on the judgment or decree and costs, shall have indulgence in like manner.

<small>Provisos.</small>

SEC. 11. *Be it further ordained,* That upon all warrants before Justices of the Peace for a demand (principal and interest) of $25 or less, should the defendant pay one-fifth to the plaintiff or to the collecting officer for his use, he shall be allowed six months to plead, and at the expiration of said six months, should he pay as aforesaid one-half of the residue, he shall be allowed six months more to plead, and at the expiration of said six months plaintiff shall have judgment and execution for the residue. Upon demands (principal and interest) of less than $60 and more than $25, the defendant shall be allowed twelve months instead of six, on each payment : *Provided,* That the plaintiff shall file his claim in writing, and if the defendant, on oath, shall deny the same, or present a counter claim, the Justice shall proceed to try the same. Upon judgment the defendant shall be allowed a stay of execution for six or twelve months, as the case may be, upon paying one-fifth, and afterwards one-half, as before judgment : *Provided,* That all Justices' judgments for $60 or more, not dormant, shall be transmitted, together with the warrant or other papers, by the Justice to Spring Term, 1867, of the Superior Court, and notice thereof shall be given the defendant at least twenty days before Court; and in the Superior Court the same proceedings shall be had as on judgments from the County Court, according to section seventh of this ordinance.

<small>Upon all warrants before Justices of the Peace for a demand of $25 or less.</small>

<small>Upon demands of $60.</small>

<small>Provisos.</small>

SEC. 12. *Be it further ordained,* That all writs of *scire facias* to subject bail, issued from the Superior or County Courts upon judgments in actions of debt, covenant, assumpsit or account, shall be returned to Spring Term, 1867, of

<small>Return of writs of scire facias.</small>

the Superior Courts, and should the tenth, fifth, and half of the judgments be paid from Spring Term to Spring Term, time to plead shall be allowed, according to section three of this ordinance.

SEC. 13. *Be it further ordained,* That this ordinance shall not apply to judgments for costs only. Judgments for costs only.

SEC. 14. *Be it further ordained,* That this ordinance shall not apply to the remedies for the collection of Town, County or State Revenue. Remedies for the collection of certain revenue.

SEC. 15. *Be it further ordained.* That this ordinance shall not apply to proceedings by attachment, unless the defendant replevy and give bail, and then and in that case the proceedings shall be subject to the provisions of this ordinance as if commenced by writ or warrant. Proceedings by attachment

SEC. 16. *Be it further ordained,* That where the action is by or on behalf of infants, still minors at the return term, and the interest exceeds one-tenth, the first payment shall be increased to the amount of interest due, not to exceed one-fifth of the whole debt. Action by or on behalf of infants.

SEC. 17. *Be it further ordained,* That the provisions of this ordinance shall not be construed to extend to any debts or demands contracted, or penalties incurred, since the first day of May, A. D., 1865, or which may be hereafter contracted or incurred, but that the remedies for the recovery of the same shall be in all respects similar to the remedies for the recovery of debts which were in force in the year 1860. Debts incurred since May 1st, 1865.

SEC. 18. *Be it further ordained,* That any creditor, attempted to be defrauded as set forth in section one, chapter fifty, Revised Code, may, without obtaining judgment at law, file his bill in Equity, and said Court is hereby authorized and empowered to direct proper issues to be made up and tried, and to make such orders and decrees as to right and justice may appertain; and said proceeding shall not affect the creditor's right to proceed at the same time at law; and any surety, before paying the debt of his principal thus attempting to defraud his creditors, may institute proceedings in equity, in like manner, to the end that he may obtain relief. Remedy in case of attempted fraud on creditors

Duty of executors and administra'rs.

SEC. 19. *Be it further ordained,* That every executor or administrator shall file, on oath, at the termination of two years from the time of his qualification, a full statement of his receipts and disbursements, and the condition of the assets, particularly setting out all money collected and how disbursed, and, on motion, the Court may allow further time to settle the estate, from year to year, not exceeding three years: *Provided,* That on each motion to extend the time, a supplemental statement shall be filed: *Provided,*

Provisos.

That any creditor or next of kin may oppose said motion, and if the statement is not full and fair, file interrogatories which the executor or administrator shall answer, before his motion for time is allowed: *Provided, further,* That the Court may also extend the time for pleading: *Provided further,* That all executors or administrators, who have heretofore qualified, shall be allowed until the County Court next after the first of January, 1867, to file their statement.

SEC. 20. *Be it further enacted,* That all acts, and parts of

Repealing clause.

acts, suspending the operation of the statutes of limitation in the Revised Code, are hereby repealed, except as herein provided: *Provided,* That the time elapsed since the first day of September, one thousand eight hundred and sixty-

Provisos.

one, barring actions or suits, or presuming the satisfaction or abandonment of rights, shall not be counted: *And provided further,* That nothing contained in this ordinance, or in the acts hereby repealed, shall be so construed as to prevent judgments from becoming dormant.

SEC. 21. *Be it further enacted,* That any Sheriff, Clerk, or other officer, failing to execute any of the provisions of

Fine of $500.

this ordinance, when the execution thereof devolves on him, or issuing, receiving, or executing any process whatever contrary to the provisions of this ordinance, shall be subject to a penalty of five hundred dollars, to be recovered by rule of Court, as penalties and fines were recovered in 1860.

SEC. 22. *Be it further ordained,* That in all actions brought by any bank or other corporation having exercised banking

Actions brought by Banks or other corporations.

privileges, or by any assignee or endorsee, or officer of said bank or corporation, it shall and may be lawful for the defendant to set off by plea or on trial any note or certificate of deposit issued by said bank or its branches, or other corporation, whether the same has been presented for payment or not, any law or usage to the contrary notwithstanding; but said plea of set off, or set off on trial, shall not avail to carry costs against the plaintiff, unless there has been a tender of such payment before suit brought: *Provided,* That should the defendant require the debt to be scaled according to the scale of depreciation of Confederate currency, then, and in that case. the said notes or certificates of deposit shall not be a set off in any manner. Proviso.

SEC. 23. *Be it further ordained,* That " An Act to change the jurisdiction of the Courts, and the rules of pleading," ratified the 11th day of September, 1861 ; an act entitled "An Act to restore the Courts and for other purposes," ratified the 14th December, 1863 ; also, an act entitled "An Act to change the jurisdiction of the Courts and the rules of pleading therein," ratified the 10th ot March, A. D., 1866, and all laws in conflict with this ordinance, be and the same are hereby repealed. Former Stay Law.

SEC. 24. *Be it further ordained,* That the General Assembly shall have no power to repeal, alter or modify this ordinance until the third Monday of November, 1868, and this ordinance shall take effect and be in force from after its ratification. Powers of Gen eral Assembly.

Adopted by the Convention, June 23d, 1866.

     EDWIN G. READE, *President.*

JAMES H. MOORE, *Secretary.*

R. C. BADGER, *Assistant Secretary.*

CHAPTER XX.

AN ORDINANCE IN RELATION TO THE ACT OF THE GENERAL ASSEMBLY, ENTITLED "REVENUE."

Taxes heretofore paid.

SECTION 1. *Be it ordained by the delegates of the people of North Carolina, in Convention assembled, and it is hereby ordained by the authority of the same,* That the act of the General Assembly, entitled "Revenue," imposing taxes on purchases, sales and receipts, shall not be construed to extend to those purchases, sales or receipts on which taxes have actually been paid, under the ordinance of the Convention, entitled "An Ordinance to provide Revenue for the year eighteen hundred and sixty-five."

Specific taxes for license.

SEC. 2. *Be it further ordained,* That where specific taxes have been imposed for license to use any article or carry on any business for the year preceding the first day of July, one thousand eight hundred and sixty-six, one-half thereof shall only be payable in those cases, where taxes were actually paid under said ordinance for the same license.

Retailers of spirituous liquors.

SEC. 3. *Be it further ordained,* That retailers of spirituous liquors, who paid the tax prescribed in section eleven of said ordinance, shall be entitled to retail for the year for which their license was granted, without further tax to the State for such retailing.

Provisions of section thirty-two, Schedule B.

SEC. 4. *Be it further ordained,* That the provisions of section thirty-two of Schedule B, of said Act of Assembly, shall only extend to the license for distilling spirituous liquors from grain.

Powers of Sheriff and Collector.

SEC. 5. *Be it further ordained,* That in all cases where taxes are payable to the Sheriff or Collector, without the subject from which they are derived being listed, such Sheriff or Collector, for the purpose of ascertaining the amount of such taxes, shall have power, and it shall be his duty, to administer an oath to the person liable to pay the same.

SEC. 6. *Be it further ordained,* That this ordinance shall be in force from its ratification.
Ratified the 12th day of June, A. D., 1866.
      EDWIN G. READE, *President.*
JAMES H. MOORE, *Secretary of the Convention.*
R. C. BADGER, *Assistant Secretary.*

CHAPTER XXI.

AN ORDINANCE CONCERNING THE CRIME OF ASSAULT, WITH INTENT TO COMMIT RAPE.

SECTION 1. *Be it ordained by the Convention of the State of North Carolina, and it is hereby ordained by the authority of the same,* That any person convicted by due course of law of an assault, with intent to commit a rape, on the body of any female, shall be punished by fine, imprisonment not exceeding two years, standing in the pillory for one hour, one or more public whippings, not exceeding thirty-nine lashes, at any one time, on his bare back, all or any of them, at the discretion of the Court, due regard being had to the nature and circumstances of the offence.   Penalties.

SEC. 2. *Be it further ordained,* That all laws and clauses of laws, which conflict with this ordinance, be and the same are hereby repealed.   Repealing clause.

SEC. 3. *Be it further ordained,* That this ordinance shall not affect the Legislative power over the subject.

SEC. 4. *Be it further ordained,* That this ordinance shall be in force from and after the first day of July next.

Ratified the 12th day of June, A. D., 1866.
      EDWIN G. READE, *President.*
JAMES H. MOORE, *Secretary of the Convention.*
R. C. BADGER, *Assistant Secretary.*

CHAPTER XXII.

AN ORDINANCE TO AUTHORIZE SUNDRY SHERIFFS TO COLLECT ARREARAGES OF TAXES.

[Grants necessary authority.

SECTION 1. *Be it ordained by the people of North Carolina, in Convention assembled, and it is hereby ordained by the authority of the same,* That William B. Campbell, late Sheriff of Beaufort county; Alexander C. Latham, late Sheriff of Craven county; Goodman Durden, late Sheriff of Washington county; and George Dill, late Sheriff of Carteret county, be, and they are hereby, authorized to collect the arrears of taxes due for the years 1860 and 1861, under the same rules, regulations and restrictions as are provided for the collection of taxes by the laws of the State: *Provided,*

Proviso.

That the authority hereby given shall not extend to persons who have removed from the county, nor to taxes which may be due by executors, administrators or guardians, or taxes due on any real estate which has been sold by the person in whose name the same was listed, nor to any person who will voluntarily swear before any Justice of the Peace of said county, that he or she verily believes that the arrears claimed of him or her have been paid.

Ratified in Convention this 23d day of June, A. D., 1866.

EDWIN G. READE, *President.*

JAMES H. MOORE, *Secretary.*
R. C. BADGER, *Assistant Secerctary.*

CHAPTER XXIII.

AN ORDINANCE EXTENDING THE TIME FOR THE SETTLEMENT OF THE PUBLIC TAXES BY THE SHERIFFS AND TAX COLLECTORS OF THIS STATE.

SECTION 1. *Be it ordained by the delegates of the people of the State of North Carolina, in Convention assembled, and it is hereby ordained by the authority of the same,* That the Sheriffs and Tax Collectors of the several counties of this State be allowed time until the first of January, one thousand eight hundred and sixty-seven, to settle their accounts with the Public Treasurer, under the same rules and regulations and restrictions, and under the same pains and penalties, as are now provided by the Revenue Laws of this State. _{Extends time to Jan. 1st, '67.}

Ratified the 22d day of June, A. D., 1866.

EDWIN G. READE, *President.*
JAMES H. MOORE, *Secretary.*
R. C. BADGER, *Assistant Secretary.*

CHAPTER XXIV.

AN ORDINANCE IN RELATION TO TAXATION BY THE COUNTY COURTS.

WHEREAS, Conflicting opinions are entertained in regard to the power and duty of the Courts of Pleas and Quarter Sessions in laying taxes for County purposes; and, _{Preamble.}

WHEREAS, Taxes have been imposed in various counties, on different constructions of the law :

Now, therefore, to settle all difficulties in regard to said powers and duties,

SECTION 1. *Be it ordained by the delegates of the people of North Carolina, in Convention assembled, as follows:* That the Courts of Pleas and Quarter Sessions of the several counties of this State (a majority of the Justices being present) shall have power during the present year to levy taxes on such subjects and persons within their counties as are now taxed for State purposes, and all levies by said Courts heretofore made are hereby validated and confirmed.

Who shall be taxed.

SEC. 2. All such Courts, whether they have heretofore levied or not, at a general or special term, may make such changes, discriminations and exemptions in the levies made by them as they may deem advisable.

Discriminations and exemptions.

SEC. 3 The powers of the County Courts shall only extend to those persons and subjects on which the taxes are payable by the Sheriffs into the Public Treasury.

Powers of county courts.

SEC. 4. The powers, regulations and penalties authorized and prescribed to enforce the payment of State taxes, shall be extended to include County taxes, and the Sheriffs and other officers shall be subject to like liabilities for failure or malfeasance in the discharge of their duties.

Regulations and penalties.

SEC. 5. Whenever the Justices of the Court of Pleas and Quarter Sessions of any county have failed to levy taxes for the support of their insane, as prescribed in the act ratified 10th day of March, 1866, entitled "An Act to secure a better government for the Insane Asylum," the Courts of said counties (seven Justices being present) may at a special or regular term levy such taxes.

Taxes may be levied by special term of county court.

SEC. 6. This ordinance shall take effect from its ratification.

Ratified the 12th of June, A. D., 1866.

EDWIN G. READE, *President.*

JAMES H. MOORE, *Secretary,*
R. C. BADGER, *Assistant Secretary.*

CHAPTER XXV.

AN ORDINANCE IN REFERENCE TO THE PAYMENT OF A PORTION OF THE PUBLIC TAXES INTO THE TREASURY OF THE STATE.

SECTION 1. *Be it ordained by the delegates of the people of North Carolina, in Convention assembled,* That so much of the public taxes as by the provision of the existing revenue laws are payable on or before the first day of July, 1866, and such as by said laws may be received by the Sheriffs or Clerks of Courts, shall be paid and transmitted to the Treasury of the State in such way and at such time as the Public Treasurer shall designate, under the same pains and penalties as are now prescribed by law. *[To be paid in such way and time as Public Treasu'r may designate.]*

Ratified the 25th day of June, A. D., 1866.

EDWIN G. READE, *President.*

JAMES H. MOORE, *Secretary.*
R. C. BADGER, *Assistant Secretary.*

CHAPTER XXVI.

AN ORDINANCE TO PAY THE PROVISIONAL JUDGES OF COURTS OF OYER AND TERMINER FOR SERVICES, UNDER "AN ORDINANCE TO PROTECT THE OWNERS OF PROPERTY AND FOR OTHER PURPOSES."

SECTION 1. *Be it ordained by the delegates of the people of North Carolina in Convention assembled, and it is hereby ordained by the authority of the same,* That the Provisional Judges of the Courts of Oyer and Terminer, who performed service under "An Ordinance to protect the owners of property and for other purposes," ratified the 18th day of Octo- *[Judges compensated at the rate of $90 per each six days service.]*

ber, 1865, be paid by the Public Treasurer, upon satisfactory proof to the Comptroller, of services performed, the sum of ninety dollars for every six days, during which such Provisional Judges were employed under the provisions of the said Ordinance, and according to that rate for any shorter time they were so employed.

Compensation to Clerk. SEC. 2. *Be it further ordained,* That for his services rendered as Clerk to the Hon. D. G. Fowle, one of the Judges aforesaid, Wm. S. Mason be allowed the sum of one hundred dollars.

SEC. 3. *Be it further ordained,* That this ordinance shall be in force from and after its ratification.

Ratified the 20th day of June, A. D., 1866.

EDWIN G. READE, *President.*
JAMES H. MOORE, *Secretary.*
R. C. BADGER, *Assistant Secretary.*

CHAPTER XXVII.

AN ORDINANCE TO EMPOWER THE JUSTICES OF THE SEVERAL COUNTIES TO BORROW MONEY IN CERTAIN CASES, AND FOR OTHER PURPOSES.

Preamble. WHEREAS, Much want and suffering exist in many of the counties of this State, from the great scarcity of provisions, and it may be deemed necessary to purchase grain or other provisions to meet the pressing need of the people; and in many cases debts have already been incurred by the counties for the relief and support of the more indigent of their citizens, and for other public purposes deemed proper by the Justices of such counties respectively; and, Whereas, in many counties it has or may become necessary to build either a Court House, jail, work-house, bridge or other public building, or to purchase a suitable farm to be used in connection with any work-house which may be established by any county:

SECTION 1. *Be it ordained by the delegates of the people of North Carolina, in Convention assembled,* That the Justices of the Peace of the several counties of this State, either at any regular term of the County Court, or at any called session, shall have power, and they are hereby authorized, to borrow, on the faith and credit of their respective counties, for any of the purposes referred to in the preamble hereto, such sum or sums of money as they may consider necessary, paying not more than eight per centum : *And provided further,* That said bonds shall not bear but eight per centum, per annum : *And provided further,* That said bonds shall not be sold at less than their par value ; and for the whole or any part of the amount so to be borrowed, bonds in the name of such county, attested by the seal of the County Court, to be signed by the Chairman and countersigned by the Clerk of that Court, shall be issued in such form and of such tenor as said Justices may determine : *Provided, however,* That the power and authority by this section granted shall in no case be exercised, unless a majority of all the Justices of the County shall concur.

<small>Justices of the Peace authorized to borrow money</small>

<small>Proviso.</small>

SEC. 2. *Be it further ordained,* That in all cases in which bonds shall have been issued by any county under the power granted by the previous section of this ordinance, it shall be the duty of the Justices of such county to provide for the payment of the accruing interest, and also for the payment of the principal money of the same, by annually laying taxes for these special purposes, on all the persons and subjects of taxation on which they may be authorized to lay taxes for county purposes ; and such taxes be laid on all such persons and subjects in the same manner and relative proportion as taxes for county purposes are or shall be required by law to be laid ; and shall be collected and specially applied to the satisfaction and discharge of the interest and principal money of such bonds ; or so much thereof as may not be required to pay such interest, and cannot be applied in discharge of the principal, shall be so invested

<small>Duty of Justices to provide for payment.</small>

SEC. 3. *Be it further ordained*, That the County Courts,

Agents for negotiation and sale of bonds to be appointed.

a majority of the Justices being present, shall appoint a suitable agent for the negotiation and sale of any bonds authorized to be issued as aforesaid, for disbursing the funds derived therefrom, and to attend to the payment of the principal and interest on the same; and they shall prescribe such rules and regulations in connection with the duties of such agent as will most certainly protect the County against loss or damage. Such agent shall enter into bond, with good and sufficient security, payable to the State, and in such sum as the Court shall deem proper, conditioned for the faithful performance of his duties, and accounting for and over to such person as may be authorized to receive the same, all such funds or securities which may be received by him as such agent. He may at any time be removed, and another agent be appointed either at a regular term of the County Court, or at a session called for that or any other purpose, a majority of the Justices being present; and he shall receive such reasonable compensation for his services as shall be fixed by a majority of the Justices.

SEC. 4. *Be it further ordained,* That the Justices of any

Powers of Justices defined.

County, a majority being present, either at the regular term of any County Court, or at any session called for any purpose whatever, shall have power to make all such orders which to them shall seem expedient, in reference to the payment and time of payment of any part or all of the taxes laid by them for County purposes during this and the next ensuing two years; and the Sheriffs of the different counties are hereby required, in all matters connected with the collection and payment of such taxes, to observe and conform to such orders as shall be made as aforesaid, under the same pains and penalties as are or may be prescribed by law in reference to the collection and payment of taxes laid for county purposes.

SEC. 5. *Be it further ordained,* That it shall be the duty

Duty of Chairman of County Court.

of the Chairman of the County Court of any county, upon the application to him in writing of any five of the Justices of his county, to call the Justices together at such time as he may deem most convenient, and to direct the Sheriff to summon the Justices to attend at the Court-House of the county at the time designated by him.

SEC. 6. *Be it further ordained,* That this ordinance shall be in force from and after its ratification, and that this ordinance only apply to the following counties, to-wit: Polk, Rutherford, Cleaveland, Davidson, Henderson, Wilkes, Cherokee, Clay, New Hanover and Martin. {To what Counties this ordinance shall apply.}

Ratified the 25th day of June, A. D., 1866.

EDWIN G. READE, *President*,
JAMES. H. MOORE, *Secretary.*
R. C. BADGER, *Assistant Secretary.*

CHAPTER XXVIII.

AN ORDINANCE TO AMEND THE CHARTER OF THE UNION MINING COMPANY, IN THE COUNTY OF ROWAN, AND THE RUDICIL GOLD MINING COMPANY, IN THE COUNTY OF MECKLENBURG, PASSED AT THE LATE SESSION OF THE GENERAL ASSEMBLY.

SECTION 1. *Be it ordained by the delegates of the people of the State of North Carolina, in Convention assembled,* That each of the charters of the said above mentioned companies be so amended as to empower the Stockholders therein to levy the assessments of money on the shares of the Stockholders, as well after they shall be paid as before, whenever the necessities of the companies shall require it, in such manner as may be prescribed by the by-laws of said corporations respectively, and the said shares to sell, in case of failure to pay said assessments, in such manner as may be prescibed by said companies respectively: *Provided,* That this ordinance shall not take effect until the said corporations shall comply with the provisions of sections first {Empowers stockholders to lay assessments on shares, &c.} {Proviso.}

and second, under Schedule C, of the Act of the General Assembly, entitled "Revenue," ratified March 12th, 1866. Ratified the 10th day of June, A. D., 1866.

EDWIN G. READE, *President.*

JAMES H. MOORE, *Secretary.*

R. C. BADGER, *Assistant Secretary.*

CHAPTER XXIX.

AN ORDINANCE TO AMEND THE CHARTER OF THE GOVERNOR'S CREEK STEAM TRANSPORTATION AND MINING COMPANY.

Alteration in name, &c.

SECTION 1. *Be it ordained by the delegates of the people of North Carolina, in Convention assembled, and it is hereby ordained,* That the Charter of the Governor's Creek Steam Transportation and Mining Company, granted at the session of the Legislature of eighteen hundred and fifty, be amended by changing the name to "The Egypt Company," and that said Company have authority to establish a foundry and machine shop; also to distil coal and other bituminous matter, for the purpose of manufacturing oil; to grind grain and make concentrated manures.

Authority to borrow money &c.

SEC. 2. *Be it further ordained,* That said Company have authority to borrow money to an extent not exceeding one hundred thousand dollars, for the purpose of completing and prosecuting their business, and to secure the payment of the same, or any part thereof, by executing a mortgage on their lands and property.

When to take effect.

SEC. 3. *Be it further ordained,* That this ordinance shall not take effect until said corporation shall comply with the provisions of sections first and second, under schedule C, of the Act of the General Assembly, entitled "Revenue," rati-

fied March 12th, one thousand eight hundred and sixty-six.
Ratified the 20th day of June, A. D., 1866.
            EDWIN G. READE, *President.*
    JAMES H. MOORE, *Secretary.*
    R. C. BADGER, *Assistant Secretary.*

CHAPTER XXX.

AN ORDINANCE TO INCORPORATE THE OCEANIC HOOK AND LADDER COMPANY, OF THE TOWN OF BEAUFORT.

SECTION 1. *Be it ordained by the delegates of the people of North Carolina in Convention assembled,* That the officers and members, who are at present, or in future may be, of "The Oceanic Hook and Ladder Company," of the town of Beaufort, Carteret county, be, and they are hereby, incorporated into a body politic and corporate, under the name and style of "The Oceanic Hook and Ladder Company," of the town of Beaufort, and, by that name, may have succession and a common seal, sue and be sued, plead and be impleaded, in any Court of record, or before any Justice of the Peace in this State: contract and be contracted with; acquire, hold and dispose of real and personal property, to an amount not exceeding ten t¹ ousand dollars; and may make all such by-laws and regulations as may be necessary for the government of said Company, and not inconsistent with the constitution and laws of this State or of the United States.

Body politic.

Powers.

Ratified the 12th day of June, A. D. 1866.
            EDWIN G. READE, *President.*
    JAMES H. MOORE, *Secretary of the Convention.*
    R. C. BADGER, *Assistant Secretary.*

CHAPTER XXXI.

AN ORDINANCE TO INCORPORATE THE WILMINGTON RAILWAY BRIDGE COMPANY.

Body politic

Style and powers.

A bridge over North-western river, and other bridges to be constructed.

Provi.

SEC. 1. *Be it ordained by the delegates of the people of the State of North Carolina in Convention assembled,* That "The Wilmington and Weldon Rail Road Company," "The Wilmington and Manchester Rail Road Company," and "The Wilmington, Charlotte and Rutherford Rail Road Company," their associates and assigns, are hereby created and constituted a body politic and corporate, for the term of ninety years, by the name and style of "The Wilmington Railway Bridge Company," and as such shall have all the rights, powers and priviliges, incident or belonging to corporations, as the same are set forth and declared in the first, second and third sections of chapter 26, entitled " Corporations," of the Revised Code of North Carolina.

SEC. 2. *Be it further ordained,* That the corporation hereby created is by this ordinance authorized and empowered to construct and erect a bridge, with one or more railway tracks, and also a track for ordinary vehicles, over the north-western branch of the Cape Fear river, and a bridge with like tracks or otherwise, over the north-eastern branch of said river, at such points or places on said branches respectively of said river as shall be deemed most judicious; and to connect the track or tracks on said bridges respectively by a rail road with one or more tracks running from one bridge to the other, and to extend and continue such a rail road, on the ea t s de of the north-eastern branch of said river, by such route as may be deemed best to form a connection within the city of Wilmington with the lines of railway belonging to the Wilmington and Weldon Rail Road Company: *Provided,* That the provisions of the Revised Code, chapter 101, section 32, shall be complied with.

SEC. 3. *Be it further ordained,* That the corporation, hereby created, shall have the same powers, rights and privileges to condemn and appropriate any land necessary or convenient for the construction and completion of said two bridges, and said rail roads, to the like extent and no more, which have been granted to the Wilmington and Weldon Rail Road Company, by the 14th section of the act of the General Assembly incorporating said Company; and the like remedies, forms of proceeding, and principles which are set forth and prescribed in said section of said act in reference to damages sustained by the owners of land, shall prevail and be observed in reference to any claim for damages to any land on account of the construction of said bridges or said line or lines of rail Road, or either of them. Power to condemn and appropriate land

SEC. 4. *Be it further ordained,* That the affairs of said corporation shall be managed by six directors, who shall elect one of their number President of the corporation; said directors shall be chosen annually, two by each of the three several Rail Road Companies before named as the corporators of the corporation hereby created; they shall be stockholders of the corporation by which they shall severally and respectively be chosen such directors, and may be members of the board of directors by which they shall be respectively elected; or should either one of said three Companies before named as corporators so prefer, three of the six directors of the corporation hereby created may be elected by said three Companies voting respectively one vote for each share of stock taken by them severally and respectively, and one of the remaining three of said directors shall be appointed by each of said three Companies or by their respective boards of directors. Management of Company's affairs.

SEC. 5. *Be it further ordained,* That the capital stock of the corporation hereby created shall not exceed four hundred thousand dollars; and said corporation, and also each of the three Companies before named as corporators, are hereby authorized and empowered, acting either jointly or severally, to borrow upon such terms as may be considered most favorable, such sum or sums of money as may be deemed necessary to complete the works contemplated by the corporation Capital stock hereby created, or may make such contracts, terms or arrangements with the contractors for building said bridges or railways, or with any other persons, as will ensure the completion of said works; and said corporation hereby created may secure the payment of any sum or sums of money so borrowed, or secure the performance of any contracts, terms or arrangements entered into with any contractor or other person aforesaid, by a lease or mortgage of the entire property and works of said corporation, or otherwise, as may be deemed most judicious.

SEC. 2. *Be it further ordained,* That this ordinance shall be in force from and after its ratification.

Ratified the 23rd day of June, A. D., 1866.

EDWIN G. READE, *President.*
JAMES H. MOORE, *Secretary of the Convention.*
R. C. BADGER, *Assistant Secretary.*

CAHPTER XXXII.

AN ORDINANCE WITH REGARD TO THE INCORPORATION OF THE TOWN OF MOCKSVILLE, IN DAVIE COUNTY.

Citizens authorized to elect Commissioners.

SECTION 1. *Be it ordained by the people of North Carolina, in Conv ntion assembled, and it is hereby ordained by the authority of the same,* That the citizens of the town of Mocksville are hereby authorized and empowered to elect Commissioners of said town, under the provisions of the acts, now existing, incorporating said town, at any time within thirty days from the passage of this ordinance.

Powers of Commission- ere.

SEC. 2. *Be it further ordained,* That said Commissioners, when elected, shall have power to levy a tax for the purposes of said town, said tax not to exceed thirty-five cents on the one hundred dollars worth of real estate, and on all other articles taxed by the State, a tax of the same proportion to the State tax as that levied upon real estate and no more.

Sec. 3. *Be it further ordained,* That this ordinance be in full force from and after its ratification, and be subject to legislative power.

Ratified the 25th day of June, A. D., 1866.

EDWIN G. READE, *President.*

James H. Moore, *Secretary of the Convention.*

R. C. Badger, *Assistant Secretary.*

CHAPTER XXXIII.

AN ORDINANCE TO INCORPORATE THE NORTH CAROLINA PETROLEUM AND MINING COMPANY.

Section 1. *Be it ordained by the Convention of North Carolina, and it is hereby ordained by the authority of the same,* That Peter Adams, Cyrus P. Mendenhall, E. P. Jones, David McKnight, L. H. Roatzhan, A. G. Brenizer, Marcus Wilty, Frank P. Cavnah, James P. Jones, Henry G. Kellogg, and their associates, successors and assigns, are hereby created and constituted a body corporate and politic, by the name, style and title of "The North Carolina Petroleum and Mining Company," for the purpose of exploring for petroleum, or rock oil, coal copper, lead, gold, iron and other minerals, metals and valuable substance, and for refining, distilling, mining, vending and smelting the same; and by that name may sue and be sued, plead and be impleaded, appear, prosecute and defend, in any Court of law and equity whatsoever, in all suits and actions; may have a common seal, and the same alter at pleasure, and may enjoy all privileges incident to mining operations; and may purchase, hold and convey real and personal estate to an amount not exceeding one million of dollars. *Body politic. Powers.*

Sec. 2. *Be it further ordained,* That the first meeting of said corporation may be called by the persons named in this ordinance, or any of them, at such time and place as *Meeting the corp tion.*

they may agree upon; and at such meetings, and at all other meetings legally notified, said corporation may make, alter and repeal such by-laws and regulations for the management of the business of said corporation as a majority of the stockholders may direct, not repugnant to the laws of this State, or of the United States.

Shares.

SEC. 3. *Be it further ordained,* That the said corporation may divide their original stock into such number of shares, and provide for the sale and transfer thereof in such manner and form, as said corporation shall, from time to time, deem expedient, and may levy and collect assessments, forfeit and sell delinquent shares, declare and pay dividends on the shares in such manner as the by-laws shall direct.

Duty of directors

SEC. 4. *Be it further ordained,* That it shall be the duty of the directors of said company, one of whom shall reside continually in the State, to have regular books of record and transfer thereof, at all times open to the inspection of the stockholders.

When to go into effect.

SEC. 5. *Be it further ordained,* That this ordinance shall not take effect until sections one and two under Schedule C, of the act of the General Assembly, entitled "Revenue," shall be complied with.

SEC. 6. *Be it further ordained,* That this corporation shall be in force ninety-nine years, and this ordinance shall continue in force from and after it passage.

Ratified the 12th day of June, A. D., 1866.

EDWIN G. READE, *President.*

JAMES H. MOORE, *Secretary of the Convention.*
R. C. BADGER, *Assistant Secretary.*

CHAPTER XXXIV.

AN ORDINANCE FOR EXCHANGING THE STOCKS OF THE STATE FOR BONDS ISSUED BEFORE THE YEAR ONE THOUSAND EIGHT HUNDRED AND SIXTY-ONE.

WHEREAS, The destruction and depreciation of taxable property in North Carolina, arising out of the late unhappy war, has greatly increased the proportion borne by the public debt to the means which the State possesses for its payment; and, whereas, the people of North Carolina are solicitous fully to discharge their just obligations at the earliest possible moment in any manner that shall be acceptable to their creditors; whereas, further, the stocks, liens and other claims upon the Rail Road Companies, and other corporations, are proceeds of the bonds of the State, issued in great part before the twentieth day of May, in the year one thousand eight hundred and sixty-one, and now outstanding; and, whereas, no regard being had as well to economy and other grave public interests as to the rights of public creditors, it were good policy to exchange for the principal of such bonds, the stocks and other property above mentioned, if such exchange can be made at par: Therefore, *Preamble.*

SECTION 1. *Be it ordained by the delegates of the people of North Carolina, in Convention assembled,* That the Public Treasurer shall advertise, in such newspapers as he may select, and invite proposals for an exchange of the principal of any bonds issued by the State prior to the twentieth day of May, one thousand eight hundred and sixty-one, for certificates of stock and other interests held by the State in various corporations; such bids shall be opened by the Treasurer upon some day (of which he shall give due notice to them) in presence of the Governor of the State and the Comptroller of public accounts, and it shall be his duty to accept those terms which may be most advantageous for the State: *Provided,* That in no event shall any of the said *Duty of Public Treasurer.*

Proviso.

stocks or other property be exchanged for less than their par value; and any premiums which may be obtained upon such exchange shall be applied either to the extinguishment of coupons or other interest (if any) due upon the particular bonds accepted in exchange, or to a further discharge of the principal due upon such other bonds; or, in case such premiums be fractional in regard to such bonds or interest, it may, as an alternative, at the discretion of the Treasurer, be paid in currency into the Treasury and charged to the public fund.

SEC. 2. *Be it further ordained*, That as soon as may be practicable after the acceptance of any bid, the Public Treasurer shall receive the bonds offered in exchange, and in the presence of the Governor and Comptroller shall cancel the same; it shall also be his duty to transfer the stocks and execute such conveyances of the other interests hereinbefore mentioned as shall be deemed necessary; such conveyances to be in a form approved by the Governor and the Attorney General: *Provided, however,* That the interest to be acquired by any such purchaser or assignee of any stock now held by the State, shall not be other than that of the holders of a like amount, in the general stock of the several and respective corporations in which the State may be a corporator.

Public Treasurer shall accept bids, &c.

Proviso.

SEC. 3. *Be it further ordained*, That it shall be the duty of the Comptroller to make a minute of what may be done by the Public Treasurer in the premises, and to make therefrom such entries in the books of his office as may secure a just accountability on the part of the Treasurer because of the transactions hereinbefore mentioned.

Duty of Comptroller.

SEC. 3. *Be it further ordained*, That the Public Treasurer shall make special reports upon the subject of this ordinance to the General Assembly at every session, and this ordinance shall be subject to repeal or modification by the General Assembly.

Special reports by Treasurer.

Ratified the 15th day of June, A. D., 1866.

EDWIN G. READE, *President.*

JAMES H. MOORE, *Secretary of the Convention.*

R. C. BADGER, *Assistant Secretary*

CHAPTER XXXV.

AN ORDINANCE CONCERNING THE BANKS OF THE STATE.

SECTION I. *Be it ordained by the delegates of the people of North Carolina in Convention assembled, and it is hereby ordained by the authority of the same,* That so much of the charters of the Banks of this State, as requires said Banks to keep on hand a certain definite proportion of their circulation in specie, be and the same is hereby repealed, so far as to allow said Banks to convert into national currency or stocks so much of their specie as they shall deem advisable: *Provided, however,* That the funds which may be thus substituted for specie, shall not be used otherwise than the specie itself could be used under their charters and the assignments made under the late act enabling the Banks of the State to close their business.

Ratified the 23d day of June, A. D., 1866.

EDWIN G. READE, *President.*
JAMES H. MOORE, *Secretary of the Convention.*
R. C. BADGER, *Assistant Secretary.*

Repeals so much of former charters as relates to keeping on hand certain am't of specie.

Proviso.

CHAPTER XXXVI.

AN ORDINANCE CONCERNING WIDOWS WHO HAVE QUALIFIED AS EXECUTRIX TO THE LAST WILL AND TESTAMENT OF THEIR DECEASED HUSBANDS.

SECTION 1. *Be it ordained by the delegates of the people of North Carolina, in Convention assembled, and it is hereby ordained by the authority of the same,* That the widow of

Widow may enter dissent.

any testator whose last will and testament has been admitted to probate in this State since the first day of January, one thousand eight hundred and sixty-two, and before the first day of May, one thousand eight hundred and sixty-five, notwithstanding such widow may have qualified to such last will and testament as executrix, be and she is hereby allowed to enter her dissent to the same, according to the same forms as are now provided by law for dissent of widows.

Rights of dower.

SEC. 2. *Be it further ordained,* That in all cases where a widow shall dissent from the last will and testament of her husband, as provided for in the foregoing section, she shall be entitled to the same rights of dower as if her husband had died intestate : *Provided however,* That no widow shall be entitled to the benefit of this ordinance unless such dissent shall be entered within six months from and after the passage of this ordinance, nor in any case where the real estate of the deceased husband has been sold subsequent to his death or has been divided between his devisees or heirs at law.

SEC. 3. *Be it further ordained,* That this ordinance shall be in force from and after its adoption.

Ratified in Convention, this 16th day of June, A. D., 1866.

EDWIN G. READE, *President.*
JAMES H. MOORE, *Secretary.*
R. C. BADGER. *Assistant Secretary.*

CHAPTER XXXVII.

AN ORDINANCE REPEALING THE PROVISIONS OF SECTION NINE, OF AN ACT OF THE GENERAL ASSEMBLY, ENTITLED "AN ACT CONCERNING NEGROES AND PERSONS OF COLOR OR OF MIXED BLOOD," AND FOR OTHER PURPOSES.

SECTION 1. *Be it ordained by the people of North Carolina in Convention assembled,* That the two provisos of the section and act above recited, be, and they are hereby, repealed: *Provided however,* That nothing herein contained shall effect the provisions of the act of the General Assembly, entitled "An Act to improve the law of evidence," or prevent the General Assembly from repealing or modifying this ordinance. [Repealing clause.] [Proviso.]

SEC. 2. *Be it further ordained,* That sections fifty-four, fifty-five, fifty-six, fifty-seven, fifty-eight and sixty-six, of chapter one hundred and seven of the Revised Code, be and the same are hereby repealed.

Ratified the 10th day of June, A. D. 1866.

EDWIN G. READE, *President.*

JAMES H. MOORE, *Secretary of the Convention.*
R. C. BADGER, *Assistant Secretary.*

CHAPTER XXXVIII.

AN ORDINANCE TO PROHIBIT THE SALE OF SPIRITUOUS LIQUORS WITHIN ONE AND A HALF MILES OF THE COMPANY SHOPS.

SECTION 1. *Be it ordained,* That no person shall sell spirituous liquors by a less quantity than a gallon, within one and a half miles of the Company Shops, and that any per- [No less quantity than a gallon to be sold.]

son violating this ordinance shall be guilty of a misdemeanor, and on conviction shall be fined not less than twenty-five dollars.

Ratified the 20th day of June, A. D., 1866.

EDWIN G. READE, *President.*
JAMES H. MOORE, *Secretary of the Convention.*
R. C. BADGER, *Assistant Secretary.*

CHAPTER XXXIX.

AN ORDINANCE TO REPEAL THE TWENTIETH SECTION OF THE FIFTY THIRD CHAPTER OF THE REVISED CODE, ENTITLED GOVERNOR AND COUNCIL.

Repealing clause

SECTION 1. *Be it ordained by the delegates of the people of North Carolina, in Convention assembled,* That the twentieth section of the fifty-third chapter of the Revised Code, entitled "Governor and Council," be, and the same is hereby, repealed.

Ratified the 20th day of June, A. D. 1866.

EDWIN G. READE, *President.*
JAMES H. MOORE, *Secretary of the Convention.*
R. C. BADGER, *Assistant Secretary.*

CHAPTER XL.

AN ORDINANCE TO GRANT TO THE CITIZENS OF THE COUNTY OF POLK THE POWER OF VOTING WITH THE DISTRICT OR COUNTY TO WHICH THEY ARE ATTACHED, IN THE ELECTION OF MEMBERS TO THE GENERAL ASSEMBLY.

SECTION 1. *Be it ordained by the delegates of the people of North Carolina, in Convention assembled, and it is hereby ordained by the authority of the same,* That in all elections hereafter to be held for the election of members of the General Assembly of said State, whether in the Senate or House of Commons, the citizens of the county of Polk shall vote with the county or district to which they are attached. Grants to citizens of Polk the power to vote with the district, &c.

SEC. 2. *Be it further ordained,* That all laws and clauses of laws coming in conflict with this ordinance, be, and the same are hereby, repealed. Repealing clause.

SEC. 3. *Be it further ordained,* That this ordinance shall be in force from and after its ratification.

Ratified the 12th day of June, A. D., 1866.

EDWIN G. READE, *President.*

JAS. H. MOORE *Secretary.*
R. C. BADGER, *Assisstant Secretary.*

CHAPTER XLI.

AN ORDINANCE TO AMEND AN ACT OF THE GENERAL ASSEMBLY, PASSED AT ITS SESSION OF 1842 AND 1843, ENTITLED AN ACT TO AUTHORIZE THE FORMATION OF A FIRE ENGINE COMPANY, IN THE TOWN OF SALEM, NORTH CAROLINA.

SECTION 1. *Be it ordained by the people of North Carolina, in Convention assembled, and it is hereby ordained by the authority of the same,* That section 1 of said Act be amend- Amends sections 1 and 5.

ed by striking out the words "seventy-five," and inserting the words "one hundred," in lieu thereof; and that section 5 of said Act be so amended as to read "Engines," instead of "Engine."

Ratified the 23d day of June, A. D., 1866.

EDWIN G. READE, *President.*

JAMES H. MOORE, *Secretary.*

R. C. BADGER, *Assistant Secretary.*

CHAPTER XLII.

AN ORDINANCE CONCERNING THE QUALIFICATION OF VOTERS FOR MUNICIPAL OFFICERS IN THE CITIES AND INCORPORATED TOWNS OF NORTH CAROLINA.

SECTION 1. *Be it ordained by the people of North Carolina, in Convention assembled,* That hereafter the voters for municipal officers in the cities and incorporated towns of the State, shall have the qualifications prescribed in section three of chapter one hundred and eleven, of the Revised Code, anything in the charter of any city or town to the contrary notwithstanding: *Provided,* That nothing in the ordinance shall be construed to affect any provision in any charter respecting evidence.

Qualifications prescribed.

SEC. 2. *Be it further ordained,* That this ordinance shall be subject to the legislative power of the State.

Ratified the 30th day of May, A. D., 1866.

EDWIN G. READE, *President.*

JAMES H. MOORE, *Secretary.*

R. C. BADGER, *Assistant Secretary.*

CHAPTER XLIII.

AN ORDINANCE TO PROVIDE FOR EXECUTING DECREES OF THE SUPREME COURT MADE AT MORGANTON.

SECTION 1. *Be it ordained by the people of the State of North Carolina in Convention assembled,* That the Clerk of the Supreme Court be and he is hereby authorized and directed to execute all unexecuted and unrescinded orders and decrees, which were made while sessions of the Supreme Court were held at Morganton, which were ordered or decreed to be executed by James R. Dodge, or the Clerk of the said Court at that place; and the same, when executed in pursuance of such decree or order, shall have like effect as if they had been duly executed in pursuance of such decrees or orders by the officer named therein.

Clerk directed to execute all unexecuted decrees, &c.

Ratified the 30th day of May, A. D., 1866.

EDWIN G. READE, *President.*

JAMES H. MOORE, *Secretary.*
R. C. BADGER, *Assistant Secretary.*

CHAPTER XLIV

AN ORDINANCE IN RELATION TO THE DEPOSIT AND PUBLICATION OF THE ORDINANCES AND RESOLUTIONS OF THE CONVENTION.

SECTION 1. *Be it ordained by the people of the State of North Carolina, in Convention assembled,* That the Secretary of this Convention deposit in the office of Secretary of State, for safe keeping, all the ordinances and resolutions passed by the Convention having the force and effect of laws; and the Secretary of State shall cause the following

Ordinances to be published.

ordinances and resolutions to be published : "An Ordinance repealing the provisions of section ninth of an act of the General Assembly, entitled 'An Act concerning negroes and persons of color or of mixed blood, and for other purposes;'" "An Ordinance concerning the crime of assault with intent to commit a rape;" "An Ordinance concerning widows, who have qualified as executrix to the last will and testament of their deceased husbands;" "An Ordinance for exchanging the stocks of the State for bonds issued before the year one thousand eight hundred and sixty-one;" "An Ordinance to change the time of elections in North Carolina, and for other purposes;" "An Ordinance extending the time for the settlement of the public taxes by the Sheriffs and tax collectors of this State;" "An Ordinance to change the Jurisdiction of the Courts and the rules of pleading therein;" "The Constitution of North Carolina as adopted by this Convention," and "The Ordinance submitting the same for ratification or rejection," in the following newspapers : *Standard* and *Sentinel*, Raleigh; and he is hereby authorized to contract for such publication at reasonable rates ; the expenses thereof shall be paid as other public printing, and it shall be sufficient for him to furnish one certified copy only, (for which he shall be paid the same fee as is now allowed him for certifying the acts of the General Assembly,) to one of the newspapers, and a printed copy to the other.

One thousand copies of the Constitution to be printed. SEC. 2. *Be it further ordained*, That the Secretary of State be required to contract for the printing of one thousand copies of the Constitution as adopted by the Convention, and the ordinance submitting the same for ratification or rejection, which he shall distribute among the several counties of the State, according to their white population.

Repealing clause. SEC. 3. *Be it further ordained*, That all laws and parts of laws coming in conflict with this ordinance are hereby repealed.

Ratified the 25th day of June, 1866.

EDWIN G. READE, *President.*
JAMES H. MOORE, *Secretary of the Convention.*
R. C. BADGER, *Assistant Secretary.*

CHAPTER XLV.

A RESOLUTION IN REFERENCE TO PAYMENT OF INTEREST ON THE PUBLIC DEBT OF THE STATE.

WHEREAS, In the present impoverished cond'tion of the people of this State, it has been deemed inexpedient to levy taxes for the payment of the interest on the entire public debt of the State : *Preamble.*

Resolved, That the Public Treasurer make no discrimination between different classes of said debt in the payment out of the Treasury of interest, until provision is made by the General Assembly for the same. *No discrimination allowed*

Ratified the 25th day of June, 1866.

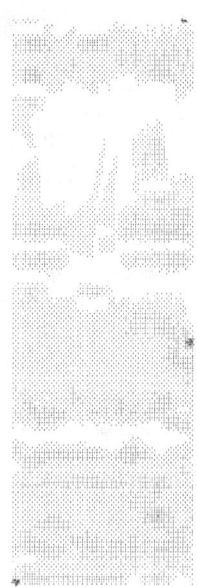

STATE OF NORTH CAROLINA,

DEPARTMENT OF STATE,
Raleigh, April 4th, 1867.

I, ROBERT W. BEST, Secretary of State, do hereby certify that the foregoing are true copies of the Ordinances of the State Convention, passed at its sessions in 1865-'66, (and ordered to be re-printed by the late General Assembly,) on file in this office.

R. W. BEST,
Secretary of State.

INDEX

TO THE

ORDINANCES,

PASSED BY THE

NORTH CAROLINA

STATE CONVENTION,

AT THE

SESSIONS OF 1865-'66.

AUTHENTICATION OF ORDINANCES—
  Ordinance in relation to   4
  Ordinance in relation to the deposit and publication of the Ordinances, &c., of the Convention,   27, 63

BANKS—
  An Ordinance concerning the Banks of the State,   57

CLERKS AND SHERIFFS—
  Ordinance for the election of   9
  Ordinance providing for compensation to Sheriffs for holding elections,   28
  Ordinance to authorize sundry Sheriffs to collect arrears,   40
  Ordinance extending time for settlement of taxes,   41

CONGRESSIONAL DISTRICTS—
  Ordinance dividing the State into seven Congressional Districts   5

CORPORATIONS—
 Ordinance to amend the charter of the Union Mining Company, in the county of Rowan, and the Rudicil Gold Mining Company, in Mecklenburg,   47
 Ordinance to amend the charter of the Governor's Creek Steam Transportation and Mining Company,   48
 Ordinance to incorporate the Oceanic Hook and Ladder Company, of Beaufort,   49
 Ordinance to incorporate the Railway Bridge Company,   50
 Ordinance with regard to the incorporation of Mocksville,   52
 Ordinance to incorporate the North Carolina Petroleum and Mining Company,   53
 Ordinance to prohibit the sale of spirituous liquors within one and a-half miles of Company Shops,   59
 Ordinance to amend Act of 1862–'63, to authorize the formation of a Fire Company in Salem,   61

COUNTIES—
 Ordinance to empower the Justices of the several counties to borrow money in certain cases, &c.,   44
 Ordinance granting to the citizens of Polk county the power of voting with the district or county to which they are attached, &c.,   61

COURTS—
 Ordinance to give jurisdiction to the Provisional Courts of Pleas and Quarter Sessions,   29
 Ordinance to change the jurisdiction of the Courts, &c.,   31
 Ordinance to pay Provisional Judges for their services, &c.,   43

DEBTS—
    Ordinance recognizing the just debts of the
      State and prohibiting the payment of those
      incurred in aid of the rebellion,   30
GENERAL ASSEMBLY—
    Ordinance providing for the election of members of, &c.,   6
    Ordinance providing for election of members
      in Cumberland and Harnett,   9
GOVERNOR AND COUNCIL—
    Ordinance repealing section twentieth, chapter fifty-three, Revised Code, entitled "Governor and Council,"   60
ORGANIZATION OF POLICE FORCE—
    Ordinance to organize a temporary force for
      the preservation of law and order,   25
ORDINANCES IN FORCE—
    Ordinance declaring what laws and ordinances
      are in force, and for other purposes,   19
ORDINANCE OF 1789—
    Ordinance declaring the same to have been
      always in full force and effect, notwithstanding the Ordinance of May twentieth, 1861,
    Ordinance submitting the ratification of the
      foregoing to the people,   10
OWNERS OF PROPERTY—
    Ordinance to protect the same,   17
PERSONS OF COLOR—
    Ordinance repealing the provisions of sec. 9, of the Act of Assembly, entitled "An Act concerning negroes, and persons of color or of mixed blood,   59
RAPE—
    Ordinance concerning the crime of assault
      with intent to commit rape,   39
RESOLUTION—
    In reference to payment of interest on the
      public debt of the State,   65

REVENUE—
 Ordinance to provide Revenue for 1865,   11
 Ordinance in relation to the act of the General Assembly entitled "Revenue,"   38
 Ordinance regulating taxation by the County Courts,   42
 Ordinance in relation to the payment of a portion of the public taxes into the Treasury of the State,   43

SLAVERY—
 Ordinance prohibiting Slavery in the State of North Carolina,   4
 Ordinance submitting the ratification of the foregoing to the people,   10

STATE CLAIMS TO PROPERTY—
 Ordinance appointing a Judge to determine the same,   23

STATE STOCKS—
 Ordinance for exchanging the Stocks of the State for Bonds issued before the year 1861,   55

SUPREME COURT—
 Ordinance to provide for executing decrees of the Supreme Court made at Morganton,   63

WIDOWS—
 Ordinance concerning Widows who have qualified as Executrix to the last will and testament of the deceased husband,   57

VACATING OFFICE—
 Ordinance declaring vacant all the offices in existence April 26th, 1865,   26

VOTERS—
 Ordinance concerning the qualification of voters in municipal elections,   63

www.ingramcontent.com/pod-product-compliance
Lightning Source LLC
Chambersburg PA
CBHW032106220426
43664CB00008B/1152